THANK YOU...

... for reading this book. I hope that you could find at least some of it useful.

PLEASE...

... email me if you have any case studies or personal experiences that you would like to share, or anything that you think can be included. I can include this in future editions.

ALSO PLEASE...

... give this book an honest review on Amazon. It will mean the world to me 😊

Copyright Disclaimer

© Yolandi Franken, 2024. All rights reserved.

No part of this book may be reproduced, distributed, or transmitted in any form or by any means, including photocopying, recording, or other electronic or mechanical methods, without the prior written permission of the author, except in the case of brief quotations embodied in critical reviews and certain other non-commercial uses permitted by copyright law. For permission requests, contact the author at yolandi@frankendipity.com

This book is a work of nonfiction. While every effort has been made to ensure accuracy, the author and publisher assume no responsibility for errors or omissions, or for any damages resulting from the use of the information contained herein. The views and opinions expressed in this book are those of the author and do not necessarily reflect the official policy or position of any other agency, organization, employer, or company.

First Edition

ACHIEVING WORK-LIFE BALANCE AND GENERAL WELLBEING IN THE SCREEN INDUSTRY

PRACTICAL STRATEGIES FOR ATL AND BTL CAST AND CREW, WITH ADDITIONAL SUPPORT FOR CARERS, PLUS ESSENTIAL ADVICE AND GUIDANCE FOR PRODUCTION COMPANIES, GUILDS, AND ORGANISATIONS.

INDEX

Foreword 8

DEFINITIONS 12

CHAPTER 1 - The Evolution of the Screen Industry 15

    History of The Screen Industry in the USA 16

    History of The Screen Industry in the UK 22

    History of The Screen Industry in Australia 28

    Box Office Data to Demonstrate Industry Growth 34

CHAPTER 2 - Influence on Current Working Conditions 37

CHAPTER 3 - Countries with Better Conditions 45

CHAPTER 4 - Independent Productions 52

CHAPTER 5 - The Reality of Working in Screen 56

CHAPTER 6 - The Impact on Physical & Mental Health 61

CHAPTER 7 - Substance Abuse 72

CHAPTER 8 - Work-Life Balance 76

CHAPTER 9 - Parenthood & Caring 78

CHAPTER 10 - Gender Disparities 101

CHAPTER 11 - Underrepresented Communities 106

    Enhancing Diversity and Inclusion in the Industry 106

    People Living With Disability 125

    People of Colour 130

    THE LGBTQIA+ Community 135

    Cisgender White Males 139

CHAPTER 12 - Movements of Change 145

CHAPTER 13 - Production-Led Solutions **165**

Implementing 4-Day Work Weeks 165

Shorter Workdays 170

Job Sharing 174

Flexible Scheduling 178

Implementing Paid Family Leave 180

Enhanced Health and Wellness Programs 187

On-Set Health Services and Wellness Facilities 199

On-Site Daycare and Family-Friendly Policies 201

Flexibility and Remote Work in Film 208

Flexible Workspaces 226

Work-Life Balance through Company Culture 227

Creating Safe and Inclusive Work Environments 230

Cultural Safety Officers 236

Access Coordinators 240

Intimacy Coordination 243

CHAPTER 14 - Personal Solutions **255**

Job-Sharing (from the employee's side) 255

Taking Your Child to Meetings and Events 255

Encouraging Walking Meetings 256

Being Outdoors 257

Separating Work and Family Time 259

Dedicated Family Days 260

Compartmentalisation of the Mind 260

Adjust Working Hours & Micromanaging Your Time 264

Using Communication Platforms Efficiently 265

Enhancing Efficiency and Eliminating Distractions 265

Staying Fit and Eating Healthy 270

Personal Mental and Emotional Health Strategies 273

Myself as a Case Study for Work-Life Balance 282

CHAPTER 15 - Unions 293

CHAPTER 16 - Future Outlook and Recommendations 297

CHAPTER 17 - Conclusion 302

WORKSHEETS & SURVEYS 303

Documenting Your Team's Accounts of Working Conditions - EXAMPLE 309

Documenting Your Personal Accounts of Working Conditions – EXAMPLE 311

Exercises for parents to document challenges and solutions . 313

Templates for creating and documenting job-sharing arrangements 319

Strategies and Templates for Flexible Scheduling on Set 324

Disclaimer

The information presented in this book is based on interviews, reaching out to the mentioned organisations, publicly available data, research studies, industry reports, and other reliable sources. Every effort has been made to ensure the accuracy and completeness of the information.

The statistics, case studies, and other data included in this book are intended for informational purposes only and should not be considered as professional advice.

The views and opinions expressed in this book are those of the author and contributors and do not necessarily reflect the views of any organisations or individuals mentioned. Any references to companies, products, or services are for informational purposes only and do not constitute an endorsement by the author or publisher.

The author and publisher shall not be held liable for any damages arising from the use or misuse of the information contained in this book. All rights reserved.

Foreword

For as long as I can remember, the film industry has been my life. It consumed almost every waking hour—days blurring into nights as I worked around the clock, pushing myself to the limit. For 20 years, I thrived on the excitement and the adrenaline that comes with non-stop working, hustling and networking. I wore my workaholism as a badge of honour. But the truth is, I crossed the line into burnout more times than I can count.

It wasn't until I became a mother that I really started to reflect on what all of this was costing me. Bringing new life into the world gave me a fresh perspective on my own. All those endless hours, the pressure, the grind—suddenly it didn't seem as noble or as important as I had always believed. I realised that this way of living was no longer an option, and I wouldn't let it affect my family, which also meant not letting it affect my own health and mental well-being.

At first, I felt so much guilt. I had conditioned myself to believe that slowing down was equivalent to failure. The film industry has this toxic culture that glorifies overwork and burnout. It's almost like we've been taught to believe that unless we're pushing ourselves to the brink, we're not truly dedicated.

As I started speaking to others, and looking at the lives of colleagues around me, it was very clear that it was not just me who was dealing with these issues of burnout, nor of trying to create some work-life balance. That realisation was both eye-opening and heartbreaking. I began to see that this isn't just a personal problem—it's a systemic issue. We've created a culture where burning out is seen as normal, even admirable. But it's not sustainable. It damages our health, strains our relationships, and, in the end, it stifles the very creativity and productivity we're chasing.

We need a real cultural shift, one that starts from the top and filters down through every level of the industry. If we start valuing health and mental well-being, we'll create a more balanced, sustainable work environment. It's not just about cutting back on hours; it's about creating spaces where people can take care of themselves and their families, and where those things are truly valued.

I'm ready to lead by example, both in my life and in my work. I believe that when we take care of ourselves, we're not just more productive—we're more creative, more engaged, and ultimately happier.

Since my shift, and in my personal life, it has taken me some time and lots of trial and error to figure out my new normal, implementing boundaries and fine-tuning how I organise my days. I feel that I have come to a good place now, and I intend to sustain this and even improve it as time goes on.

As a producer and film industry member, I am determined to offer better conditions for my teams, and to create opportunities for those who need it, like people who are re-entering the workforce or need to work untraditionally.

This book is my call to action—for myself and for everyone in the film industry. It's time to create a new way of working, one that values well-being as much as creativity and dedication. By making these changes, we can build a brighter, healthier future for ourselves and for the industry we love so much.

YOUR UNIQUE SITUATION

What everyone needs for their life, happiness, and well-being is unique to them, so the method—or set of methods—that works will differ from person to person. It's up to each of us to do some internal digging, to really understand what balance looks like for us individually, and to apply what works best for our own circumstances. Really assess what is important for us and where things sit on the priority ladder. Even if you've found a good balance, there will be times when things get a bit more difficult. Sometimes it's just a temporary situation, and you know there's an end date. Other times, you might find you've been swept up by life and circumstances, losing sight of that balance. In those moments, it's crucial to bring yourself back, which is why regular self and life check-ins are so important. They help us stay grounded and ensure that we're living in a way that truly supports our well-being.

TYPES OF SITUATIONS

As I was researching this book and talking to people, I identified a few different groups of people with unique sets of problems, relevant to the topic of this book:

- Individuals who are overworked and burned out.
- Individuals who are overworked, burned out AND stressed about future work.
- Parents and carers who need a more realistic work-life balance.
- Parents and others who want to re-enter the workforce.
- People in general who want to have a more realistic and sustainable work-life balance.
- People who, based on personal criteria, find it even harder to thrive and be happy in the industry.
- And everyone in between.

DEFINITIONS

WHAT IS

WORK-LIFE-BALANCE

Work-life balance refers to the equilibrium between personal life and professional work, where an individual effectively manages the demands and responsibilities of both areas without one overwhelming the other.

Studies on work-life balance often emphasise the **quality** of time spent in each area rather than strictly quantifying the hours needed. However, **general guidelines** suggest the following:

Family Life: Spending at least **1-2 hours daily** on family activities or meaningful interactions is recommended. For working parents, dedicating weekends or at least one full day a week to family activities can also significantly improve work-life balance. Quality family time strengthens bonds, provides emotional support, and is crucial for long-term well-being.

Health and Fitness: Engaging in physical activity for **30 minutes to 1 hour daily**, at least 3-5 times a week, is ideal for maintaining physical and mental health. Regular exercise reduces stress, boosts energy, and improves overall health, which is essential for sustaining work-life balance.

Relaxation and Mental Health: Allocating **30 minutes to 1 hour daily** for relaxation or mental health activities such as meditation, reading, or simply unwinding is advisable.
Consistent relaxation time is crucial for stress management and preventing burnout.

Social Life: Spending **1-2 hours weekly** on social activities or connecting with friends, though this can vary based on personal needs and social preferences. Social interactions provide emotional support and can improve mood and reduce stress.

Personal Development: Devoting **a few hours weekly** to learning new skills, or personal growth activities can be beneficial. The exact amount varies based on individual goals and interests. Continuous personal development contributes to a sense of fulfilment and long-term happiness.

Leisure Activities: Allocating **a few hours weekly** for leisure activities such as hobbies, entertainment, or travel. A full day on weekends is often recommended for complete relaxation. Leisure activities provide necessary breaks and help rejuvenate the mind and body.

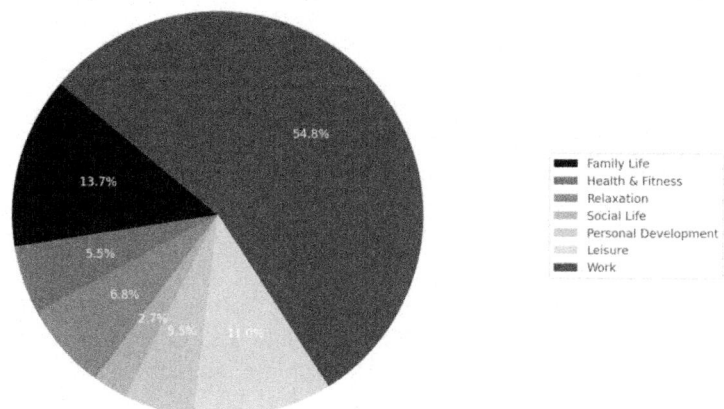

While the specific time spent on each aspect of your personal life can vary depending on individual circumstances, the emphasis should be on balancing time across these areas in a way that meets personal needs and maintains overall well-being. And I'll say this again because all my research on this topic pointed out that prioritising quality over quantity is key to achieving an effective work-life balance.

WHAT IS

GENERAL WELLBEING

General well-being refers to the overall state of an individual's health, happiness, and life satisfaction. It encompasses multiple dimensions, including physical health, mental and emotional stability, social connections, and a sense of purpose and fulfilment. General well-being is often considered a holistic measure of how well a person is thriving in various aspects of life, balancing personal, professional, and social needs.

Key components of general well-being, ordered by importance according to experts and studies:

Mental and Emotional Health: The ability to manage stress, maintain a positive outlook, experience emotions in a healthy way, and cope with life's challenges. Mental and emotional health is foundational for overall well-being and influences other areas of your life.

Physical Health: The state of being free from illness, having good physical fitness, and maintaining healthy bodily functions. Physical health is closely linked to mental well-being and is crucial for a high quality of life.

Social Well-being: Having strong, supportive relationships with family, friends, and community, and feeling a sense of belonging and connection. Social connections are vital for emotional support and happiness.

Purpose and Fulfillment: Engaging in meaningful activities, pursuing personal goals, and feeling that your life has purpose and direction. A sense of purpose is essential for long-term satisfaction and motivation.

Economic Stability: Having financial security and the ability to meet basic needs and enjoy a reasonable standard of living. Economic stability supports other aspects of well-being by reducing stress and enabling access to resources for health and social engagement.

These components interact dynamically, and maintaining a balance among them is key to achieving and sustaining general well-being.

CHAPTER 1

The Evolution of the Screen Industry

The film industry, as we know it today, has a rich and fascinating history. From its humble beginnings in the late 19th century, it has grown into a global powerhouse, shaping culture and society in ways few other industries can claim. Understanding the evolution of the film industry provides a vital context for exploring the work-life balance issues faced by its professionals today.

Early History and Development:

The story of cinema begins in the late 1800s with the invention of motion pictures. The Lumière brothers, Thomas Edison, and other pioneers played crucial roles in developing the technology that made moving pictures possible. These early films were short, silent, and often documentary-style, capturing everyday life or staged events. Despite their simplicity, they captivated audiences and sparked a new form of entertainment.

As technology advanced, so did the art of filmmaking. The introduction of narrative storytelling, special effects, and the first "stars" marked the transition from mere novelty to a burgeoning industry. Silent films became increasingly sophisticated, with directors like D.W. Griffith pushing the boundaries of the medium. The 1920s saw the rise of Hollywood as the epicentre of the global film industry, thanks to its favourable weather and a growing pool of talent. And as time went on, the industry just kept expanding.

It's important to recognise that the history and circumstances of cinema vary greatly from country to country. Because of this, I've made a point to separate certain areas of discussion in this book to reflect those differences. However, when it comes to solutions and future trends, you'll notice that many of these ideas become more universal across the board.

For now, let's dive into the history of screen in some of the major Western territories. I've chosen not to cover non-Western territories in this book, as I don't feel qualified to provide the depth and perspective those territories deserve.

History of The Screen Industry in the USA

The history and growth of the U.S. film industry is one of the most significant cultural and economic developments of the 20th century, shaping global entertainment and culture. From its early experimental stages to becoming the largest and most influential film industry in the world, the American film industry has seen various milestones.

Early Beginnings (1890s - 1920s)

1890s – The Birth of Cinema:

Thomas Edison and the Kinetoscope: The first film technology in the U.S. was pioneered by Thomas Edison, who created the Kinetoscope in 1891, a device for viewing moving pictures. Edison's studios produced early short films that could be viewed individually through the Kinetoscope.

1894: The first public demonstration of the Kinetoscope took place in New York City, giving birth to an early interest in moving images.

1900s – The Rise of Narrative Filmmaking:

1903 - "The Great Train Robbery": Directed by Edwin S. Porter, this 12-minute film is considered the first American narrative film. It introduced continuity editing and was one of the first "blockbusters" of the silent era.

1908 - The Edison Trust (MPPC): The Motion Picture Patents Company (MPPC), also known as the Edison Trust, was formed to control the early film industry and restrict competition. However, independent filmmakers resisted and eventually relocated to Hollywood to escape the trust's legal influence.

1910s – The Move to Hollywood:

1910 - First Hollywood Film: "In Old California," directed by D.W. Griffith, was the first film made in Hollywood, marking the beginning of Los Angeles as the centre of American filmmaking.

1915 - "The Birth of a Nation": Directed by D.W. Griffith, this controversial film was a technological and storytelling breakthrough. It pioneered techniques like cross-cutting and large-scale battle scenes. However, it was also criticised for its racist portrayal of African Americans.

1915 - The Fall of the Edison Trust: The MPPC was declared a monopoly by U.S. courts, leading to its dissolution and paving the way for independent filmmakers to thrive.

1920s – The Silent Film Era and Studio System:

The Rise of Major Studios: By the 1920s, major studios like Warner Bros., Paramount Pictures, MGM, and Universal Pictures were founded, giving rise to the "studio system," which dominated American cinema for decades.

1927 - The Jazz Singer: Warner Bros. released "The Jazz Singer," the first feature-length film with synchronised sound, marking the end of the silent film era and the beginning of the "talkies."

The Golden Age of Hollywood (1930s - 1940s):

1930s – The Studio System and Sound Films:

The Great Depression and Film: Despite the economic hardships of the Great Depression, cinema thrived as an affordable form of escapism. The studio system became more established, controlling all aspects of film production, distribution, and exhibition.

The Hays Code: Implemented in 1930, the Motion Picture Production Code (Hays Code) introduced moral guidelines for films, restricting what could be shown in terms of violence, sex, and other moral issues.

1939 - "Gone with the Wind" and "The Wizard of Oz": These two films, released in 1939, became cultural milestones, showcasing the power of Technicolour and epic storytelling in cinema. "Gone with the Wind" became one of the highest-grossing films of all time.

1940s – World War II and Its Aftermath:

Hollywood during WWII: The U.S. government collaborated with Hollywood to produce propaganda films during the war, boosting morale and promoting the war effort. Films like "Casablanca" (1942) became iconic for their war themes and patriotism.

The Rise of Film Noir: Post-war America saw the emergence of film noir, a genre characterised by dark, cynical tones and morally ambiguous characters, with films like "Double Indemnity" (1944) and "The Maltese Falcon" (1941).

Post-War Expansion and Decline of the Studio System (1950s - 1960s)

1950s – The Advent of Television and CinemaScope:

Television's Impact: The rise of television in the 1950s posed a major threat to the film industry as audiences shifted to home entertainment. In response, studios adopted new technologies like CinemaScope and 3D to attract viewers with larger-than-life cinematic experiences.

1956 - Paramount Consent Decrees: In 1948, the U.S. Supreme Court ruled against the major studios in United States v. Paramount Pictures, leading to the dismantling of the studio system and the end of vertical integration. Studios could no longer own theatres, and independent producers gained more power.

1960s – The Rise of Independent Filmmakers:

New Hollywood: The 1960s saw the decline of the studio system and the rise of independent filmmakers who challenged traditional filmmaking. Directors like Stanley Kubrick, Sidney Lumet, and John Cassavetes pushed the boundaries of storytelling with more artistic freedom.

"Bonnie and Clyde" (1967) and **"The Graduate" (1967)**: These films marked the beginning of a new era in American cinema, with more experimental narratives and the embrace of counterculture themes.

New Hollywood and the Blockbuster Era (1970s - 1990s)

1970s – The New Hollywood Movement:

Auteur Filmmakers: The 1970s is often referred to as the era of "New Hollywood," where filmmakers like Martin Scorsese, Francis Ford Coppola, and Steven Spielberg gained creative control over their projects, emphasising artistic vision over studio mandates.

1972 - "The Godfather": Directed by Francis Ford Coppola, this film became a cultural touchstone and is still considered one of the greatest films of all time. It symbolised the shift toward more complex, character-driven storytelling.

1975 - "Jaws": Directed by Steven Spielberg, this was the first film to be widely considered a "summer blockbuster." Its immense commercial success revolutionised the marketing and distribution strategies of Hollywood, leading to the rise of the modern blockbuster.

1980s – The Blockbuster Boom:

1980 - "Star Wars" Franchise: George Lucas's "Star Wars" (1977) became a global phenomenon, revolutionising the film industry with its special effects, merchandising, and franchise-building model. The 1980s saw the dominance of the blockbuster film, with franchises like "Indiana Jones," "Star Wars," and "Back to the Future."

Rise of Home Video: The advent of VHS and Betamax in the 1980s led to a new revenue stream for the film industry, as films could now be viewed at home, allowing studios to capitalise on home video sales and rentals.

1990s – CGI and the Birth of the Modern Franchise:

1993 - "Jurassic Park": Directed by Steven Spielberg, "Jurassic Park" pioneered the use of computer-generated imagery (CGI) to create realistic dinosaurs, revolutionising special effects and shaping the future of visual storytelling in film.

1995 - "Toy Story": Pixar's "Toy Story" was the first fully computer-animated feature film, leading to the rise of CGI animation in filmmaking.

The Digital Revolution and Globalisation (2000s - Present)

2000s – Digital Cinema and Franchise Domination:

The Rise of Superhero Films: The 2000s saw the explosion of superhero franchises, with Marvel Studios dominating the box office. Films like "Spider-Man" (2002) and "The Dark Knight" (2008) reshaped the blockbuster landscape.

Digital Filmmaking: The 2000s also marked the transition from film to digital cinema, with films like "Avatar" (2009) using cutting-edge motion capture and 3D technology to create immersive cinematic experiences.

Franchise-Driven Model: Studios increasingly relied on established intellectual properties (IP) and franchises, such as Marvel's Cinematic Universe (MCU), "Harry Potter," and "The Lord of the Rings" series, which became global cultural phenomena.

2010s – Streaming and the Decline of Theatrical Dominance:

The Rise of Streaming: Platforms like Netflix, Amazon Prime, and Hulu disrupted the traditional film distribution model, offering original content and reshaping how audiences consumed movies. By the late 2010s, streaming had become a dominant force in the industry.

Diversity in Filmmaking: There was a growing emphasis on diverse voices in the industry, with films like "Black Panther" (2018) and "Crazy Rich Asians" (2018) marking important milestones in representation.

2020s – The COVID-19 Pandemic and Its Impact:

COVID-19 and Streaming's Expansion: The COVID-19 pandemic accelerated the shift toward streaming, as movie theatres closed worldwide. Studios released films directly to digital platforms, signalling a major change in film distribution models.

The Future of Theatrical Releases: While theatrical releases have begun to recover post-pandemic, the industry continues to grapple with the balance between streaming and traditional cinema, and the future of large-scale film distribution remains in flux.

The U.S. film industry has undergone numerous transformations, from the silent film era and the golden age of Hollywood to the rise of independent filmmakers and the blockbuster-driven model. Today, it continues to evolve, facing new challenges and opportunities with the digital revolution, globalisation, and the increasing dominance of streaming platforms. The industry's influence on global culture and entertainment is unparalleled, and it remains one of the most important and innovative sectors in the world.

History of The Screen Industry in the UK

The UK film industry has a rich and diverse history, marked by periods of innovation, decline, resurgence, and global influence. From the early days of silent cinema to modern-day blockbusters, the UK has played a key role in shaping the global film landscape. Below is an overview of the history and growth of the UK film industry, along with its major milestones.

Early Beginnings and Silent Film Era (1890s - 1920s)

1890s – The Birth of British Cinema:

1895: The UK was one of the early adopters of motion pictures. The first known British film was shot by Birt Acres, titled "Rough Sea at Dover," in 1895. This was just a year after the Lumière brothers' public film screening in Paris.

1896: Robert W. Paul, one of the pioneers of British cinema, showcased "The Derby," which depicted a horse race. His work laid the groundwork for early filmmaking in the UK.

1901 - "Scrooge, or, Marley's Ghost": One of the earliest narrative films, this adaptation of Charles Dickens' "A Christmas Carol" became a significant step in narrative storytelling.

1900s – The Silent Film Boom:

1903 - "Alice in Wonderland": Directed by Cecil Hepworth, this early silent film adaptation of Lewis Carroll's story became one of the notable British films of the period.

1905 - "Rescued by Rover": Directed by Cecil Hepworth, this short film is considered a landmark in narrative filmmaking for its use of continuity editing and storytelling.

1910s - World War I: British cinema was greatly affected by World War I. However, filmmakers like Alfred Hitchcock began their careers during this period, setting the stage for future British cinema.

1920s – Decline and Competition from Hollywood:

British cinema faced stiff competition from Hollywood productions, which had higher budgets and more advanced technology. Although silent films remained popular in the UK, Hollywood films dominated British screens by the 1920s.

1927 - "The Jazz Singer": Although American, this film marked the end of the silent era globally, as sound films, or "talkies," became the new standard.

The Golden Age of British Cinema (1930s - 1940s)

1927 – The Cinematograph Films Act:

The British government introduced the Cinematograph Films Act to protect the domestic industry. The act imposed a quota that required British cinemas to show a certain percentage of British-made films, encouraging the growth of the industry.

1930s – British Film Industry Flourishes:

1930 - First British "Talkie": Alfred Hitchcock's "Blackmail" became the first British sound film, marking a significant milestone in UK cinema.

1933 - British International Pictures: The studio began producing successful films that competed with Hollywood productions. Directors like Alexander Korda and Michael Powell rose to prominence.

1939 - "The Four Feathers": Directed by Zoltan Korda, this Technicolour adventure film became a significant achievement in British cinema.

World War II and Propaganda Films:

1940s - Wartime Cinema: The British government used cinema as a tool for propaganda during World War II. Films like "In Which We Serve" (1942), co-directed by Noël Coward and David Lean, were designed to boost morale and promote patriotism.

1944 - "Henry V": Directed by and starring Laurence Olivier, this Shakespearean adaptation was both a critical and commercial success, elevating British cinema's cultural status.

Post-War Decline and Revival (1950s - 1960s)

1950s – Challenges and Resurgence:

Television Competition: The rise of television in the 1950s led to a decline in cinema attendance in the UK. Many British studios struggled to compete with this new form of entertainment.

Ealing Studios: Famous for its comedies, Ealing Studios produced some of the UK's most beloved films during this period, including "The Ladykillers" (1955) and "Kind Hearts and Coronets" (1949).

1956 – The British New Wave:

Free Cinema Movement: Filmmakers like Lindsay Anderson, Tony Richardson, and Karel Reisz spearheaded the British New Wave, characterised by a focus on social realism and working-class life. Films like

"Look Back in Anger" (1959) and "Saturday Night and Sunday Morning" (1960) exemplified this trend.

Hammer Horror: Hammer Film Productions found success with its horror films, such as "Dracula" (1958) and "The Curse of Frankenstein" (1957), establishing a new genre in British cinema.

The 1960s - The Swinging Sixties and International Success

1960s – Global Success and the Birth of James Bond:

James Bond Franchise: The release of "Dr. No" (1962), the first James Bond film, marked the beginning of one of the most successful franchises in cinematic history. The Bond series became a global phenomenon, showcasing British talent and locations.

"Lawrence of Arabia" (1962): Directed by David Lean, this epic film won seven Academy Awards and is considered one of the greatest films of all time, highlighting the global impact of British cinema during this period.

The Swinging Sixties: The 1960s saw a vibrant cultural revolution in the UK, and British cinema reflected this with films like "A Hard Day's Night" (1964), "Alfie" (1966), and "Blow-Up" (1966), which tapped into the counterculture and new social freedoms of the era.

The Decline of the Studio System and the Rise of Independent Cinema (1970s - 1980s)

1970s – Decline of Traditional Studios:

Studio Closures: Many British film studios struggled financially in the 1970s, with the rise of television and the decline of traditional cinema attendance. However, independent filmmakers gained prominence during this period.

Monty Python: The release of "Monty Python and the Holy Grail" (1975) and "Life of Brian" (1979) brought a new era of British comedy to international audiences, cementing the legacy of the Monty Python comedy troupe.

1980s – Channel 4 and the Revival of British Cinema:

Channel 4: Launched in 1982, Channel 4 played a critical role in funding and promoting British films. The channel invested in filmmakers and productions that would not otherwise have been made, supporting independent cinema.

"Chariots of Fire" (1981): This film, based on the story of British athletes at the 1924 Olympics, won four Academy Awards, including Best Picture. It was a milestone in British cinema's resurgence during the 1980s.

1980s – Merchant Ivory Productions: Films like "A Room with a View" (1985) and "Howard's End" (1992) were part of the successful Merchant Ivory Productions, which became known for its period dramas based on British literary works.

Modern Era and Global Influence (1990s - Present)

1990s – International Recognition:

Working Title Films: The 1990s saw the rise of Working Title Films, a production company that produced several successful films, including "Four Weddings and a Funeral" (1994), "Notting Hill" (1999), and "Bridget Jones's Diary" (2001). These films became international hits, with their unique mix of British charm and global appeal.

1996 - "Trainspotting": Directed by Danny Boyle, this film became an instant cult classic and put British cinema back in the spotlight. Its bold narrative style and raw depiction of youth culture reflected a new era of British filmmaking.

"The Full Monty" (1997): This comedy-drama about unemployed men turning to stripping became a surprise international hit, winning critical acclaim and commercial success.

2000s – British Cinema Goes Global:

Harry Potter Franchise: Beginning with "Harry Potter and the Philosopher's Stone" in 2001, this film series became one of the highest-grossing franchises of all time. It marked the global influence of British cinema and its ability to produce large-scale, internationally successful films.

Danny Boyle's Success: Danny Boyle's "Slumdog Millionaire" (2008) became a worldwide hit, winning eight Academy Awards, including Best Director and Best Picture.

2010s – The Rise of Streaming and Co-Productions:

Streaming Platforms: The rise of streaming platforms like Netflix and Amazon Prime has transformed the British film industry, with UK-based productions increasingly gaining international audiences through digital distribution.

Diversity in Filmmaking: The 2010s saw an increase in diversity in British cinema, with films like "The Favourite" (2018), directed by Yorgos Lanthimos, and "12 Years a Slave" (2013), directed by British filmmaker Steve McQueen, winning critical acclaim.

2020s – Post-COVID Challenges and Opportunities:

COVID-19 Pandemic: Like other film industries globally, the UK film industry faced significant challenges due to the COVID-19 pandemic, with production halts and cinema closures. However, the shift to digital platforms and streaming has opened new opportunities for filmmakers to reach global audiences.

The UK film industry has evolved over the years, adapting to changing technologies, social trends, and economic pressures. From its early beginnings to the golden age of British cinema, the rise of independent filmmakers, and its current position as a global powerhouse in cinema, the British film industry continues to play a vital role in shaping global film culture. Through iconic films, innovative filmmakers, and lasting contributions to world cinema, the UK remains a key player in the global entertainment industry.

History of The Screen Industry in Australia

The Australian film industry has a rich history that dates back to the late 19th century, marked by significant growth, challenges, and milestones. Here's an overview of its history and key milestones:

Early Beginnings (1890s - 1910s)

1896: The first film screenings took place in Australia, just one year after the Lumière brothers' first public screening in Paris.

1900: Australia was among the first countries to produce narrative films, with titles like "The Story of the Kelly Gang" (1906), considered the world's first full-length feature film. It ran for over an hour and was based on the story of the infamous Australian outlaw, Ned Kelly.

1900s-1910s: This period saw a boom in Australian filmmaking, with over 150 narrative films produced between 1906 and 1911. Early filmmakers were experimenting with narrative structures and themes that explored Australian identity, landscapes, and cultural stories.

The Silent Era and Decline (1920s - 1930s)

1920s: While the silent film era thrived in Australia, the arrival of Hollywood films began to dominate the market. Australian filmmakers found it increasingly difficult to compete with the high production values and star power of American films.

1930: The introduction of sound ("talkies") in films marked a significant technological shift. However, the cost of adapting to sound technology was prohibitive for many Australian filmmakers, leading to a decline in local production.

1930s: The Great Depression further impacted the industry, with fewer films being produced. During this time, the British government introduced the "quota quickie" system, which encouraged low-budget films from the British Empire, including Australia, to meet requirements for British cinemas.

Post-War Resurgence and Challenges (1940s - 1950s)

1940s: World War II saw the Australian government commission war documentaries and newsreels, keeping some production activity alive. The war years also witnessed a rise in patriotic films.

1945-1950s: Post-war Australia experienced a rise in feature films, though the industry still struggled against Hollywood imports. However, notable films like "The Overlanders" (1946) directed by Harry Watt, received international attention.

Revival and Government Support (1960s - 1980s)

1960s: There was a cultural push for a distinct Australian film identity, driven by the New Wave movement globally. This period saw a demand for films that reflected Australian stories and perspectives.

1970s: The Australian government played a crucial role in revitalising the industry by establishing the Australian Film Development Corporation (1970), later known as the Australian Film Commission. The funding led to the emergence of the Australian New Wave cinema.

Milestone Films: Key films from this era include "Wake in Fright" (1971), "Walkabout" (1971), "Picnic at Hanging Rock" (1975), and "Mad Max" (1979). These films gained international recognition and highlighted unique aspects of Australian culture and landscape.

1980s: The success continued with critically acclaimed films such as "Gallipoli" (1981), "The Man from Snowy River" (1982), and "Crocodile Dundee" (1986), the latter becoming a massive international hit and putting Australian cinema on the global map.

International Success and Diversification (1990s - 2000s)

1990s: Australian filmmakers began gaining recognition internationally, with directors like Baz Luhrmann and George Miller making their mark. Films such as "Muriel's Wedding" (1994), "Babe" (1995), and "The Adventures of Priscilla, Queen of the Desert" (1994) showcased the diversity and creativity of Australian cinema.

2000s: This decade saw continued international collaboration, with Australia becoming a preferred location for major Hollywood productions due to its landscapes, skilled workforce, and competitive costs. Films like "Moulin Rouge!" (2001) and "Happy Feet" (2006) were critically acclaimed, with the latter winning an Academy Award for Best Animated Feature.

Recent Developments (2010s - Present)

2010s: Australia continued to produce a mix of blockbuster and independent films. International co-productions increased, and the country became a popular destination for filming due to tax incentives, state-of-the-art studios, and diverse locations.

Milestone Films: Films like "The Great Gatsby" (2013), directed by Baz Luhrmann, "Mad Max: Fury Road" (2015), directed by George Miller, and "Lion" (2016), based on a true story, received global acclaim.

Streaming and Global Reach: The rise of streaming platforms like Netflix, Amazon Prime, and Stan opened new opportunities for Australian content creators, leading to international distribution and recognition of Australian series and films.

Diversity and Indigenous Storytelling: Recent years have seen a stronger emphasis on diverse stories and Indigenous perspectives. Films such as "Samson & Delilah" (2009) and "The Sapphires" (2012) have showcased

Indigenous talent and stories. Indigenous filmmakers like Warwick Thornton and Rachel Perkins have gained prominence.

2020s and Beyond: The Australian film industry continues to thrive, balancing local storytelling with global appeal. The COVID-19 pandemic presented challenges, but Australia's relatively successful management of the virus early on allowed it to become a hub for international productions.

The Australian film industry has evolved from its pioneering beginnings to become a significant player on the global stage. With ongoing government support, international collaborations, and a strong emphasis on diverse and Indigenous storytelling, the industry continues to grow, balancing commercial success with artistic integrity.

Comparison:

Category	UK	US	Australia
Early Beginnings	**1895**: Birt Acres and Robert Paul shoot early films.	**1891**: Thomas Edison develops the Kinetoscope.	**1906**: "The Story of the Kelly Gang," first feature film.
First Major Film	**1903**: "Alice in Wonderland" (silent).	**1903**: "The Great Train Robbery," first narrative film.	**1906**: "The Story of the Kelly Gang," the world's first feature film.
First Sound Film	**1930**: Alfred Hitchcock's *Blackmail* becomes the first British "talkie."	**1927**: "The Jazz Singer," first synchronised sound film.	**1931**: "Diggers" becomes the first Australian sound film.

Golden Age of Cinema	**1940s-1960s**: Ealing Studios comedies, WWII propaganda films, and the rise of James Bond.	**1930s-1940s**: Studio System dominates; Hollywood becomes global centre.	**1970s-1980s**: Resurgence of Australian cinema with New Wave directors.
Iconic Films of the Era	**1939**: "The Four Feathers"; **1962**: "Lawrence of Arabia"; **1962**: "Dr. No" (James Bond).	**1939**: "Gone with the Wind"; **1941**: "Citizen Kane"; **1972**: "The Godfather."	**1979**: "Mad Max"; **1986**: "Crocodile Dundee"; **1995**: "Babe."
Post-War Decline & Resurgence	**1950s-1960s**: The rise of independent filmmakers (Free Cinema and British New Wave).	**1950s**: Television impacts box office; **1970s**: New Hollywood movement (Scorsese, Coppola).	**1970s-1980s**: Australian New Wave, government funding boosts local cinema.
Modern Blockbuster Era	**1990s-present**: *Harry Potter* franchise (2001); **1996**: "Trainspotting."	**1975**: "Jaws" begins the modern blockbuster era; **1990s-present**: Rise of franchise films (MCU, Star Wars).	**1990s-present**: "The Adventures of Priscilla, Queen of the Desert" (1994); *Happy Feet* (2006); "The Great Gatsby" (2013).
Key Milestones	**1927**: Cinematograph Films Act (Quota Act); **1982**: Channel 4 funds indie films.	**1948**: Paramount Consent Decrees break up studio monopoly;	**1970s**: Australian Film Commission established;

			1975: "Jaws" revolutionises marketing and summer blockbusters.	1979: "Mad Max" goes global.
Influential Figures		Alfred Hitchcock, David Lean, Ken Loach, Danny Boyle.	D.W. Griffith, Steven Spielberg, Martin Scorsese, Quentin Tarantino.	Peter Weir, George Miller, Baz Luhrmann.
Impact of Streaming		2010s-present: Increased international reach through platforms like Netflix and Amazon Prime.	2010s-present: Netflix, Disney+, Amazon reshape distribution; Hollywood continues franchise dominance.	2010s-present: Australian productions gain global exposure through streaming platforms.
Current Challenges		COVID-19: Impact on cinemas and shift to streaming; diversity in film and global co-productions.	COVID-19: Accelerated shift to streaming; balancing traditional cinemas and digital.	COVID-19: Impact on cinemas, rise of streaming, maintaining local production with global competition.

Box Office Data to Demonstrate Industry Growth

Box Office Data: US, UK, and Australia (in 10-Year Increments)

Year	US Box Office (USD)	UK Box Office (GBP)	Australian Box Office (AUD)
1900s	Early nickelodeons, no consistent tracking	Small local theatres, minimal tracking	Early screenings, few cinemas, no tracking
1910s	**1915**: "The Birth of a Nation" grosses ~$10 million USD domestically	Dominated by Hollywood imports, local films struggling	Limited cinema growth, box office mostly untracked
1920s	**1927**: "The Jazz Singer" grosses ~$2.6 million USD	Limited box office tracking, dominated by Hollywood	Small market, few local productions making impact
1930s	**1939**: "Gone with the Wind" grosses ~$390 million (adjusted)	Limited UK cinema dominated by imports, small local impact	Small local films; **1935**: "Robbery Under Arms" performed modestly
1940s	**1946**: Highest cinema attendance year in US (~4 billion tickets sold)	**1946**: Highest cinema attendance year in UK (~1.6 billion tickets sold)	Small but growing market, local films beginning to develop

1950s	**1956**: "The Ten Commandments" grosses ~$122.7 million USD domestically	**1955**: "The Dam Busters" a major UK hit	Growing local production; **1955**: "Jedda" one of the early successes
1960s	**1965**: "The Sound of Music" grosses ~$286 million USD domestically	**1962**: "Dr. No" (James Bond) grosses ~£6 million GBP	Local production remains modest; **1969**: "They're a Weird Mob" grosses well
1970s	**1977**: "Star Wars" grosses ~$775 million USD globally	**1977**: "Star Wars" grosses ~£20 million GBP in the UK	**1979**: "Mad Max" grosses ~$100 million globally
1980s	**1982**: "E.T." grosses ~$435 million USD domestically	**1981**: "Chariots of Fire" grosses ~£19 million GBP	**1986**: "Crocodile Dundee" grosses ~$47 million AUD domestically
1990s	**1997**: "Titanic" grosses ~$600 million USD domestically	**1997**: "Titanic" grosses ~£80 million GBP	**1994**: "The Adventures of Priscilla, Queen of the Desert" grosses ~$16 million AUD
2000s	**2009**: "Avatar" grosses ~$760 million USD domestically	**2009**: "Avatar" grosses ~£94 million GBP	**2001**: "Moulin Rouge!" grosses ~$27 million AUD

2010s	**2019**: "Avengers: Endgame" grosses ~$858 million USD domestically	**2019**: "Avengers: Endgame" grosses ~£90 million GBP	**2015**: "Mad Max: Fury Road" grosses ~$21 million AUD domestically
2020s	**2022**: "Top Gun: Maverick" grosses ~$718 million USD domestically	**2022**: "Top Gun: Maverick" grosses ~£83 million GBP	**2022**: "Elvis" grosses ~$22 million AUD domestically

The box office trends in the US, UK, and Australia reflect the growth of cinema from small, early exhibitions to the global entertainment giants we see today. The US has consistently led in box office figures, but the UK and Australia have made significant contributions through major international hits, particularly with iconic franchises like *James Bond* and *Mad Max*. The 21st century has seen the dominance of franchises, blockbusters, and the rise of streaming as a new frontier for box office revenue.

CHAPTER 2

Influence on Current Working Conditions

The historical development of the film industry has shaped the working conditions faced by its professionals today. The studio system of early Hollywood, with its rigorous schedules and demanding expectations, established a culture of long hours and intense work environments. This culture, though evolved, persists in various forms, from the pressure to deliver blockbusters to the hectic schedules of film festivals and award seasons.

Understanding this history is crucial as we delve deeper into the realities of working in the film industry. It provides context for the challenges faced by those working behind the scenes and in front of the camera, setting the stage for discussions on the issues in the screen industry.

Financial Pressures and Budget Constraints:

Financial pressures play a significant role in shaping the working conditions in the film industry. Productions often operate under tight budgets, and any delays or unforeseen expenses can have a substantial impact on the bottom line. This financial constraint often leads to cost-cutting measures, such as reducing the length of the shooting schedule or minimising the number of crew members, which can increase the workload for those involved.

In many cases, the financial backers of a project—be they studios, investors, or distributors—place immense pressure on producers and directors to deliver the product on time and within budget. This pressure can trickle down to all levels of production, resulting in a work environment where long hours and intense work schedules are seen as necessary to meet financial goals.

Working Hours:

Historical Reasons for Long Hours

As previously discussed, the tradition of long working hours in the film industry dates back to its early days. The nature of film production often requires a significant amount of work to be completed within tight deadlines. From the silent film era to the golden age of Hollywood, studios were driven by a relentless schedule to produce content for an ever-growing audience. This pressure often resulted in extended working hours for everyone involved, from actors to crew members.

Early studio heads and producers often saw long hours as a necessary sacrifice for the sake of creative and commercial success. The belief that hard work and dedication were essential to achieving high-quality films became ingrained in the industry's culture. This mindset has been passed down through generations, becoming an unwritten rule that long hours are simply part of the job.

Average Working Hours in the Film Industry: 1950s to Today (USA, UK, and Australia)

1950s - 1970s

Country	Studio/Union Productions (1950s-1970s)	Independent Films (1950s-1970s)
USA	8-10 hours/day (unionised), 5-6 days/week	10-12+ hours/day, fewer regulations
UK	8-10 hours/day, 5 days/week	10-12 hours/day, with frequent overtime
Aus	8-10 hours/day (growing regulation)	10-12 hours/day, less structured

USA (1950s - 1970s):

Studio/Union Productions: By the 1950s, labour unions like IATSE in the USA regulated working hours for unionised productions, which typically involved 8-10 hour workdays. The typical workweek was 5-6 days.

Independent Films: For independent productions, working hours were generally much longer, with 10-12+ hour days being common due to lower budgets and less regulation. Freelancers had less protection, and longer hours were expected to save costs and meet tight schedules.

UK (1950s - 1970s):

Studio/Union Productions: In the UK, the major studios adhered to union rules that helped keep workdays around 8-10 hours. However, overtime was common when tight schedules needed to be met.

Independent Films: Independent films in the UK often operated on low budgets, leading to longer working hours for cast and crew. Independent filmmakers often worked 10-12 hours a day, sometimes more, to get the job done on time and within budget.

Australia (1950s - 1970s):

Studio/Union Productions: During this period, Australia's film industry was still developing. The industry was influenced by UK and US practices, with typical unionised working hours of around 8-10 hours per day.

Independent Films: Independent films in Australia typically saw long workdays, often reaching 10-12 hours, with fewer regulations to protect crew members. Independent films were largely passion projects with limited oversight, leading to longer hours.

1980s - 2000s

Country	Studio/Union Productions (1980s-2000s)	Independent Films (1980s-2000s)
USA	10-12 hours/day (unionised), 5-6 days/week	12-14+ hours/day, little regulation
UK	10-12 hours/day, 5-6 days/week	12-14+ hours/day, variable
Aus	10-12 hours/day (growing union presence)	12-14+ hours/day, variable

USA (1980s - 2000s):

Studio/Union Productions: Unionised crew members in major productions saw their hours rise to 10-12 hours/day as the industry ramped up the scale and ambition of filmmaking. However, overtime pay and safety regulations were in place.

Independent Films: Independent films continued to have less protection for workers, with 12-14+ hour days being typical. Indie filmmakers operated on tight budgets and pushed schedules to the maximum to save money.

UK (1980s - 2000s):

Studio/Union Productions: UK film industry unions such as BECTU set limits on working hours, but crew members often worked 10-12 hours per day on unionised sets.

Independent Films: In the UK, independent productions frequently required cast and crew to work longer hours, sometimes exceeding 12-14 hours per day due to limited budgets and tight deadlines.

Australia (1980s - 2000s):

Studio/Union Productions: By the 1980s, Australia's industry was growing, with unionised films requiring 10-12 hour workdays. Productions adhered more closely to labour laws as the Australian Film Commission grew in influence.

Independent Films: Independent productions in Australia continued to see long working hours, often reaching 12-14+ hours a day, similar to the US and UK independent sectors.

2010s – Present

Country	Studio/Union Productions (2010s-Today)	Independent Films (2010s-Today)
USA	10-14 hours/day (unionised), 5-6 days/week	14-16+ hours/day, some improvements
UK	10-12 hours/day, 5-6 days/week	12-14+ hours/day, some improvements
Aus	10-12 hours/day (unionised), 5 days/week	12-14+ hours/day, some improvements

USA (2010s - Present):

Studio/Union Productions: On major Hollywood productions, crew members typically work 10-14 hours a day. While unions such as IATSE regulate working conditions and overtime pay, the nature of the film industry continues to push long hours.

Independent Films: Independent productions continue to have longer workdays, often stretching to 14-16 hours. There is increasing awareness of the need for better work-life balance, but the lack of union oversight means conditions vary widely.

UK (2010s - Present):

Studio/Union Productions: In the UK, major film sets see 10-12 hour days. Unions like BECTU regulate working conditions, ensuring overtime pay and reasonable turnaround times between shifts.

Independent Films: Independent filmmakers in the UK still face long hours, sometimes exceeding 12-14 hours a day, but there has been growing attention to improving conditions, particularly for smaller productions.

Australia (2010s - Present):

Studio/Union Productions: Major productions in Australia follow regulated work hours, with crew members typically working 10-12 hour days, and overtime being compensated. Unions like the MEAA (Media, Entertainment & Arts Alliance) help ensure that working hours are fair.

Independent Films: Independent productions in Australia still tend to push longer hours, often 12-14+ hours per day. However, with growing awareness and labour rights, conditions are gradually improving.

Summary of Trends

Studio/Union Productions: Across all three countries (USA, UK, Australia), studio or unionised productions tend to follow regulated working hours, typically ranging from 10-12 hours/day, though the US sometimes pushes this to 14 hours or more. Unions play a key role in ensuring compensation for overtime and enforcing safety protocols, especially as productions become larger and more complex.

Independent Films: Independent productions in all three countries consistently have longer working hours due to budget constraints and lack of strict regulation. Crew members in indie films can often expect to work 12-16 hours a day. In recent years, there has been more awareness of the need for better conditions, but the disparity between indie and unionised studio films remains significant.

Despite these long hours, many indie filmmakers continue to work in challenging conditions due to the creative and collaborative nature of independent cinema. However, advocacy for better working conditions, particularly in independent filmmaking, is growing across the industry globally.

Factors Contributing to Increased Hours

Project Complexity: Modern film projects often involve more complex special effects, intricate set designs, and detailed scenes, which can require longer hours to complete. The increasing demand for high-quality visual and special effects, as well as the use of cutting-edge technology, often extends production timelines.

Budget and Scheduling Pressures: To meet tight deadlines and stay within budget constraints, production schedules have become more demanding. This pressure often pushes crew members to work longer hours to ensure that projects are completed on time and within financial limits. This is a well-documented issue within the industry and is highlighted by organisations such as **UNI Global Union.**

Technological Advances: While technological advancements have streamlined many aspects of production, they have also raised expectations for faster turnaround times and higher quality output. These heightened expectations can add pressure on crew members to work longer hours to meet the increasingly ambitious goals set by production teams. This paradox is often discussed in industry analyses.

The Impact of Long Working Hours on Workers

Health and Safety: Extended work hours in the film industry have been linked to increased incidents of fatigue-related accidents, both on set and during commutes. The physical and mental health of workers is significantly impacted, with higher rates of exhaustion and burnout reported. Fatigue is a major concern in any industry with long working hours, and the film industry is no exception, with fatigue contributing to accidents and health problems.

Work-Life Balance: The demanding schedules typical in the screen industry leave little room for personal time, which negatively affects family life and personal relationships. Many workers have reported that the long hours are detrimental to their social lives, family lives and overall well-being. This is a well-documented issue in discussions about industry working conditions, as noted by sources such as Film Stories and UNI Global Union.

CHAPTER 3

Countries with Better Conditions

The working conditions for film crews in European countries like Germany, Sweden, Denmark, France, Norway, and the Netherlands are generally considered favourable due to strong labour laws, union involvement, and cultural emphasis on work-life balance. These factors contribute to better working hours, flexibility on set, and support for families and carers. Here's a detailed look at how these countries operate.

Working Hours and Overtime: Across countries like Germany, Sweden, Denmark, France, Norway, and the Netherlands, labour laws ensure structured working hours, though the film industry often demands longer hours during production periods. In most of these countries, the standard workweek ranges from 35 to 48 hours, with Denmark at 37 hours and Sweden at 40. While extended hours are common during shoots, strict regulations govern overtime pay and ensure adequate rest periods between shifts. For instance, Germany mandates 11 hours of rest between shifts, and all countries require mandatory meal and rest breaks. Overtime is consistently compensated at higher rates across these territories, which helps manage worker fatigue and ensures safety on set.

I might just add that what I found to be very interesting is that even though their meal and rest breaks are not that different, their guidelines are generally stricter adhered to than in the US, UK and Australia and crew really do have proper breaks instead of working breaks and do demand their space during those times.

Flexibility on Set: Flexibility is a key feature in film production across these countries, although it's implemented differently based on cultural norms. Scandinavian countries like Sweden, Denmark, and Norway emphasise work-life balance and mutual respect between employers and employees. As a result, film sets are often flexible, accommodating personal needs and unforeseen circumstances. Similarly, in Germany, productions are well-organised and efficient, incorporating flexibility into shooting schedules while adhering to labour laws. In France and the Netherlands, while professionalism and adherence to schedules are valued, there is room for adjustment when personal situations arise, reflecting a culture of collaboration and respect for work-life balance.

Support for Families and Carers: One of the standout features of these countries is their robust family support systems, which extend to the film industry. Generous parental leave, subsidised childcare, and benefits for caregivers are common across all these regions. Sweden leads the way with up to 480 days of parental leave, while Denmark offers up to 52 weeks, and Norway provides 49 weeks at full pay or 59 weeks at 80% pay. These family-friendly policies are reflected on film sets, where flexible working arrangements are often available, such as adjusted schedules, part-time work, or even on-set childcare in some productions. This level of support allows film crew members to balance intense production schedules with family obligations, contributing to a healthier work environment.

Strong Union Presence and Collective Bargaining

Active Unions: Unions play a significant role in advocating for workers' rights in these countries. Film industry unions like Ver.di in Germany, BECTU in the UK, Teaterförbundet in Sweden, and others are well-organised and influential. They negotiate collective bargaining agreements that include provisions for working hours, safety standards, health benefits, and family leave.

Industry Standards: Unions help set industry-wide standards that ensure consistent working conditions across different productions. They provide a platform for workers to voice concerns and collectively negotiate better terms, leading to improved conditions over time.

Enforcement and Advocacy: Unions actively monitor compliance with labour laws and agreements. They advocate for changes when necessary and support workers in disputes with employers, providing a strong layer of protection against exploitation.

Cultural Emphasis on Work-Life Balance and Well-Being

Cultural Norms: In many of these countries, there is a strong cultural emphasis on work-life balance, quality of life, and well-being. This cultural attitude permeates the workplace, including the film industry, leading to practices that prioritise reasonable working hours, adequate rest, and respect for personal and family time.

Social Expectations: Societal expectations around health, safety, and family responsibilities influence workplace practices. Employers are often expected to provide a supportive work environment, which includes considerations for employees' personal lives and mental health.

Well-Being Initiatives: There is an increasing awareness of mental health and well-being in the workplace. Productions may include wellness programs, mental health support, and stress management initiatives to support crew members.

Government Support and Social Welfare Systems

Social Safety Nets: These countries have strong social welfare systems that provide comprehensive support for workers, including unemployment benefits, healthcare, and pensions. This safety net reduces financial pressure on workers and allows them to prioritise health and well-being.

Family Support Policies: Generous parental leave, subsidised childcare, and support for carers are standard in these countries. These benefits make it easier for film crew members to balance work and family responsibilities. Government policies actively support these provisions, creating a supportive environment for working parents and carers.

Funding and Incentives: Government funding for the film industry often comes with conditions that ensure fair working conditions. Film funds and incentives, such as those provided by the German Federal Film Fund (DFFF) and the Swedish Film Institute, may require compliance with labour standards, contributing to improved conditions on set.

Economic Models and Industry Funding

Public Funding and Subsidies: Many European countries provide substantial public funding for film production, which helps stabilise the industry and ensures that working conditions are maintained. Publicly funded films are often required to adhere to strict labour regulations, which improves overall conditions for cast and crew.

Sustainable Production Models: The emphasis on quality and sustainability over quantity helps ensure that productions are planned and executed within reasonable timeframes, reducing the pressure on cast and crew to work excessive hours. This approach fosters a more balanced and humane working environment.

High Levels of Education and Training

Skilled Workforce: These countries have well-established education and training programs for film and media professionals, which lead to a highly skilled workforce. Skilled workers are better able to negotiate fair working conditions and are often more aware of their rights, contributing to a culture of respect and professionalism in the industry.

Professional Standards: Education and training programs emphasise professional standards, including the importance of safe working conditions and ethical practices. This awareness is carried into the industry, promoting better working environments.

In conclusion, the favourable working conditions for film crews in countries like Germany, Sweden, Denmark, France, Norway, and the Netherlands result from a combination of strong legal frameworks, active union involvement, cultural values that emphasise well-being and work-life balance, comprehensive social support systems, and sustainable economic models. These factors create an environment where workers' rights are respected, safety and well-being are prioritised, and family responsibilities are supported, leading to better working conditions and overall quality of life for those in the film industry.

Here is a quick side-by-side comparison of a few contributing factors:

Country	Average Work Hours	Rates of Pay	Unemployment Rate in Film Industry	Mental Health Support	Employee Benefits
Germany	10-12 hours/day	Moderate to high; varies by role and project, approx. €15-€30/hour for crew	Low to moderate	Strong support, including counselling services	Generous parental leave, health insurance, retirement plans
Sweden	8-10 hours/day	Moderate; approx. SEK 150-250/hour for crew	Low	Excellent support, government-funded mental health programs	Generous parental leave, subsidised childcare, health benefits
Denmark	8-10 hours/day	Moderate; approx. DKK 150-300/hour for crew	Low	Good support, access to mental health resources	Comprehensive parental leave, healthcare, and family support

France	10-12 hours/day	Moderate; approx. €15-€25/hour for crew	Moderate	Strong support through national health services	Generous family leave, health insurance, retirement plans
Norway	8-10 hours/day	High; approx. NOK 200-350/hour for crew	Low	Excellent mental health support programs	Extensive parental leave, high-quality healthcare, retirement plans
Netherlands	8-10 hours/day	Moderate; approx. €15-€25/hour for crew	Low to moderate	Strong mental health awareness and support services	Good family support, health insurance, retirement benefits
USA	12-14 hours/day	High; approx. $25-$50/hour for union crew members	Moderate to high	Growing awareness, union-negotiated mental health programs	Health insurance often through unions, variable parental leave

UK	10-12 hours/day	Moderate to high; approx. £12-£25/hour for crew	Moderate	Increasing support, industry organisations offer mental health resources	National health service access, limited paid family leave
Australia	10-12 hours/day	Moderate to high; approx. AUD 25-50/hour for crew	Low	Growing mental health support initiatives	Medicare coverage, parental leave, and other employee benefits

CHAPTER 4

Independent Productions

Working conditions, benefits, and adherence to regulations can vary significantly between large, unionised productions and smaller, independent film projects. While strong labour laws, union involvement, and cultural attitudes towards work-life balance create a foundation for good working conditions, the reality for independent crew members can be quite different, even in countries with robust protections.

Challenges Faced by Independent Film Crews

Lack of Union Protection: Independent productions often operate outside the framework of union regulations, which means crew members may not benefit from the same protections regarding working hours, overtime pay, health benefits, and safety standards. Without union representation, these workers might lack the bargaining power to negotiate fair conditions.

Budget Constraints: Independent films typically have smaller budgets, which can lead to cost-cutting measures that impact crew working conditions. This often results in longer working hours, fewer breaks, and limited compensation for overtime. Small productions may not be able to afford the same benefits and may not strictly adhere to labour laws, especially if enforcement is weak.

Variable Enforcement: Even in countries with strong labour laws, enforcement can vary, especially in the independent film sector. Regulatory bodies might not have the resources to monitor every production, allowing some independent filmmakers to bypass standard practices. Crew members may feel pressured to accept poor conditions due to the competitive nature of the industry and the desire to gain experience or complete projects.

Freelance Nature of Work: Film crew members often work as freelancers, which can limit their access to benefits such as healthcare, retirement plans, and parental leave. In independent productions, crew members might work on a project-by-project basis, making it difficult to qualify for or maintain consistent access to benefits that are more readily available in permanent or long-term employment.

The Reality of Independent Productions

Scale of Production: As we have seen, smaller productions often face different economic realities, which impact their ability to follow industry standards strictly. While laws and union guidelines provide a framework, not all productions can or do comply, especially when operating on tight budgets and schedules.

Industry Experience: Newer or less experienced crew members might accept lower standards of working conditions in exchange for experience, networking opportunities, or credits. This can perpetuate a cycle where poor working conditions become normalised in the independent sector.

Informal Agreements: In independent filmmaking, informal arrangements are common. Crew members might agree to work under conditions that are less than ideal, either due to personal relationships with filmmakers or a passion for the project.

In conclusion, while strong labour laws, union guidelines, and cultural attitudes provide a foundation for good working conditions, the reality for independent film crews can be quite different. In countries like the US, UK, and Australia, the guidelines exist but are not always followed, especially in independent productions. This discrepancy also exists, albeit to a lesser extent, in European countries known for better working conditions. Understanding these dynamics is crucial for acknowledging the challenges faced by independent film crews and for advocating for improved standards across all types of productions.

Differences in Independent Productions Across Countries

USA: In the United States, independent productions frequently operate without union agreements, especially if budgets are below certain thresholds. While guidelines exist, they are not always followed, leading to long hours and fewer protections for crew members. Unionised crew often have better conditions, but independent crews may experience inconsistent adherence to safety, overtime pay, and benefits.

UK: Similar to the US, the UK has strong union protections through organisations like BECTU. However, independent productions may not always comply with these standards. Crew members on indie projects might face longer hours and fewer benefits due to budget constraints and the lack of strict enforcement. Freelancers in the UK film industry might not receive the same level of support as those working on union-regulated projects.

Australia: Australia has solid labour laws and union protections, but independent productions can still see varying levels of adherence. The Media, Entertainment & Arts Alliance (MEAA) offers guidance, but smaller productions may not always follow these guidelines due to budgetary or logistical challenges. As in other countries, crew members may face longer hours and less access to benefits when working on independent projects.

European Countries (Germany, Sweden, Denmark, France, Norway, Netherlands): While these countries generally offer better overall working conditions, independent productions may still operate outside the full scope of regulations. However, the strong cultural emphasis on work-life balance and well-being can mean that even independent productions strive to maintain reasonable conditions. Enforcement may be more consistent, and there is often a higher baseline of respect for labour laws. Nevertheless, independent crew members might not have access to the same benefits as those working on larger, government-funded projects or those with strong union involvement.

Here's a comparative table of **current working hours** (over the past 20 years) for film crew members in both **studio/union productions** and **independent productions** across various countries, including the **UK**,

USA, **Australia**, and key European countries such as **Germany**, **Sweden**, **Denmark**, **France**, **Norway**, and the **Netherlands**.

Current Working Hours (Past 20 Years)

Country	Studio/Union Productions (Avg Hours/Day)	Independent Productions (Avg Hours/Day)
USA	10-14 hours/day, 5-6 days/week	14-16 hours/day, 6-7 days/week
UK	10-12 hours/day, 5-6 days/week	12-14+ hours/day, 6-7 days/week
Australia	10-12 hours/day, 5-6 days/week	12-14+ hours/day, 6-7 days/week
Germany	8-10 hours/day, 5-6 days/week	10-12+ hours/day, 5-6 days/week
Sweden	8-10 hours/day, 5 days/week	10-12+ hours/day, 5-6 days/week
Denmark	8-10 hours/day, 5-6 days/week	10-12+ hours/day, 5-6 days/week
France	8-10 hours/day, 5-6 days/week	10-12+ hours/day, 5-6 days/week
Norway	8-10 hours/day, 5-6 days/week	10-12+ hours/day, 5-6 days/week
Netherlands	8-10 hours/day, 5-6 days/week	10-12+ hours/day, 5-6 days/week

CHAPTER 5

The Reality of Working in Screen

The allure of the screen industry often conjures images of glamorous premieres, red carpets, and celebrities basking in the limelight. However, as we have seen in the chapters above, it is far from it. This chapter explores the typical working conditions on film sets, the impact on those involved, and the unique challenges faced by various roles.

Typical Working Conditions

Apart from the long hours, burnout and lack of work-life balance the screen industry offers, on-set environments can also be physically demanding. Whether it's setting up complex scenes, managing heavy equipment, or performing physically challenging roles, the work can be strenuous. The need to capture the perfect shot can mean repetitive tasks and prolonged exposure to the elements, whether it's filming in extreme heat, cold, or unpredictable weather conditions. And for those involved from development through post-production, the long hours and burnout extend far beyond just the production phase.

Case Studies and Personal Accounts

To illustrate these realities, consider the experiences of various industry professionals. For example, a gaffer might describe the exhaustion of setting up lighting for long hours, often under tight deadlines. Similarly, a production assistant might recount the pressures of managing logistics and running errands, all while trying to anticipate the needs of the cast and crew.

Actors, too, face unique challenges. They might be required to perform intense scenes repeatedly or spend hours in makeup and costume. The psychological toll of embodying different characters, especially in emotionally demanding roles, can be significant.

Moreover, the instability of freelance work in the industry adds to the stress, with many professionals constantly seeking their next job.

Let's have a look at what some of the industry greats and crew have to say about their experiences:

Ava DuVernay, Director and Producer: *"The long hours on set can be grueling, and it's easy to lose sight of your personal life. I've had to make a conscious effort to set boundaries and make time for myself and my family."* (Source: Interview with The Hollywood Reporter, January 2020).

Christopher Nolan, Director and Screenwriter: *"Working in the film industry often means sacrificing personal time. There are days when you hardly see your family, and that can be incredibly tough."* (Source: The Guardian, March 2018).

Viola Davis, Actress and Producer: *"The hours are insane. There have been times when I've had to choose between a family event and a late-night shoot. It's a constant struggle to balance both worlds."* (Source: Variety, November 2019).

Kathryn Bigelow, Director and Producer: *"I remember the first time I missed a significant family event because of a shoot. It was heartbreaking, and it made me realise how much this career demands from your personal life."* (Source: Vanity Fair, July 2017).

Guillermo del Toro, Director and Producer: *"The film industry is relentless. The long hours and intense schedules can leave you feeling disconnected from your loved ones. It's important to find a balance, but it's not always easy."* (Source: Empire Magazine, October 2018).

Reese Witherspoon, Actress and Producer: *"Balancing a film career and personal life is challenging. There are days when I'm on set for 14 hours,* and it's hard not to feel guilty about missing time with my children." (Source: People Magazine, February 2019).

Steven Spielberg, Director and Producer: "I've missed countless family dinners and special moments due to the demanding nature of this industry. It takes a toll on your personal relationships." (Source: TIME Magazine, December 2017).

Mindy Kaling, Actress and Producer: "Filmmaking is a passion, but it often comes at the expense of your personal life. The long hours can be draining, and finding time for yourself becomes a luxury." (Source: The New York Times, August 2018).

Zoe Saldana, Actress: "There are times when I'm away from home for weeks, and it's hard to stay connected with my family. The long hours make it difficult to maintain a work-life balance." (Source: Entertainment Weekly, April 2019).

Ryan Coogler, Director and Screenwriter: "The long hours and intense pressure of the film industry can be overwhelming. It's important to take breaks and prioritise personal time to avoid burnout." (Source: Rolling Stone, June 2018).

Alex Russell, Sound Recordist: I've been working as a sound engineer for nine years, and while I love the job, the reality is exhausting. The hours are long, often 12 or more each day, and the work is unpredictable. I'm often moving from one production to the next without much of a break in between. The uncertainty of the gig economy means I never know when the next job will come, so I feel compelled to take every offer, even when I'm completely worn out.

Then there are times when I didn't have work for months, and the stress and anxiety during those periods can be overwhelming. I'm either overworked or I'm anxious about where the next paycheck is coming from, and that's been the pattern for years. The lack of stability makes it difficult to find any real balance in my life.

It's also taken a toll on my personal life, especially relationships. I've found it hard to maintain anything long-term because I'm either too busy to commit time to someone or too anxious when I'm not working. As a result, most of my relationships have been short-lived.

This is the reality of working in the gig economy, especially in the film industry. It's hard to feel secure or settled, but despite all the challenges, I'm still passionate about what I do. The passion keeps me going, even when the rest of my life feels unstable.

Unique Challenges Faced by Different Roles

Different roles in the industry come with their own set of challenges. Apart from the long hours and crazy schedules, for instance, crew members such as camera operators, sound technicians, and grips often have to work with heavy and intricate equipment. Their roles are physically taxing and require precision and focus, which can be difficult to maintain over long periods.

Directors are among the hardest-working roles on set, with typical working hours ranging from 16-18 hours per day, especially during the intense periods of pre-production, principal photography, and post-production. Their role involves overseeing all creative aspects of the film, requiring a significant time commitment.

Producers often work extensive hours throughout the entire lifecycle of a film, from development to release. Working 16-18 hours per day is common, especially during critical phases such as principal photography and post-production. Their role involves constant coordination, problem-solving, and decision-making, leading large teams to highly irregular and demanding schedules. Being a producer generally also involves working without a fee, often for years, to develop and get a project off the ground, and producers often have to sacrifice their fees, invest in their films, or reinvest their fees to fill finance gaps. And keeping in mind that there is hardly ever a backend profit for independent producers.

Actors face the dual pressures of performance and public scrutiny. The demands of maintaining a certain image, coupled with the uncertainties of the industry, can be overwhelming. Moreover, the nature of their work often requires them to be away from home for extended periods, which can strain personal relationships and family life. Their work includes not just time on set, but also preparation, makeup, rehearsals, and downtime between scenes.

Impact on Health and Well-being

The demanding nature of the job can have serious implications for both physical and mental well-being, leading to chronic fatigue, musculoskeletal issues, and mental health concerns like stress, anxiety, and burnout. Additionally, the unpredictable schedules in the industry can disrupt sleep patterns and create further lifestyle challenges. Understanding these harsh realities is key to addressing the widespread work-life balance issues that plague the industry. Let's discuss this more in the next chapter.

CHAPTER 6

The Impact on Physical & Mental Health

The film industry presents a variety of physical health concerns due to the demanding nature of the work, long hours, and often unpredictable conditions on set. While mental health issues like stress and burnout are well-documented, physical health risks can also significantly affect industry professionals. Below are some of the primary physical health concerns, risks, and relevant statistics in the film industry:

Physical Health Issues

Musculoskeletal Issues

Many jobs in the film industry involve repetitive physical tasks, heavy lifting, or prolonged standing. This is especially true for crew members like camera operators, grips, lighting technicians, and sound mixers. Repeated strain on the body, coupled with long hours without adequate rest, can lead to chronic conditions such as:

- Back pain
- Neck and shoulder injuries
- Repetitive strain injuries (RSIs)

These issues are exacerbated by the fact that film sets often require workers to move and carry heavy equipment, sometimes in awkward positions or under tight time constraints. For instance, camera operators may spend hours holding heavy equipment or maintaining uncomfortable postures to get the right shot. Inadequate ergonomic setups and irregular breaks further contribute to musculoskeletal disorders.

Sleep Deprivation and Fatigue

Sleep deprivation is a widespread issue in the film industry due to extended working hours, irregular shifts, and nighttime shoots. The lack of consistent sleep can lead to both short-term and long-term health issues, such as:

- Chronic fatigue
- Impaired cognitive function
- Increased risk of cardiovascular disease

Sleep deprivation not only affects personal health but also increases the risk of accidents on set. Studies show that sleep-deprived workers are significantly more prone to making mistakes or having accidents, which can be dangerous on fast-moving and sometimes hazardous film sets.

Injury Risks on Set

Working on film sets often comes with physical risks. Large equipment, complex stunts, and rapidly changing environments can create hazardous conditions. Workplace injury rates in the film industry are notably higher than in other industries. Some of the common risks include:

- Falls from heights (especially for grips, electricians, and set builders)
- Injuries from moving heavy equipment

- Accidents involving special effects or stunts

According to a report by the U.S. Bureau of Labor Statistics, film and TV production has an injury rate of 1.5 per 100 full-time workers, higher than the national average across all industries. Stunt performers are especially at risk, with serious accidents sometimes leading to hospitalisations or worse. While safety regulations have improved, the rush to stay on schedule can sometimes lead to corners being cut in terms of safety protocols.

Exposure to Hazardous Conditions

Film industry professionals, particularly those working in special effects, makeup, and production design, can be exposed to hazardous materials or environments. Common exposures include:

- Toxic chemicals (used in special effects, makeup, and props)
- Fumes from pyrotechnics
- Dust and mould on sets

While protective gear and ventilation systems are often used, consistent exposure over time can lead to respiratory issues, skin irritation, or long-term health problems. In a survey of film industry workers, over 40% reported exposure to potentially harmful substances during the course of their work.

Cardiovascular Health

The combination of high stress, long working hours, and poor lifestyle habits (such as irregular eating schedules or reliance on fast food) can contribute to cardiovascular issues among film professionals. The long hours and physical strain can lead to:

- Increased blood pressure
- Higher risk of heart disease
- Obesity due to lack of physical activity or unhealthy eating habits

According to a study published by the Journal of Occupational Health, film industry workers are at a higher risk of developing cardiovascular diseases compared to those in less demanding professions, largely due to lifestyle and work-related stress.

Heat-Related Illnesses

Outdoor film shoots, especially in extreme weather conditions, pose risks of heat exhaustion or heatstroke, particularly for crew members who work long hours in full sun or with limited hydration. Locations in hot climates or confined spaces with poor ventilation can increase these risks. According to a report from OSHA, heat stress is a serious issue on sets, with over 20% of outdoor set injuries linked to heat-related causes.

Nutrition and Eating Habits

The irregular and long working hours of the film industry often result in unhealthy eating habits. Catering on film sets sometimes offers convenience foods that are high in calories but low in nutritional value, especially on lower budget independent productions. I have recently heard of the 'wheels of death' served on sets – this of course is pizza. In addition, time constraints often mean that workers skip meals or eat on the go, which can contribute to:

- Weight gain
- Nutrient deficiencies
- Digestive issues

Poor nutrition can further exacerbate stress, fatigue, and other health problems, making it harder for film workers to maintain their physical and mental well-being.

Substance Abuse

Due to the stressful nature of the industry, there has historically been a higher risk of substance abuse among film professionals. Workers may turn to alcohol or drugs to cope with stress, long hours, or the emotional toll of their work. A report by the National Institute on Drug Abuse found that industries with high stress and irregular hours, such as entertainment, are more prone to substance misuse. This can further deteriorate physical health and safety on set, increasing the risk of accidents and long-term health problems.

In conclusion, the physical health risks in the film industry are pervasive, and the nature of the work amplifies the potential for injury and long-term health issues. From musculoskeletal disorders to cardiovascular problems, the physical demands of filmmaking can take a toll on professionals at every level. While improvements have been made in workplace safety, more attention is needed to protect the health and well-being of those who work behind the scenes. Addressing these risks with better support systems, safety protocols, and promoting healthier working conditions will be crucial in reducing the physical health challenges that many in the industry face.

Mental Health Problems

As we have discussed, the film industry is notorious for its high-pressure environment, long hours, intense competition, and a yet long list of unexplored challenges, all of which contribute to a range of mental health challenges for its professionals. Mental health issues are pervasive in the industry, yet they are often overlooked or stigmatised, creating a culture where workers are expected to endure stress and burnout as part of their craft. Below are some of the primary mental health concerns, risks, and statistics related to the film industry.

Prevalence of Anxiety and Depression: A significant portion of employees in the screen industry report experiencing moderate to high levels of stress, often attributed to heavy workloads and demanding schedules. Some reports indicate that up to 77% of industry workers face such challenges.

Impact on Younger Workers: Younger employees, particularly those aged 18-29, are more likely to report mental health issues. Around 34% of this age group have considered quitting their jobs due to the impact of work on their mental health.

Gender Differences: Women in the film industry are more likely than men to experience mental health challenges, such as anxiety and depression.

Mental Health Services Utilisation: Despite the high levels of stress and mental health issues, many employees do not utilise available mental health services. Only a small percentage of employees feel comfortable using their company's mental health resources, with significant barriers such as stigma, concerns about confidentiality, and lack of awareness contributing to underutilisation.

The Culture of Overwork and Burnout

Burnout is a significant issue in the film industry, with many workers experiencing high levels of stress and exhaustion. This is due to the demanding nature of the work, long hours, and high-pressure environments. Compared to many other industries, burnout rates are notably higher in film. The culture of overwork is deeply embedded, driven by the concept of "paying your dues," where both newcomers and seasoned professionals are expected to work long hours to prove their dedication and passion. This mindset is reinforced by the competitive nature of the industry, where the fear of missing out on future opportunities often pushes individuals to work beyond reasonable limits.

The collaborative nature of filmmaking also plays a role. Since the work of one department impacts others, any delays or issues in one area can create a domino effect, leading to extended hours for multiple teams. The unpredictability of creative work, with frequent changes and adjustments, further adds to the pressure. In fact, recent surveys indicate that around 60% of film industry workers believe that working long hours is essential for career advancement. This perception, combined with the demands of production schedules, makes burnout a widespread issue that requires serious attention within the industry (Future of Jobs Report 2023, Pew Research Centre, ADP Research Institute).

Age: Younger workers, particularly those in the 18-24 age group, are among the most affected by burnout. Studies indicate that this age group, along with Millennials and Gen Z, reports high levels of burnout, with some sources suggesting rates as high as 85% among the youngest workers.

The reason why this age group tends to experience higher rates of burnout are for several reasons. Many of them are just starting their careers and often face intense pressure to prove themselves in a competitive industry like film. This age group is also more likely to work in lower-paying, entry-level jobs with long hours and less job security, adding to the stress. Additionally, the rise of the gig economy and freelance culture in the film industry means that younger workers may have less stability and fewer boundaries between work and personal life, making it harder to maintain a healthy work-life balance. Social media and the constant connectivity of the digital age can further contribute to burnout by blurring the lines between work and rest, leaving them feeling like they're always "on."

Gender: Women in the film industry are more likely to experience burnout compared to men.

Women in the film industry are more likely to experience burnout than men due to a combination of factors that are both industry-specific and reflective of broader societal trends. In the film industry, women often face additional pressures, including gender bias, limited representation in leadership roles, and the challenge of breaking through in male-dominated spaces. This can lead to a sense of needing to constantly prove themselves or work harder to gain recognition and opportunities.

On top of that, women are more likely to juggle multiple roles outside of work, including caregiving responsibilities, which can make it harder to achieve a sustainable work-life balance. The lack of flexible working arrangements in the film industry, particularly for those with family obligations, can further intensify stress. Studies also suggest that women are more prone to experiencing emotional exhaustion because they often take on more of the emotional labour in both their professional and personal lives, contributing to higher levels of burnout.

Anxiety

Anxiety in the film industry is a widespread issue across the globe, with professionals in the US, UK, and Australia experiencing significantly higher levels of anxiety compared to other sectors. While anxiety exists in nearly all professions, it is particularly pronounced in the film industry, where the fast-paced, high-pressure environment exacerbates the problem.

United States: In the US, anxiety is especially prevalent within the film and television industry. According to a report by the University of Southern California, up to 64% of US film and TV workers report experiencing regular anxiety, which is well above the national average for other industries, which tends to be around 40%. The American Psychological Association has also noted that anxiety disorders are disproportionately higher in creative industries, including film. Many US professionals report frequent feelings of unease, often leading to symptoms like panic attacks and chronic stress.

United Kingdom: In the UK, the situation is similarly troubling. The British Film Institute (BFI) conducted a comprehensive survey, which revealed over 60% of UK film industry workers experience ongoing anxiety, which is significantly higher than the UK's national average of 30-35%. The study also highlighted how anxiety affects both on-set and off-set lives, as workers find it difficult to separate the intense pressures of their jobs from their personal lives.

Australia: In Australia, a study by Entertainment Assist and Victoria University found that mental health issues, particularly anxiety, are alarmingly prevalent in the entertainment industry, with film workers being among the most affected. Their research showed that 70% of Australian screen industry professionals experience anxiety at rates far higher than the national average of 20% for other sectors. Many Australian professionals cite the unpredictable nature of the industry and its impact on mental health, leaving them with little time to recover between projects.

Depression

Depression is another significant issue in the film industry, affecting professionals across all levels. In the US, UK, and Australia, depression rates among film workers are far higher than in many other industries, driven by the intense demands, job instability, and creative pressures that come with the territory. The prevalence of depression in the film industry is alarming and continues to be a growing concern.

United States: In the US, depression rates in the film and television industry are notably higher than the national average. According to a study by the American Psychological Association, nearly 50% of film industry professionals report experiencing symptoms of depression at some point in their careers, compared to 22% of the general US workforce. This stark difference highlights the significant mental health burden faced by those working in film. The high-pressure, project-based nature of the work, combined with long periods of unemployment between gigs, leaves many feeling isolated and emotionally drained.

United Kingdom: In the UK, the situation is equally troubling. A survey conducted by the British Film Institute (BFI) revealed that 57% of UK film industry workers experience symptoms of depression, more than double the national average of 17%. The BFI study also found that the constant pressure to secure work, combined with long and irregular hours, exacerbates feelings of hopelessness and emotional exhaustion in UK film professionals. Depression in the UK film industry is widespread, with workers often feeling that there are limited resources or support systems available to help them cope.

Australia: In Australia, a report by Entertainment Assist and Victoria University found that depression rates among screen industry professionals are alarmingly high. Their research showed that 44% of Australian film industry workers suffer from depression, compared to the national average of 15% for other sectors. This study emphasised the long-term effects of irregular work schedules and job insecurity, which leave many workers in a constant state of emotional fatigue. The Australian film industry, while vibrant, lacks adequate mental health support structures, leaving many individuals to manage depression on their own.

Imposter Syndrome and Performance Pressure

The film industry is highly competitive, and many professionals feel intense pressure to prove themselves. This pressure can contribute to imposter syndrome, where individuals doubt their abilities or feel undeserving of their success. Imposter syndrome is particularly common in creative fields, where the subjective nature of success makes it easy to feel like a fraud, even when achieving outward success.

The constant evaluation and scrutiny by peers, critics, and audiences can heighten feelings of inadequacy and contribute to anxiety and low self-esteem. Many workers internalise these feelings, which can lead to longer-term mental health struggles like depression and chronic stress.

Emotional Vulnerability

The creative aspects of the film industry can also contribute to mental health challenges. Writers, directors, actors, and other creatives often pour their emotions into their work, making themselves more vulnerable to criticism and rejection. This emotional investment, while essential for storytelling, can be mentally exhausting and leave professionals feeling emotionally drained.

The pressure to constantly deliver innovative and successful work can lead to emotional burnout, where the passion for the craft begins to fade. Over time, this can result in creative block, a phenomenon that contributes to feelings of inadequacy and anxiety, especially in a field where one's creativity is directly tied to their livelihood.

Positive Developments

While mental health challenges remain a significant concern, there have been positive developments in recent years. Some production companies are beginning to recognise the importance of addressing mental health issues and have implemented initiatives, which we will discuss later on.

In conclusion, mental health concerns in the film industry are widespread, driven by a combination of high-pressure work environments, long hours, job insecurity, and the emotional demands of the craft. Anxiety, burnout, depression, and substance abuse are common, yet support systems remain limited, particularly for freelance professionals. However, with increasing awareness and proactive measures from some companies, there is hope that the industry will continue to evolve toward better mental health practices. Prioritising mental health and fostering a culture of openness and support will be essential for ensuring the long-term well-being of film industry professionals.

CHAPTER 7

Substance Abuse

We've now explored the history of the screen industry, the realities of working in both studio and independent productions and how these factors impact both physical and mental health. We've discussed burnout, long working hours, and their toll on industry professionals. Now, let's delve into additional factors that contribute to the ongoing health and mental health challenges within the screen industry—issues that make it increasingly unsustainable for many who work in it.

Substance abuse in the film industry is a significant issue that has been present for decades, fueled by the high-pressure environment, long hours, and frequent social aspects of the job. Whether it's alcohol, prescription drugs, or recreational substances, the temptation to self-medicate is all too common in an industry known for its intensity. While the glamorous image of Hollywood or film premieres may dominate public perception, the behind-the-scenes reality often involves professionals struggling to cope with stress in unhealthy ways.

United States:

In the US, the film industry has a well-known history of substance abuse, and it's not just limited to actors or high-profile directors. Crew members, writers, and other professionals are equally affected. According to a report from the National Institute on Drug Abuse, the entertainment industry, including film, has higher rates of substance abuse compared to the national average. An estimated 10-12% of workers in the film industry struggle with some form of substance abuse, compared to 8% of the general US workforce.

Alcohol is one of the most common substances, often used as a way to cope with stress or unwind after long days on set. The fast-paced, project-based nature of the job also contributes to irregular routines, which can increase the reliance on alcohol or other substances as a form of relaxation. Prescription drug misuse, particularly stimulants like Adderall or anti-anxiety medications like Xanax, is also rising. These drugs are sometimes used to help workers keep up with demanding schedules or manage the anxiety that comes with unstable employment.

The US film industry's culture often normalises this behavior. Social events, after-parties, and networking gatherings frequently involve alcohol, and the lines between professional obligations and social drinking can blur easily. For many, what begins as casual drinking or stress relief can escalate into dependency.

United Kingdom:

The situation is similar in the UK, where substance abuse is also a significant issue within the film industry. A survey by the British Film Institute (BFI) found that over 50% of UK film industry professionals have used alcohol or drugs to cope with the pressures of their work. This is far higher than the national average of 26% of adults in the UK who report using alcohol or drugs as a coping mechanism for stress.

The BFI's research also highlighted that many film industry workers turn to substances to handle the unpredictable and often unstable nature of their careers. Long gaps between jobs, financial uncertainty, and irregular hours contribute to a culture of escapism through substance use. Cocaine use is particularly prevalent in some parts of the UK's film industry, as workers seek to stay alert and energised during long shoots.

The high-pressure, all-consuming nature of the industry in the UK has led to increased awareness of mental health and substance abuse issues in recent years, but many professionals still feel there is a lack of support when it comes to seeking help. The stigma around admitting to a substance abuse problem in such a competitive environment can prevent people from getting the assistance they need.

Australia:

In Australia, the problem of substance abuse in the film industry is equally concerning. A study by Entertainment Assist and Victoria University revealed that 29% of Australian entertainment industry workers, including those in film, have a substance abuse problem. This is significantly higher than the general workforce, where around 13% report similar struggles.

The Australian film industry, like its counterparts in the US and UK, is highly competitive and often involves long hours, irregular work schedules, and high levels of stress. These factors make professionals more susceptible to turning to drugs or alcohol as a way to cope. The research also found that substance abuse is closely linked to mental health struggles, with many workers using substances to manage anxiety, depression, or burnout.

Interestingly, the study also highlighted the social aspect of substance use in Australia's film industry. Alcohol is frequently present at industry events, on set, or even during after-hours bonding sessions. While this can create a sense of camaraderie, it also normalises drinking and drug use as a way to manage the stresses of the job.

Common Themes Across All Three Countries:

Across the US, UK, and Australia, one of the main drivers of substance abuse in the film industry is the lack of stability and support. The transient nature of film work means professionals often feel disconnected or isolated, which can lead to self-medicating with drugs or alcohol. The industry's emphasis on networking and socialising frequently involves alcohol, further blurring the lines between casual use and problematic behaviour.

Moreover, the culture of overwork and perfectionism in the film industry often leaves little room for addressing mental health concerns openly. Many feel that admitting to a substance abuse problem could harm their reputation or future career prospects. As a result, the stigma surrounding addiction in the film industry remains strong, making it difficult for professionals to seek help.

Solutions and Initiatives:

While the issue of substance abuse in the film industry is significant, there are efforts to address it. In the US, organisations like Entertainment Industry Foundation and MusiCares offer mental health and substance abuse support for entertainment workers, including those in film. Similarly, the BFI in the UK has launched initiatives to provide mental health resources and raise awareness about the dangers of substance abuse.

In Australia, Entertainment Assist provides similar services, offering support and guidance for those struggling with substance use. However, despite these initiatives, there is still much work to be done to reduce the stigma and make it easier for industry professionals to access help without fear of judgment or career repercussions.

In conclusion, substance abuse in the film industry is a widespread and growing concern, affecting professionals in the US, UK, and Australia at significantly higher rates than the general population. While some progress has been made in addressing the issue, the film industry's high-pressure environment, coupled with a culture of overwork and social drinking, continues to fuel the problem. Increasing awareness, reducing stigma, and offering better access to mental health and addiction support are essential steps toward improving the well-being of those working in this demanding field.

CHAPTER 8

Work-Life Balance

Work-life balance in the film industry has long been a complex and challenging issue for professionals at all levels. Whether it's actors, crew members, or directors, the intense demands of the job make it incredibly difficult to maintain a healthy balance between work and personal life. The industry's long hours, project-based nature, and high-pressure environment create unique challenges that often leave little room for rest, family time, or personal well-being.

Filmmaking schedules make it incredibly hard for professionals to find time for their personal lives, including family commitments, social activities, or even basic self-care.

Adding to this challenge is the project-based, gig economy structure of the industry. Many film professionals work on short-term contracts, jumping from one project to the next with little downtime in between. While this may seem like an opportunity to recharge, the reality is often filled with anxiety about when or if the next job will come. This instability can blur the lines between work and personal time, as workers feel constant pressure to stay connected and hustle for their next opportunity. The lack of consistent income and job security only exacerbates this issue, making it difficult for many professionals to switch off and truly enjoy their personal time.

Just to repeat what I previously said, the culture within the film industry often glorifies overwork. The idea of "paying your dues" is deeply embedded, with long hours and non-stop commitment seen as necessary to succeed. For many, the fear of losing out on future work or being seen as less dedicated keeps them pushing past reasonable limits. This mentality contributes significantly to poor work-life balance, as professionals feel compelled to sacrifice their well-being to prove their worth.

Despite these challenges, there are some efforts within the industry to improve work-life balance. Movements advocating for shorter hours, better conditions, and more support for mental health are gaining traction, with some production companies implementing family-friendly policies like flexible schedules or on-set childcare. However, these changes are still the exception rather than the rule, and much of the industry continues to operate in a way that prioritises productivity over personal well-being.

Ultimately, work-life balance remains a significant challenge for those in the film industry. While there is growing awareness around the issue, more systemic changes are needed to truly address the problem. This could include stronger labour protections, more consistent mental health support, and a cultural shift that values both the creative process and the well-being of those behind it. For many, finding a sustainable balance in the film industry is still a work in progress, but the hope is that awareness and advocacy will lead to meaningful improvements in the future.

In future chapters, we will talk about how the issue of work-life-balance can be addressed and improved.

See Worksheet: Evaluating Personal Work-Life Balance

See Survey: Work-Life Balance Survey for Film Industry Professionals

CHAPTER 9

Parenthood & Caring

Parenthood is challenging in any profession, but the film industry's demanding schedules and unpredictable nature add unique hurdles for parents. This chapter explores the impact of these challenges on parents in the film industry, and how these pressures can affect both professional and family life.

78% of parent carers in the Western Film Industry are women and 21% are men.

63% of Film Industry Workers work freelance, are self-employed and are financially insecure.

Impact of Schedules on Parenting

One of the most significant challenges for parents in the film industry is the erratic and often gruelling schedules, long hours that sometimes extend well beyond a standard workday, and can include weekends and nights. This unpredictability makes it difficult for parents to establish and maintain a consistent routine, which is crucial for managing family life.

For example, shooting schedules can change with little notice, requiring parents to scramble for childcare or adjust plans. The necessity to travel for location shoots can also be disruptive, often requiring parents to be away from home for extended periods. This can strain relationships with children and other family members, leading to feelings of guilt and anxiety.

Percentage of Parents Missing Significant Family Events Due to Work Schedules

United States: Around 38% of working parents in the U.S. film industry report missing significant family events, such as birthdays or school plays, due to demanding work schedules.

United Kingdom: In the UK, approximately 79% of parents in the film industry state that their caregiving roles negatively impact their professional lives, including missing significant family events.

Australia: For Australia, about 74% of parents in the film industry report lacking adequate support for childcare, leading to missed significant family events due to long and unpredictable work hours.

These statistics highlight the significant impact of demanding work schedules on family life for parents in the film industry across the U.S., UK, and Australia.

Challenges for Single Parents

The challenges are even more pronounced for single parents, who often lack the support network that can help manage these disruptions. Single parents in the film industry must juggle their professional responsibilities with their roles as primary caregivers, often without the benefit of a partner to share the load. This dual burden can be overwhelming and lead to burnout.

Without sufficient support, single parents may face tough choices, such as whether to take on certain projects that require long hours or travel. These decisions can impact their careers, as turning down work can lead to fewer opportunities in a highly competitive industry. The financial pressures of raising a family on a single income also add to the stress.

In the US, UK, and Australia, the attrition rates among single parents in the film industry are notably high, ranging between 45% and 50%. These high turnover rates are driven by demanding and unpredictable work schedules, lack of adequate support for balancing work and family life, and the financial instability associated with freelance or project-based work. (McKinsey & Company, Screen Daily)

Lack of Support and Resources

The film industry has been slow to adapt to the needs of working parents. There is often a lack of support systems, such as on-set childcare or flexible working arrangements, which could alleviate some of the pressures faced by parents. Many productions do not offer parental leave, and the freelance nature of much of the work in the industry means that even basic benefits like health insurance can be inconsistent.

Moreover, the culture of the film industry often discourages discussion of family responsibilities. There can be a stigma attached to being a parent, with some fearing that admitting to family commitments might make them appear less dedicated or capable. This can lead to parents hiding their struggles or avoiding seeking help, further compounding the challenges they face.

Percentage of Film Sets Providing Childcare Support

In the film industry, the provision of on-set childcare support is significantly limited. According to available data, less than 5% of film sets offer any form of childcare support. This figure highlights a substantial gap in the support provided to working parents within the industry, making it challenging for parents to balance their work and family responsibilities effectively.

The cost of setting up and maintaining childcare facilities on film sets is a significant barrier. The other barrier is the project-based and freelance nature of many film industry jobs and adds to the complexity, as consistent childcare support becomes harder to sustain across different locations and productions.

Emotional and Psychological Effects on Families

The demanding nature of the film industry can have significant emotional and psychological effects on families. For parents, the pressure to succeed and provide for their families, coupled with the fear of missing important moments in their children's lives, can lead to stress, guilt, and anxiety. This stress can spill over into family life, affecting relationships with partners and children.

Children of parents in the film industry may also feel the effects of their parents' demanding work schedules. They might miss having a parent present for important events or daily routines, which can lead to feelings of neglect or insecurity. In some cases, the frequent absences and long hours can impact the child's emotional well-being and development.

Between 35% and 40% of children of film industry workers in the US, UK, and Australia experience stress and anxiety related to their parents' demanding work schedules.

Mothers and Primary Caregivers: The Double Burden

The unpredictable and demanding nature of film work can be particularly challenging for those with primary caregiving responsibilities. Mothers often face a "motherhood penalty," where they are perceived as less committed to their careers or capable of handling demanding roles. This bias can limit their opportunities and advancement in the industry. Moreover, there is often a lack of support systems, such as on-set childcare or flexible working arrangements, which can make it even more difficult for women with families to sustain their careers.

My honest opinion

Here is an opinion piece I wrote when I had a newborn that was published in IF.com.au in which I share my personal story:

I have always wanted two things in life: to be a successful film producer, and to be a mum, a good one. It never occurred to me how unsuited the film industry is to have these two goals simultaneously. With the long and irregular hours, it is virtually impossible to foster an environment in which you can be a good mother and flourish in your career as a filmmaker. I guess the same could be said about fatherhood, or about single parents, and other industries too, but I cannot speak to that.

I used to think that I could easily do both. After all, isn't that what babysitters and childcare are for? I am a producer, and multi-tasking and project management are my strengths. Having a child would just be another project to incorporate, right? Oh boy, how wrong I was!

When my little one arrived, I started reading about the mother-child relationship and how vital the mother's presence and attention are to a child's happiness, security, and development, and how important those things are in raising confident, secure and healthy children. I then realised that there was no way that I will be able to be the best mum I could be for my baby girl while also working as a filmmaker.

I can either be the best mum I can be, or I can be an average mum with a career. But to be honest, I personally cannot imagine putting my career over the little person I created. I didn't just want to be a mother so I have an extra mouth to feed while someone else raises my child and spends their time with her. I wanted to be a mother so I could live the full experience and be there for this little person. Besides, kids are young only for so long and missing out on those years would just be heartbreaking to me. But I still need to work too, and let's face it, female filmmakers always had to, and still have to, work much harder than their male counterparts to achieve the same.

This situation really saddened me for so many reasons. Firstly, I empathised with all the other female filmmakers before me; those who had to choose not to have kids, and those who couldn't be the mothers they wanted to be at the expense of their kids, just to build a career or put food on the table.

The second reason it saddened me was because I knew I had to make a choice and either let go of my career, or compromise on what is best for my child. Being a filmmaker, I have worked extremely hard to try and make a success of my career and I had finally reached a point where I felt I was making significant progress when I became pregnant.

As these realisations set in, so did the panic. What if I take some time off to focus on my child? Will all the work I did to build my career be for nothing? What if I am forgotten about and have to start all over again? What if I fall out of touch with current trends and industry practices? Imagine the connections I will lose! Was all the work I did for the last 20 years for nothing, because let's face it, our industry is all about staying in the know, staying connected and networking?

One day I saw a wonderful film by filmmaker Jane Castle called 'When the Camera Stopped Rolling'. The film is about Jane's mother who was one of the only female filmmakers in Australia back in the day. She had to work two, three times harder than her male colleagues and at times even omitted the fact that she was female to get a job. The effect that it had on Jane was described in the film, and without giving anything away, her mother's filmmaking career really affected how Jane and her sister grew up. The film really touched me and I could only put myself in Jane's mother's shoes. I wondered if she had the same thoughts as I have now. And if she did and she chose to make a go at her career regardless, I can only imagine the conflict and guilt she must have felt.

The way the business world in general is set up is not conducive to motherhood. The system was created a long time ago by men whose wives stayed at home and raised the children. In today's world where women want more than that, it's not fair to have to choose between your career/dream job/contributing to the family income and being a mother and having a family (and populating the earth).

Of course, some mothers might prefer to fit into the current system and leave their little ones in the care of someone else, and that is totally fine too, but what about those who don't want to? Isn't it time for the system to adjust in a way that will allow mothers to still be able to build a career and *have a good job, while being a mother? Or better yet, to take some time off and be welcomed back to continue where you left off. Why not?*

After much thought and emotional commitment to this problem I decided that I am going to try my level best at being the best for my little girl that I can be, and still keep my career on track. I might not be able to be the workaholic that I used to be, but I can certainly still try to maintain some of what I have worked so hard for. And I will not be guilt-tripped or manipulated into anything else. Not by the system and not by anyone in it.

I saw another female filmmaker, Ruby Challenger, on social media with her newborn and older daughter at Cannes Film Festival where her film was selected, and then I saw her sitting in the cinema breastfeeding her baby. And I was inspired! She didn't let motherhood stand in the way of her career nor did she let her career stand in the way of motherhood! It made me realise that perhaps it is possible to juggle both balls, hard as it might be, but it didn't seem impossible anymore.

To implement my plan, I've undergone significant lifestyle changes. While I can maintain the same level of work quality, I now manage fewer projects simultaneously. I've trimmed unnecessary commitments, focusing on being present with my daughter during her awake hours and working during her naps and after her bedtime. Of course, I do still take meetings during the day, but I limit them, and I make sure they are spaced out enough. I've also learnt to avoid overcommitting and to set realistic boundaries, declining certain meetings, using emails more than phone calls and I even take my littly with me to meetings. I will keep adapting the way I do things as she gets older and her needs change.

The good news is that I have been able to mostly be the mother to my daughter that I want to be, and I have also been able to continue my career. Yes, at a slightly slower pace, but at least I didn't need to leave it behind completely. All it took was for me to set the boundaries and for me to align myself with, and work with people and companies that respect and understand this. I took on a contract office job for four months where I managed to negotiate working from home and working in the hours that suit me, which was 8pm to 2am – baby's sleep time. The job was completed successfully, and all the work got done and with praise.

If it wasn't for the company's understanding and respect for my role as mother, it never could have worked. And if I never asked, I never would have known that I could still have the job and have it in a way that works for me. And no, the person who employed me was not female.

I was also midway through early pre-production of a film I am producer on, Carmen & Bolude, when I fell pregnant. Lucky it is a female-led project, and I was able to comfortably express my need for proper time off to spend with my newborn and that my work methods will be very different moving forward. My team, especially the creator of the project and co-producer, Michela Carattini, have been great in understanding my new way of working. In fact, many people on our team are mothers and fathers of young children and we have made some major adjustments in how our set is run. We have even implemented job sharing for some of the roles and we will be shooting 4-day weeks so that there is a better work-life balance.

Meanwhile, during the release of my previous film Streets of Colour in cinemas, I've been truly touched by the warm and understanding support I've received from director Ronnie S. Riskalla and the team regarding my flexible schedule. Now, we primarily use WhatsApp for communication, except for emergencies. This way, I can check and respond during the day when I have short breaks, while handling the rest of the work during nighttime.

I don't know how my career will be affected moving forward, and I don't know how many people, companies and projects will be accommodating to my requirements, but I know that there are enough opportunities to at least maintain a large portion of my career.

I might need to juggle fewer projects, and I won't always be readily available, but prioritising being the best mum for my daughter is a worthwhile compromise. Perhaps over time, the system can evolve to support parents and caregivers, giving the outdated approach a much-needed update. It's like a wise little person once said: Porque no los dos?

I know that as a producer I want to create an environment for my teams in which they can balance work with what is important to them. Working differently doesn't mean working any less good or any less hard. A happy workplace is a constructive and successful workplace!

⊞ **See Worksheet: Exercises for parents to document challenges and solutions**

I have gathered some more real-life stories of people from the industry to hear first-hand what their experience of working in the film industry is, particularly relating to parenthood:

Ronnie S. Riskalla, Writer & Director: *As an independent screenwriter and director, one of the biggest challenges I face is the lack of income during the crucial stages of writing, development, and pre-production of a film. Unlike other professions, there's no steady paycheck coming in for the countless hours spent crafting a story, refining a script, or preparing for production. This financial void creates a difficult choice: either maintain a separate job to support my family, which eats up all my free time and leaves little for writing and directing duties or focus entirely on my film projects at the cost of putting financial strain on my family.*

The reality is that when I'm not at my paying job, I have to dedicate all my remaining time to my film work, often resulting in neglecting my family. The alternative—quitting my job to focus solely on my film projects—means enduring the stress of financial insecurity, knowing that my efforts won't be compensated until the film turns a profit, if it ever does.

This is where the support of my wife has been invaluable. She's had to put her own career on hold to care for our three children, allowing me to pursue my dreams in the film industry. Without her unwavering support, it simply wouldn't be possible for me to work in this field. But the sacrifices are immense. The long hours of writing, principal photography, and editing mean that I'm often away from my family, missing important milestones and moments.

The burden of working on unpaid projects, in the hopes that they will eventually be successful, is a heavy one. This is the curse of independent filmmaking—until you've built a strong reputation and secured financial backing, you're often working for free just to prove your skills and worth. The stress of this situation has taken a toll on my health, with anxiety and depression creeping in as I struggle to balance the demands of my career with the needs of my family.

If there were more funding available for the development of projects and financial support for independent filmmakers, it would make a world of difference. It would relieve some of the financial pressure and allow filmmakers like me to focus on our craft without sacrificing our well-being or the well-being of our families. The journey of an independent filmmaker is a challenging one, and greater financial support could help ease the burden and enable us to continue creating the stories we're passionate about.

Kirsty Stark, Producer: So, I think work-life balance became a significant issue for me primarily after I became a parent. I had my son, who's now three and a half, in October 2020. I was producing at the time. We had finished and released season one of First Day, and we had gone through the development of season two. My intention was to finish all of our financing, send off all of the funding applications, go on maternity leave, and then come back in time to shoot in June or July the following year.

Unfortunately, five days after my son was born, we had one of our financing partners fall through, and so I was hormonal, crying on the call, going, "why have you taken our funding away?" Quite funny in hindsight, but that essentially meant that within the week after he was born, I was back to work in breaks when he was asleep and trying to complete our finance plan and make the show happen.

When he was about seven or eight months old, we filmed the second series of First Day. From a work-life balance perspective, I had another producer on the project, Kate Butler, who I brought on, knowing that I probably wouldn't be able to produce at full capacity or at least be on set full-time. Kate has kids as well; she has two, and I have one. So, we tag-teamed the producing responsibilities. Generally, one of us was on set in the morning, and the other was on set in the afternoon, and we would cross over in the middle of the day to make that work. We shared the role but focused on our respective strengths and weaknesses, which was fantastic.

Kate had been a co-producer on the first series, so she knew the project well and was a fantastic person to have on the team. She stepped up and, I believe, got her first long-form producing credit on that series.

Throughout pre-production, my parents were around as my son's caregivers. They would usually come to the production office, and we had a little room set aside for them where he could come back to feed since I was breastfeeding. They would go for walks and visit the park, have fun with him, and then bring him back to me in the office for feeds. He ended up attending several production meetings and became a familiar presence around the office, which was really lovely. On set, he would occasionally come and spend time, more around the unit base than on set itself, so I could feed him during the day. It was fantastic to have him around, thanks to the amazing support from my parents. People on set often said that at the end of a long or tough shoot day, it was so nice to have a baby to cuddle. It was great to have him as part of that experience and to have him be part of my film and working life.

Adam Bridges, Crew: *After years of navigating the Camera Department, including stints at Camera Rentals, I finally secured a consistent on-set role as a Video Split Operator and 2nd Assistant Camera for streaming series, beyond the occasional commercial. During this time, my wife was pregnant, and we wrapped just before our first child arrived. I found immense joy in our new family and realised I couldn't return to the grueling on-set demands—10-hour days, plus lunch, pre-call, tight schedules, extensive travel across Sydney, and inevitable overtime. The job's pay wasn't enough to support our family, meaning my wife would also need to work, while I'd be largely absent.*

Faced with the choice, I decided to step back into a Rental House, putting my on-set dream on hold, perhaps permanently. If I could work on set and still be a present parent and partner, I would do it in a heartbeat, but unfortunately, that isn't an option right now.

Ashleigh Murray, Actor: *Re-entering the industry as an actor now I'm a parent of a young infant/toddler has been interesting. It has saddened me to hear how many people I've spoken to along the way that dropped out of acting once they had kids because it was too hard. I know full well that if it wasn't for my partner and mother supporting me and minding our child so I can go and do jobs that I wouldn't be capable of working in the industry either. It sure does take a village.*

We live on the south coast to which this village has 11-page waitlists for daycare with kids under the age of 2. So right now, daycare isn't an option for us. Equally with the commute time to a set in Sydney I would be leaving and getting back before childcare opens and after it closes. So really the only option is my mother (Who still works part time mind you) or a professional Nanny service which is VERY expensive and not subsidised by the government. And we all know the consistency and pay for acting in Australia isn't quite sustaining a private nanny lifestyle just yet. Equally you can't just have a Nanny on call on the occasion that you land a gig. Generally, they will want set days and consistent work otherwise you will lose them to a family who can offer that. So, your option for any on call work is leave your child with an unvetted casual nanny who you haven't met nor does your child have a rapport with, which is very distressing for both Mumma and child.

Right now, TVCs are my best option as they pay well and require minimal days. Another challenge with the industry is call sheets getting them the day before your shoot, so trying to organise care for say a half day but not sure what half of the day yet until you get the call sheet the night before is difficult. I just end up having to get someone for an entire day even if a shoot perhaps is only a couple of hours.

When I was still breastfeeding I showed up to an TVC with breast pumps and thankfully the organiser saw them in my suitcase and was a mother herself and said the nicest most supportive gesture of saying "any time you need to pump, you just stop us and go and do it, please do not feel like you are wasting our set time and don't be afraid to ask" I could have cried with how kind that was. I absolutely was going to just hold it in in pain and hope to do it on the lunch break without anyone knowing and I sure as hell was concerned to share that with anyone in case it was seen as unprofessional or a nuisance. I don't know how it would have been received had the staff been majority men. I am so grateful to the woman who took notice and made a safe space for me.

Equally with trying to re-enter the industry I wanted to scrub up on the latest acting courses and wanted to consider prestigious schools. As a parent with a mortgage to pay and a mouth to feed I cannot pick up and fly to WAAPA or attend NIDA full time for 3 years not sustaining an income and there are ZERO scholarships targeted at the minority of actors who are parents nor is there a degree offered online. It became abundantly clear there were scholarships for all sorts of minority groups but nothing to help support parents.

ever-growing life experiences with them are expanding my creative pool to draw upon.

But more to the realities of juggling the two—the practicalities—of being both parent and artist, especially as the main carer. We now have two children—one 15 and one 10. The nature of my work in the arts is gig-by-gig, contract-based. This allows me to be very present for the kids, especially when there are no gigs, no work—which is a financial strain on the family but a well-being benefit for the kids.

I'm lucky—very lucky—that my partner isn't in the industry. My partner holds a stable job, with regular hours and pay. This allows us to function as a family unit, each bringing benefits that complement the other. This isn't always the case for everyone.

Where it gets really tricky is turning down jobs that intrude too heavily into main carer duties. Turning down jobs because I want to be emotionally present in my kids' lives. Turning down jobs out of guilt. It raises issues such as a lack of support for parents in or returning to the industry, a lack of understanding about juggling parenting with a creative life, and a lack of options and alternatives for creatives who are also parents.

In the end, being a parent in the arts and film industry is a balancing act—one that requires constant adjustments, sacrifices, and, most importantly, love for both your family and your craft. It's a journey that never really stops, but I wouldn't have it any other way.

Tsu Shan (pronounced Suzanne) Chambers, Actor/Writer/Producer: *Well, hello there! I'm Tsu Shan Chambers (pronounced Suzanne), a former Optometrist and Senior Executive turned Actor/Writer/Producer,*

passionate about bringing awareness to issues that matter through telling provoking stories.

After having three children, I decided to wait until my youngest child was one years old before starting to do the work, I've always wanted to do in the entertainment industry. However, transitioning from having a stable income with a family and existing financial commitment was a challenge and still is a juggling act, ten years later. Working in the industry often involves incredibly long hours, high pressure work environments and irregular income. It is not surprising that our industry is known to have high divorce rates and a large percentage of workers with mental health issues. Fortunately, whilst it hasn't been easy on the family, I have had the support from my husband and looking back, it has made us stronger as a team.

Particularly over the past few years, my career and work became more demanding and the responsibilities that my husband and I held in the family changed. Rather than me look after the kids primarily, my husband took on more of that role. My work as a production accountant and producer carries a lot of responsibility which can be stressful. Acting also requires a lot of emotional and mental focus. So consequently, when I'm finally at home, I need to switch off from everyone and everything for a while. For me, that entails doing yoga every day, going for a long walk or diving into my latest romance book. Fortunately, my husband takes over during this time and my children have developed a wonderful, close relationship with him. Sometimes, I am jealous of the connection they now have and the time he gets to spend with them, but it is a choice we made for now as I am the main income earner and have crazy, big dreams.

There has been a lot of life lessons over the past decade, and I am sure there will be more. One of them is having the discipline to be true to my core values which in turn, helps me prioritise my work. Family and altruistic work were surprisingly my top two values on equal par with each other. This comes with its own challenges. For example, in this industry, relationships are important, and we must network. However, because of my family, I am very selective about which screenings, industry events, and social gatherings I attend. I do not go out a lot compared to others because I would rather spend time with my family. This can be a disadvantage to my career but, it is what feels right for me. When I do go out, I really make the most of it.

Being a parent has also taught me that, no matter how I try to be diligent and punctual, things can be just out of your control. I've learnt to accept this and be kinder to myself when things don't go according to plan. Open communication, flexibility and patience are my friends and when you find the same attributes in others, I don't let them go!

Choosing the right business partners has been another game-changer for me and often not an easy one to navigate. I've made very expensive mistakes in working with the wrong people for me, but the lessons have been invaluable. Like most people, we want to work with those who have emotional maturity, share our values, have a good work ethic, business acumen and integrity. I've learnt that it's important to have a partner with complementary skills at a similar level to you where everyone is contributing equally. I always learn a lot about someone when they are under high levels of stress and how they deal with money.

Saying "no" has also become a necessary skill and something I do believe women (as care givers) have more of an issue doing. When I was an emerging filmmaker and artist, I used to say "yes" a lot more. However, after being exploited way too many times, and with family on the forefront of my mind, I now find it much easier to walk away from jobs, people or situations that are not aligned.

Having said that, it can be challenging when most of us seek financial stability, and our industry is mostly project/contractual work where we go from gig to gig. As an independent Producer, we can work for years putting our own money into development and not be paid at all. Producers are the ones that are paid last (if at all) and often need to reinvest our fees into projects to ensure they are green-lit. We often have to work "day jobs" to make ends meet in the interim. There have been countless times where I have had to say "no" to an acting or writing gig because of my commitments to my "day job". It took a while to find the right "day job" and people to work for that allows me the flexibility and income that meets my needs. It's been a journey in understanding and valuing my own worth.

Balancing work and life in the screen industry isn't easy. However, by prioritising my values, being selective about my commitments, working with the right people and taking care of myself, I'm probably now in the best position in my life where I am grateful for what has been, where I am right now and what is to come. I love what I do and look forward to doing this work for the rest of my life.

Ruby Challenger, Art Department & Director - *From a young age, I always knew I wanted to be a director, but like many women in the creative industries, I struggled with imposter syndrome. I started in the film industry at 19, working in the art department, which I loved, but directing was always my real goal. Despite making a successful short film that was shown at festivals around the world, I just didn't have the confidence to apply for the competitive AFTRS Masters in Directing. I convinced myself I wasn't good enough.*

At the same time, I was also going through several years of infertility. The long hours working in the art department were taking a toll, so we made the decision for me to step back from work to see if that would help. While I didn't fall pregnant immediately, I used that time to write a script—something I'd been putting off for years. IVF eventually worked, and I was lucky enough to get pregnant.

After my baby was born, something inside me shifted. When my child was about three months old, I experienced this incredible surge of confidence and creativity. As fate would have it I was at AFTRS supporting a friend during the Open Day and I felt irrepressibly called to spend the next month *writing my application for the directing Masters. I applied to AFTRS and was thrilled to be accepted.*

By the time classes started, my baby would only be eight months old. To be able to balance film school and my baby, my husband and I made lots of compromises to our lifestyle - the largest was having my mother-in-law come over from Canada to live in our tiny 2 bedroom apartment to be the primary caregiver to our daughter. Two months into classes and COVID hit. Oddly enough, the timing worked in our favour. Classes moved online, and my mother-in-law could pass me the baby so I could breastfeed while attending class, a situation that, in hindsight, was a blessing for my daughter (but not without the pain of hearing her sometimes crying at the door for me to come out and be with her).

During film school, I collaborated with my peers and we developed a project that was very close to my heart—a short film called MumLife, a drama musical about postpartum anxiety. I also wrote my major paper on the representation of motherhood both in front and behind the camera. The experience helped me shift my focus toward how motherhood is portrayed on screen, our societal view of motherhood. I also became passionate about the challenges that working mothers face, especially when trying to return to work after having children. With many women taking huge hits to the success of their career, or sacrificing their family connections.

Upon concluding the Masters I was expecting my second child. I had seen another woman finish the Masters 2 years before me, heavily pregnant. As they say 'of you can see it you can be it'. So it had always been the plan to fall pregnant with our second child in the last quarter of the Masters. Once again, IVF was a part of the journey, and so my plan worked perfectly (except for battling first-trimester exhaustion and sickness while finishing my film and studying!). By the time I was 38 weeks pregnant, I was in the middle of production on our project Next, and we received the exciting news that MumLife had been accepted into Cannes. It was a stressful time—trying to balance family, pregnancy, filming, and the preparations for Cannes. I was nervous about the baby's timing — if it arrived too early it would disrupt the shoot, too late and I wouldn't be able to attend Cannes.

We filmed this incredibly low-budget project while I was 38 weeks pregnant and then embarked on the 43-hour journey to Cannes when my newborn was 5 weeks old.

Thankfully, it all worked out, but again, only through the huge support of my family. I went to Cannes with my husband, toddler, newborn, and mother-in-law. Without them, the experience I had would have been impossible. I managed to fulfil all my festival duties while running back to breastfeed and take care of my children. Having never attended Cannes before, we accidentally stayed very far from the Palais and so I gave myself long-lasting foot damage from running back and forth in flat shoes on the cobblestones several times a day to breastfeed. Despite the distance and other challenges, I was still able to attend networking events, walk the red carpet, and made sure to utilise the breastfeeding area in the Palais.

After Cannes, I faced another major decision: similar to so many, we were victims of the cost of living, so we moved to the Central Coast to create a better lifestyle for our children. Initially, I was (very) hesitant because of the impact it would have on my career. I worried about missing out on networking opportunities, and the ability to take meetings because when living in Sydney my mother was able to be a huge support and take the kids while I took a meeting.

The careful web of childcare and career I had built crumbled when I moved away from the city. Against my desire to lean full throttle into my career, I found myself leaning into motherhood more deeply. I took the children out of daycare and dedicated more of my time to them.

This shift was profound for me. For so long, my identity had been wrapped up in my career, but through the move, and the pain of realising my career would have to take a new shape, I was able to put things in perspective. I realised that this time with my children was precious. They grow up so quickly, and, through much soul searching, I decided that my career could kick into a slower gear. I continued working remotely for a film company, but I started to see that the 9-to-5 lifestyle wasn't sustainable for our family. The toll it was taking on all of us wasn't worth it, so we made a decision: I would focus on motherhood and my personal creative projects, where I could have control over my time and output. We decided that living on one income was worth it if it meant preserving our family's well-being.

Throughout this journey, I've become increasingly focused on balancing motherhood with a creative career. I even started a podcast called Mums in Film, where I speak with other mothers about their experiences navigating the industry. It's been an incredible way to connect with others who are going through the same challenges—juggling creative aspirations with raising a family. And it has been encouraging hearing how listeners have felt comforted by hearing other women's journeys and struggles.

As was always the plan and hope, I'm currently expecting my third baby.

Over time, my advocacy has shifted. Early on, I pushed for the idea that women could and should do both—be mothers and filmmakers, with the industry embracing that (hello Disney Studios in Sydney - where is your casual drop off daycare? Why do we not have day care available for large film productions? I have a healthy list of changes in our industry could work towards). But now, my focus has evolved. I believe that mothers should have the freedom to fully embrace motherhood without feeling pressured to balance it all at once. We need to support women in re-entering the workforce when their children are older, instead of forcing them to maintain an impossible balance.

The reality in the film industry is that if you don't make a film every couple of years, people start to assume you're not serious about your career. There's this real threat that you'll be forgotten, and worse - an assumption you will have (somehow) forgotten your craft. But I don't believe that taking time away for motherhood doesn't take away from your skills or your experience. The challenge now is breaking that perception and ensuring there's space for women to come back to their careers when the time is right, without the fear of being left behind.

PS: It must be said that it is not without extreme trepidation that I embark on this new chapter of motherhood and personal creative work. I have no guarantee I will be able to pick up where I left off after AFTRS and Cannes. But I have faith the world is evolving.

Support for Parent Caregivers in the Film Industry: Data and Statistics

Percentage of Parent Caregivers Reporting Inadequate Childcare Support:

United States: Approximately 79% of parent caregivers in the U.S. film industry report that they do not have adequate support for childcare. This lack of support is a significant barrier, impacting their ability to participate fully in the industry.

United Kingdom: In the UK, around 72% of parent caregivers working in the film industry feel they do not receive sufficient support for childcare. This is exacerbated by long working hours and the freelance nature of many jobs in the industry.

Australia: In Australia, about 74% of parent caregivers in the film industry express that they do not have adequate childcare support. The challenges include irregular work hours and the high cost of quality childcare, making it difficult for many mothers to sustain their careers.

CHAPTER 10

Gender Disparities

The film industry, like many others, has long been dominated by men. Despite progress in recent years, significant gender disparities persist, affecting opportunities, treatment, and recognition of women. This chapter delves into the statistics that highlight these disparities, the unique challenges faced by women, and personal stories that illustrate the impact of these issues on their careers and lives.

Statistics on Gender Representation:

The numbers tell a stark story. Studies consistently show that women are underrepresented in almost every facet of the film industry, from directing and writing to technical roles. For instance, women directed only about 10-15% of the top-grossing films annually in recent years. Similarly, women make up a small fraction of cinematographers and editors in Hollywood and other major film industries worldwide.

On-screen representation also shows significant imbalances. Female characters are often underrepresented, and when they do appear, they are frequently depicted in stereotypical roles or portrayed with less depth compared to their male counterparts. This lack of diversity behind the scenes contributes to a limited range of stories and perspectives, which in turn affects the types of characters and narratives that audiences see on screen.

Gender Breakdown in Key Film Industry Roles – United States:

Directors: Percentage of Women: In 2023, women accounted for 16% of directors working on the top 250 grossing films.

Producers: Percentage of Women: Women made up 26% of producers on the top 250 grossing films in 2023.

Executive Producers: Percentage of Women: Women represented 24% of executive producers in 2023.

Writers: Percentage of Women: Women constituted 17% of writers working on the top 250 grossing films.

Cinematographers: Women account for about 6% of cinematographers in the U.S. film industry.

Editors: Women represent approximately 21% of editors.

Production Designers: Women hold around 23% of production designer roles.

Sound Technicians: Women are significantly underrepresented, with only about 5% working as sound technicians.

Gender Breakdown in Key Film Industry Roles – United Kingdom:

Directors: Percentage of Women: 13.6% of directors in the UK film industry over the last decade were women. Only 14% of UK films had at least one female director.

Producers: Percentage of Women: 25.7% of producers of UK films are women.

Writers: Percentage of Women: 14.6% of screenwriters on UK films are women.

Executive Producers: Percentage of Women: The data specific to executive producers was not separately detailed, but overall women are significantly underrepresented in senior roles across the industry.

Cinematographers: Women make up less than 10% of the cinematographers in the UK.

Editors: Approximately 22% of editors in the UK are women.

Production Designers: Women hold about 25% of production designer positions.

Sound Technicians: Similar to the U.S., women are underrepresented in sound roles, making up around 7%

Gender Breakdown in Key Film Industry Roles – Australia:

Directors: Estimated Percentage: Around 17% of directors are women, based on broader studies of film industry representation in comparable markets.

Producers: Estimated Percentage: Approximately 30% of producers are women. Australian statistics often show better representation in producing roles compared to directing or technical roles.

Executive Producers: Percentage of Women: Women represent approximately 28% of executive producers in the Australian film industry.

Writers: Estimated Percentage: Similar to the UK, around 15-20% of screenwriters are women, indicating an underrepresentation that impacts the types of stories being told.

Cinematographers: Women account for around 7% of cinematographers in Australia.

Editors: Women represent approximately 20% of editors.

Production Designers: About 26% of production designers are women.

Sound Technicians: Women in sound technician roles are underrepresented, with figures similar to the UK and U.S., at around 6%

Challenges for Women in the Industry:

Women in the film industry face a myriad of challenges, starting with access to opportunities. There are well-documented biases that can hinder women's careers, such as the assumption that they are less capable of handling large budgets or directing action films. This often leads to a "glass ceiling" effect, where women find it challenging to progress beyond certain roles or budgets.

Even when women do secure positions, they often face additional scrutiny and have to work harder to prove themselves. The pressure to succeed can be immense, with the success or failure of one woman's project sometimes seen as a reflection on all women in the industry. This can lead to a hostile work environment where women feel they have to constantly prove their worth, leading to increased stress and burnout.

The pay gap is another significant issue. Women in the film industry, including high-profile actors, often earn less than their male counterparts for similar roles and responsibilities. This pay disparity extends beyond the stars to behind-the-scenes roles, where women frequently earn less than men in similar positions.

The Women in Film (WIF) survey provides critical insights into gender discrimination experienced by women in the film industry. Here are the key statistics:

Approximately 50% of women in the film industry reported experiencing some form of gender discrimination on set. This includes discrimination in hiring, promotion, and day-to-day interactions (Women In Film) (UCLA).

Microaggressions and Bias: The survey revealed that women often face microaggressions and biased behaviour more frequently than their male counterparts. About 34% of women reported witnessing or experiencing biased behaviour directed towards them over the past year, which is significantly higher compared to the 12.5% reported by men in similar roles (McKinsey & Company) (UCLA).

Barriers to Promotion: The survey highlighted that 27% of women believe their gender has hindered their ability to receive promotions or raises, compared to only 7% of men. Additionally, 35% of women expect their gender to continue being a barrier to their advancement in the future (McKinsey & Company).

Women of Colour: The discrimination is more pronounced for women of colour, who are less represented in leadership roles. For example, while white women hold 22% of C-suite positions in media and entertainment, women of colour hold only 4% (McKinsey & Company) (UCLA).

Personal Stories and Experiences:

Personal stories from women in the industry highlight the human impact of these challenges. Many recount experiences of being overlooked for projects, facing harassment or discrimination, and having their creative contributions undervalued. For example, female directors have shared stories of having to fight for control over their projects or being dismissed by crew members who are unaccustomed to working under a woman.

These stories are not just anecdotal; they reflect systemic issues within the industry. Women often have to navigate a complex landscape of sexism, racism, and other forms of discrimination, making their journey in the film industry uniquely challenging. However, they also highlight resilience and a growing movement toward change, with more women pushing back against these barriers and advocating for greater inclusion and equality.

CHAPTER 11

Underrepresented Communities

Enhancing Diversity and Inclusion in the Industry

Diversity and inclusion remain critical issues in the film industry. Despite some progress, many groups, including women, people of colour, people with disability and LGBTQIA+ individuals, continue to be underrepresented and face systemic barriers to success.

Policies and Practices to Promote Diversity and Inclusion

Promoting diversity and inclusion requires intentional policies and practices. These can include setting diversity targets, implementing bias training, and creating mentorship programs for underrepresented groups. Productions should also strive to create inclusive environments where all individuals feel valued and respected.

Supporting Underrepresented Groups in the Film Industry

Supporting underrepresented groups involves not only providing opportunities but also ensuring that these opportunities are accessible. This might include offering scholarships or grants, creating pathways for entry-level positions, and actively seeking to work with diverse talent both on-screen and behind the scenes. Several programs have successfully supported underrepresented groups in the film industry by offering scholarships, grants, and creating pathways for entry-level positions. Here are some notable examples:

Programs Making a Positive Difference:

UNITED STATES:

ACADEMY GOLD PROGRAM

The Academy Gold Program was launched by the Academy of Motion Picture Arts and Sciences. It is designed as an internship enhancement and mentorship program specifically aimed at supporting individuals from underrepresented communities in the film industry. The program's goal is to increase diversity and inclusion within Hollywood by providing opportunities and resources to participants who might otherwise face barriers to entry in the industry.

The program offers a variety of resources to its participants, including educational workshops, mentorship opportunities, and networking events. These elements help participants gain valuable insights into the industry, build professional connections, and develop the skills needed to succeed in Hollywood. The Academy Gold Program has been instrumental in providing a pathway for many young talents from diverse backgrounds to enter the film industry. By offering access to industry professionals and creating a supportive network, the program has helped to broaden the pipeline of talent entering Hollywood, contributing to greater diversity in the industry.

SUNDANCE INSTITUTE'S DIVERSITY INITIATIVES

The Sundance Institute is committed to fostering diversity and inclusion through several dedicated programs. While the term "Diversity Initiative" may be used broadly, the Institute has multiple programs aimed at supporting underrepresented voices in filmmaking, including Women at Sundance and other initiatives that focus on diversity across various dimensions such as race, ethnicity, gender, and sexual orientation.

These initiatives provide a range of support mechanisms, including fellowships, grants, and workshops, which are designed to help filmmakers from diverse backgrounds develop their projects and advance their careers. The Women at Sundance program is specifically aimed at supporting female filmmakers. It offers mentorship, financing, and professional development opportunities to help women in the industry overcome barriers and succeed in their filmmaking endeavours. This program has been instrumental in elevating the voices of women in film, providing them with the resources and networks necessary to thrive in a traditionally male-dominated industry.

GHETTO FILM SCHOOL (GFS)

GFS is a non-profit organisation that provides young people from underrepresented communities with the resources and training needed to pursue careers in film and media.

GFS offers intensive courses that cover various aspects of filmmaking, including screenwriting, directing, and editing. The program provides hands-on training with professional-grade equipment and software, giving students practical experience in the field. Additionally, GFS provides mentorship from industry professionals, which helps students build valuable connections and gain insights into the film industry. Alumni of the program have gone on to successful careers in filmmaking, which demonstrates the effectiveness of GFS's approach. Many graduates have worked on major film and television projects, and some have even been recognised with awards for their work.

NBCUniversal's DIVERSITY, EQUITY & INCLUSION INITIATIVES

NBCUniversal is committed to increasing diversity and inclusion within the entertainment industry. The company has established a range of programs aimed at supporting this goal. Among these are the NBCUniversal Launch and the Talent Infusion Program (TIPS).

- NBCUniversal Launch is a diversity, equity, and inclusion brand that encompasses various initiatives designed to identify and develop talent from underrepresented communities. This program includes efforts across different areas of the company, focusing on both in front of and behind-the-camera roles.
- Talent Infusion Program (TIPS) is another key initiative within NBCUniversal that seeks to infuse diverse talent into the company's productions and departments, enhancing the overall inclusivity of the media content they produce.

These initiatives provide fellowships, internships, and mentorship opportunities for individuals from diverse backgrounds. The programs focus on nurturing talent both in front of and behind the camera, contributing to a more inclusive industry.

FILM INDEPENDENT'S PROJECT INVOLVE

Project Involve is Film Independent's signature diversity program, dedicated to increasing diversity within the film industry by supporting filmmakers from underrepresented backgrounds.

The program offers fellowships that provide a comprehensive package of support, including mentorship from experienced industry professionals, workshops designed to develop the fellows' skills and knowledge, and networking opportunities to help them build connections within the industry. Project Involve has a strong track record of success, with fellows producing award-winning films that have been recognised at major film festivals such as Sundance, Cannes, and others. This underscores the program's effectiveness in fostering diverse talent and helping participants gain visibility and recognition in the industry.

DISNEY'S LAUNCHPAD: SHORTS INCUBATOR

Disney's Launchpad is a program specifically designed to create opportunities for diverse filmmakers to produce short films with the support of Disney. The program focuses on emerging filmmakers from underrepresented backgrounds, aiming to amplify diverse voices and stories within the entertainment industry.

The program provides funding, resources, and mentorship to its participants. These emerging filmmakers are given the opportunity to develop and produce their short films under the guidance of experienced Disney professionals. The short films created through the program are distributed on Disney platforms, such as Disney+, giving the filmmakers significant exposure and career advancement opportunities. This platform allows their work to reach a wide audience, helping to propel their careers in the film industry.

AUSTRALIA:

SCREEN AUSTRALIA

Screen Australia has implemented several initiatives aimed at promoting diversity and inclusion within the Australian screen industry. Two of its notable programs are:

Gender Matters: As discussed in an earlier chapter.

Indigenous Department: This department is dedicated to supporting Indigenous filmmakers and the telling of Indigenous stories. It provides funding, resources, and support to projects that reflect the diversity and richness of Indigenous cultures and perspectives. This department has been instrumental in supporting films and TV shows that bring Indigenous stories to the forefront. Through funding and development support, it has enabled the production of critically acclaimed works that showcase Indigenous perspectives. This has contributed to a richer and more diverse

Australian screen landscape, fostering greater understanding and appreciation of Indigenous cultures.

CREWHQ

CrewHQ is an Australian platform dedicated to improving the career sustainability of film and TV crew, including contributing to improving the working conditions and well-being of film crew members where possible. Recognising the demanding nature of the industry, CrewHQ provides resources and tools that support work-life balance, mental health, and career transitions, particularly for those returning to work after an extended leave, such as parental leave.

Services and Features:

Job Matching:

Customisable Job Availability: CrewHQ allows users to set up a profile and be searchable for jobs that suit their preferences, including location, production type, and working hours, helping crew members find roles that align with their personal needs and schedules.

Part-Time and Freelance Opportunities: The platform offers part-time and freelance positions, enabling crew members to manage their workload while balancing personal responsibilities.

Support for Job Sharing and Career Re-entry:

Job Sharing: CrewHQ facilitates job-sharing arrangements, where two individuals share the responsibilities of a single role by working on different days, half-days, or alternating weeks. This helps professionals maintain a career while balancing personal needs.

Career Re-entry: CrewHQ supports those returning to the industry after a break, such as parental leave, by offering flexible roles, job-sharing opportunities, and resources to help ease the transition back into work.

Mental Health and Wellness Support:

CrewHQ provides resources for crew to assist them in accessing mental health, financial, health & safety and wellbeing information and services, including from organisations who provide specific support to the film and television industry.

The platform also aims to address some of these issues at their core, by helping crew to build sustainable careers that work alongside the other important aspects of their life, and to ease some of the challenges of freelancing, such as the 'feast or famine' nature of work, time away from family and friends, long hours and the likelihood of burnout.

Community Building and Networking:

Online Community: CrewHQ fosters a supportive online community where industry professionals can network, share experiences, and offer mutual support, helping to alleviate the isolation that can come with freelance work.

Annual Conference: CrewHQ also offers a national online conference, CrewCon, for crew to come together, accelerate their careers and be part of the discussion around major issues that affect them across the industry.

Impact on Work-Life Balance and Well-Being:

Improved Work-Life Balance: CrewHQ's promotion of flexible work and job-sharing opportunities helps crew members manage their work-life balance more effectively, reducing the pressures of long hours and providing more time for personal activities and family life.

Support for Career Re-entry: CrewHQ's focus on career re-entry is particularly beneficial for professionals returning to work after extended leave. The platform's flexible roles and job-sharing options make it easier for individuals to transition back into the workforce while balancing new responsibilities.

Enhanced Mental Health: The mental health support and wellness resources provided by CrewHQ help crew members connect with organisations that can help them cope with the stressors of working in the industry, leading to improved mental health outcomes and reduced burnout.

Stronger Support Networks: CrewHQ's community-building efforts create a supportive network for crew members, fostering a sense of belonging and shared understanding, which is crucial for long-term career sustainability.

CrewHQ plays a vital role in improving work-life balance, supporting career transitions, and enhancing the overall well-being of film crew members in Australia. Through its flexible job opportunities, mental health support, and community-building initiatives, CrewHQ helps create a more sustainable and supportive working environment in the film industry, benefiting both individuals and the industry as a whole.

CrewHQ is also partnered with The Everyone Project which you can read about below.

THE EVERYONE PROJECT

The Everyone Project: This project recognises the significant impact that media representation has on public perceptions, cultural narratives, and societal norms. By focusing on the film and TV industry, The Everyone Project seeks to ensure that storytelling reflects the true diversity of society, both on-screen and behind the scenes.

The key aspects of the Everyone Project are as follows:

Advocacy for Diverse Representation: The Everyone Project is committed to advocating for broader representation of diverse voices in film and television. This includes promoting stories that accurately reflect different races, genders, sexual orientations, abilities, and other underrepresented groups. The project believes that by showcasing a variety of experiences and perspectives, media can foster empathy, understanding, and inclusivity.

Support for Creatives from Diverse Backgrounds: The project provides support to filmmakers, writers, directors, and other creatives from diverse backgrounds. This support can take the form of mentorship programs, networking opportunities, and resources that help individuals navigate the film and TV industry, which has traditionally been challenging for underrepresented groups.

Collaboration with Industry Stakeholders: The Everyone Project collaborates with production companies, studios, broadcasters, and other key industry stakeholders to promote diversity and inclusion. These collaborations can include developing guidelines for inclusive hiring practices, encouraging diverse storytelling, and creating environments where all voices are valued and heard.

Public Awareness and Education: Part of The Everyone Project's mission is to raise public awareness about the importance of diversity in media. Through campaigns, events, and educational initiatives, the project aims to educate both the industry and the audience about why diverse representation matters and how it can positively influence society.

Research and Data Collection: The project emphasises the importance of research and data in understanding the current state of diversity in the film and TV industry. By collecting and analysing data on representation, employment practices, and audience perceptions, The Everyone Project can highlight areas for improvement and track progress over time.

Commitment to Authentic Storytelling: The Everyone Project encourages the film and TV industry to engage in authentic storytelling, where stories are told by people who have lived the experiences being depicted. This approach not only enhances the authenticity of the narrative but also provides opportunities for marginalised voices to tell their own stories.

How The Everyone Project Operates:

Workshops and Training: The project offers workshops and training sessions aimed at educating industry professionals about diversity, equity, and inclusion. These sessions are designed to increase awareness and provide practical tools for implementing inclusive practices.

Resource Hub: The project provides a resource hub where industry members can access information, tools, and guidelines for fostering diversity and inclusion within their organisations and productions.

Partnerships and Endorsements: The Everyone Project works with industry partners to endorse projects and productions that align with its mission of promoting diversity. These partnerships can help amplify the impact of initiatives that align with The Everyone Project's goals.

Impact of The Everyone Project:

The Everyone Project aims to create a more inclusive and representative media landscape, where diverse voices are heard, and stories from all parts of society are told. By pushing for changes both in front of the camera and behind the scenes, The Everyone Project hopes to challenge stereotypes, break down barriers, and promote a more equitable industry that reflects the diversity of the world we live in.

Through its comprehensive approach involving advocacy, education, research, and support, The Everyone Project is making strides towards a film and TV industry that not only entertains but also educates and enriches society by reflecting its true diversity.

SCREEN VIXENS

Screen Vixens is a professional body of women screen producers dedicated to supporting and empowering women working across all sectors of the screen industry with a specific focus on producing. Founded by Leonie Marsh in 2015, at a time when Screen Australia was actively focused on the despairing gender inequality in the local industry, Vixens are a dynamic and active community of female-identifying professionals. Their membership includes weekly and monthly networking opportunities - online and face to face, professional development, encouragement of strong health and well-being boundaries and advocacy for better work-life balance. The organisation plays a crucial role in addressing gender disparities in the industry and promoting the well-being of women in screen.

Services and Features

Networking and Community Building: Regular Meetups and Events: Screen Vixens organises regular networking events, including meetups, pep talks, masterclasses, industry experts, and panel discussions. These events allow women in the industry to connect, share experiences, and build professional relationships, fostering a strong community of support.

Professional Development

Monthly Online Meetings: Screen Vixens hosts regular online workshops and training sessions tailored to the needs of women in producing roles.

Career Advancement Resources: The organisation offers resources and guidance on career advancement, peer to peer mentoring to help women overcome barriers to progression in the industry, such as gender bias and unequal opportunities.

Advocacy for Work-Life Balance

Promoting Flexible Work Arrangements: Screen Vixens advocates for flexible working hours and job-sharing opportunities to help women manage their careers alongside personal and family responsibilities. The organisation highlights the importance of such arrangements in retaining female talent in the industry especially when leading their own shoots.

Raising Awareness and Visibility

Showcasing Women's Achievements: Screen Vixens actively promotes the work and achievements of women in producing roles, helping to increase their visibility in the industry. This includes featuring success stories, awards, and notable projects led by women.

Screen Vixens plays a pivotal role in empowering women and promoting work-life balance in the global industry. By addressing the challenges faced by women in the industry and advocating for policies that support work-life balance, Screen Vixens contributes to the well-being and career advancement of female professionals in screen. www.screenvixens.com

SCREEN DIVERSITY AND INCLUSION NETWORK (SDIN)

The Screen Diversity and Inclusion Network (SDIN) is a coalition of Australian broadcasters, screen agencies, and industry organisations that are collectively committed to improving diversity and inclusion within the Australian screen sector. SDIN's primary focus is on promoting diversity across all aspects of the industry, from content creation to hiring practices.

The network works on sharing best practices, implementing inclusive policies, and measuring progress in diversity and inclusion efforts. These activities are designed to ensure that the screen industry becomes more representative of Australia's diverse society.

SDIN also publishes annual reports that document the progress made by its members in achieving diversity and inclusion goals. These reports serve as a tool for accountability and help to identify areas where further improvements are needed.

SDIN has successfully fostered a collaborative approach to diversity within the Australian screen industry. By bringing together various stakeholders, the network has helped to create a more unified and strategic approach to diversity and inclusion.

This collaboration has led to more inclusive hiring practices and greater representation of diverse communities on screen. Through the efforts of SDIN and its members, the screen industry in Australia is becoming increasingly reflective of the country's multicultural population.

The biannual reports produced by SDIN are crucial for tracking improvements and highlighting areas where additional focus is needed. These reports provide valuable insights into the effectiveness of diversity initiatives and guide future actions to enhance inclusion.

UNITED KINGDOM:

BAFTA ELEVATE

The BAFTA Elevate program is an initiative by the British Academy of Film and Television Arts (BAFTA) aimed at supporting individuals from underrepresented groups within the film, television, and games industries. The program is designed to help these individuals advance their careers through a range of supportive measures.

BAFTA Elevate offers mentoring, networking opportunities, and professional development workshops. These resources are tailored to help participants overcome barriers that may have hindered their career progression and to provide them with the tools and connections needed to succeed in their fields.

Participants in the BAFTA Elevate program have indeed reported increased opportunities and visibility within the industry. The program has been effective in helping bridge gaps in career progression for many individuals from underrepresented groups, including women, people of colour, LGBTQ+ individuals, and people with disabilities.

By providing targeted support and creating opportunities for exposure and networking, BAFTA Elevate has contributed to the advancement of diverse talent within the industry. The program is recognised as a significant initiative in promoting diversity and inclusion within the UK's creative sectors.

BFI DIVERSITY STANDARDS

The British Film Institute (BFI) Diversity Standards were introduced to ensure that diversity and inclusion are central to the projects funded by the BFI. These standards are mandatory for all BFI-supported film and TV projects.

The standards focus on four key areas:

- **On-screen representation**: Ensuring diverse characters and narratives are represented.
- **Creative leadership**: Promoting diversity in key creative roles such as directors, writers, and producers.
- **Industry access and opportunities**: Providing pathways for underrepresented groups to enter and progress in the industry.
- **Opportunities for training and development**: Ensuring that projects offer opportunities for skill development and career progression for people from diverse backgrounds.

The standards have significantly increased diversity in funded projects, ensuring that a wider range of voices and stories are represented in British media. This initiative has set a benchmark for the industry and encouraged other organisations to adopt similar policies.

CREATIVE ACCESS

Creative Access is a UK-based organisation dedicated to improving diversity in creative industries. It provides paid internships, mentoring, and training programs for individuals from underrepresented backgrounds.

Creative Access has placed hundreds of trainees in leading creative companies, facilitating long-term careers in the industry. The organisation has also raised awareness about the importance of diversity, influencing hiring practices across the sector.

These programs demonstrate the importance and impact of targeted support for underrepresented groups in the film industry. By providing scholarships, grants, mentorship, and networking opportunities, these initiatives help to create a more diverse and inclusive industry where all voices can be heard and valued.

Creating Sustainable Career Paths:

The film industry is known for its project-based nature, which can make it challenging to build a stable, long-term career. Addressing this issue involves creating sustainable career paths that offer stability and opportunities for growth.

Career Development and Continuous Learning Opportunities:

Providing opportunities for continuous learning and career development is key to sustainability. This might include offering training programs, workshops, and mentorship opportunities. Productions can also support career transitions, helping individuals move between different roles or departments within the industry.

To address the challenge of building stable, long-term careers in the project-based film industry, many organisations offer career development programs worldwide, including Australia. These programs focus on continuous learning, training, workshops, and mentorship opportunities. Here is an overview of the availability and impact of these programs:

Impact of Career Development Programs:

Increased Job Satisfaction and Retention: Studies indicate that career development programs lead to higher job satisfaction and retention rates among participants. For example, a survey by the Entertainment Industry Foundation found that 70% of participants in their career development programs reported increased job satisfaction.

Career Advancement and Mobility: Participants in career development programs often experience faster career advancement and greater mobility within the industry. The Directors Guild of America reported that members who participated in their career development programs were 50% more likely to be promoted within two years compared to those who did not participate.

Skill Enhancement and Adaptability: Training programs and workshops help individuals develop new skills and adapt to industry changes. The Motion Picture Association found that 80% of participants in their training programs reported improved skills that directly contributed to their career growth.

Diversity and Inclusion: Career development programs have a significant impact on promoting diversity and inclusion within the industry. Screen Skills' diversity initiatives have resulted in a 30% increase in the number of participants from underrepresented backgrounds entering the film industry.

Programs to Support Career Transitions and Growth

Supporting career transitions might involve providing resources for skill development or facilitating networking opportunities. For example, a lighting technician might transition to a director of photography role with the right training and mentorship. Encouraging cross-departmental learning can also help individuals build versatile skill sets, making them more resilient to industry changes. Successful career transition programs in the film industry provide resources for skill development, training, mentorship, and networking opportunities, facilitating smooth transitions between different roles. Here are some examples from the UK, US, and Australia:

UNITED KINGDOM:

FILM SKILLS FUND

The Film Skills Fund offers funding for training and development across various departments within the film industry. This fund supports professionals at different stages of their careers, providing access to training that helps them develop the skills needed to advance.

The Film Skills Fund is designed to help industry professionals transition to higher roles. For example, a lighting technician might use this funding to gain the skills needed to become a director of photography. The program provides access to specialised training courses and workshops that focus on both technical skills and leadership development, which are essential for career progression.

Participants in the Film Skills Fund have indeed transitioned into new roles through these funded training programs. The training typically focuses on areas like technical skills, leadership, and department-specific knowledge, enabling participants to move into more senior positions within their field.

BFI NETWORK

BFI NETWORK offers funding, mentorship, and development support to new and emerging filmmakers. The program is designed to nurture talent and help individuals build sustainable careers in the film industry. Support is provided through grants, workshops, and one-on-one mentoring, among other resources.

The program is particularly effective in helping individuals from various roles within the industry, including technical positions, transition into creative roles such as directing and producing. By offering short film funding and professional development opportunities, the BFI NETWORK helps these individuals gain the experience and confidence needed to take on more creative responsibilities.

Emerging filmmakers benefit from mentorship provided by experienced industry professionals. This guidance is invaluable in helping them navigate career transitions, develop their craft, and make informed decisions about their creative paths. The program has a track record of successfully aiding filmmakers in moving from technical or entry-level positions into more senior and creative roles.

UNITED STATES:

AMERICAN FILM INSTITUTE (AFI)

The AFI Conservatory provides a comprehensive education that combines practical experience with mentorship from industry professionals. The program is designed to prepare students for careers in the film industry by immersing them in the craft and providing opportunities to work on real-world projects. Each discipline is taught by experienced faculty and mentors, many of whom are successful professionals in the industry.

The AFI Conservatory equips its fellows (students) with the skills and knowledge necessary to succeed in various roles within the film industry. The program is particularly effective in helping professionals transition between roles, whether they are moving from a technical position to a creative leadership role or refining their expertise in a specific discipline.

Graduates of the AFI Conservatory have indeed successfully transitioned from technical roles to creative leadership positions. The program's emphasis on hands-on training, combined with its strong network of industry connections, provides graduates with the tools they need to advance their careers. Many alumni have gone on to become prominent directors, producers, cinematographers, and other key creative figures in the film industry.

SUNDANCE INSTITUTE

Sundance Ignite provides a comprehensive support system for young filmmakers, offering them mentorship from experienced industry professionals, opportunities for internships, and training that covers various aspects of filmmaking. The program also includes access to Sundance events, such as the Sundance Film Festival, where participants can network with industry leaders and gain valuable exposure.

The program is effective in helping young professionals transition into higher roles within the film industry. By providing access to Sundance mentors and industry events, Sundance Ignite offers participants the guidance and opportunities they need to move from entry-level positions to more advanced roles, such as directing and producing.

Participants in the Sundance Ignite program have successfully transitioned from entry-level positions to more advanced roles in the industry. The mentorship and resources provided by the program play a crucial role in helping these emerging filmmakers gain the experience and confidence needed to take on greater responsibilities in directing, producing, and other key creative roles.

AUSTRALIA:

SCREEN AUSTRALIA

The program, Enterprise People, provides funding for tailored professional development plans. These plans can include mentorships, training, and other activities that are specifically designed to help individuals develop new skills, transition to different roles, or enhance their expertise in their current roles.

Enterprise People supports career transitions by funding professional development that is often cross-departmental, enabling participants to gain new skills and experience in different areas of the screen industry. This can help professionals move from roles like assistant directors to lead directors or shift from technical positions to more creative ones.

Professionals have used the Enterprise People program to make significant career transitions. For example, an assistant director might leverage this program to gain the necessary skills and mentorship to become a lead director. Similarly, someone in a technical role might use the program to transition into a creative role, such as a producer or screenwriter, through targeted training and mentorship opportunities.

AUSTRALIAN FILM, TELEVISION AND RADIO SCHOOL (AFTRS)

Their industry certificates offered by AFTRS can provide upskilling opportunities for professionals who are looking to advance in their careers or transition to new roles. These programs are typically focused on specific industry needs and offer practical, hands-on training that aligns with current industry standards.

The Industry Certificates help individuals gain the expertise needed to move between departments or advance within their current field. By completing these programs, professionals can acquire new technical skills, industry knowledge, and connections that are crucial for career progression.

A lighting technician might enroll in a certificate program in cinematography to develop the skills required to transition into a director of photography role. The program would provide both the technical training and industry networking opportunities necessary to make this career shift.

People Living with Disability

People living with disability face significant barriers within the screen industry, both in front of and behind the camera, across the U.S., UK, and Australia. Despite increased attention to diversity and inclusion, the industry still struggles to create equitable opportunities for individuals with disabilities, leading to systemic challenges in representation, access, and employment.

Key Challenges:

Lack of On-Screen Representation:

In all three countries, people with disabilities are severely underrepresented in film and TV. While people with disabilities make up a significant portion of the population—26% in the U.S. (according to the CDC), 22% in the UK (according to the Department for Work and Pensions), and 18% in Australia (according to the Australian Institute of Health and Welfare)—this is not reflected on screen.

In the U.S., the 2021 GLAAD "Where We Are on TV" report found that only 3.5% of characters in scripted television had a disability. In the UK, the Creative Diversity Network's 2021 report revealed that just 8.2% of on-screen roles were filled by people with a disability, a significant underrepresentation given the population. Similarly, in Australia, research from the Australian Film, Television and Radio School (AFTRS) in 2020 showed that only 6% of main characters in Australian dramas had a disability, again falling short of representing the actual disabled population.

Limited Roles and Stereotyping:

Even when people with disabilities are represented, they are often portrayed through harmful stereotypes—either as people to be pitied, or as "inspirational" figures overcoming their disability. These narrow portrayals not only reinforce negative societal views but also limit the complexity of stories being told about people living with disabilities.

Additionally, disabled roles are frequently given to able-bodied actors. In the U.S., UK, and Australia, there is still a trend of "cripping up," where able-bodied actors play disabled characters, which takes away opportunities from actors with disabilities and perpetuates inauthentic portrayals.

Physical Accessibility Barriers:

Many film and TV sets, production facilities, and studios are not accessible to people with physical disabilities. This lack of accessibility limits the participation of actors, crew, and creatives living with disabilities. For instance, in the UK, 78% of disabled respondents in the Creative Diversity Network's survey said they had faced accessibility barriers at work.

Similar issues are prevalent in Australia and the U.S., where many sets, audition spaces, and training facilities do not meet accessibility standards, making it difficult for people with physical disabilities to gain entry into the industry.

Lack of Inclusive Hiring Practices:

In all three countries, people living with disabilities face significant barriers to employment in the screen industry. A 2019 study by Screen Australia found that only 10% of people living with disabilities working in the industry felt their workplace was inclusive. Similarly, in the UK, a report from the British Film Institute (BFI) found that only 4.5% of the workforce in film and TV production had a disability.

In the U.S., data from RespectAbility shows that only 2.3% of all working actors living with disabilities in the industry had secure, full-time employment, indicating that opportunities for sustained careers in the industry are extremely limited.

Challenges Behind the Camera:

People living with disabilities are not just underrepresented on screen but also behind the camera. In roles such as directors, writers, and producers, there is a lack of individuals with disabilities, which limits the variety of stories told and the perspectives shared in film and TV.

In the UK, a report from the Creative Diversity Network highlighted that only 5.2% of off-screen roles were held by disabled individuals, and in Australia, the Screen Diversity and Inclusion Network (SDIN) found similar trends, with disabled people holding less than 3% of key creative roles behind the camera.

Potential Solutions:

Improved On-Screen Representation: Ensuring that characters with disabilities are written into scripts authentically and that actors with disabilities are cast in those roles is a crucial first step. Production companies can prioritise casting actors with disabilities to reflect the diversity of the population accurately.

Accessible Production Environments: Making and hiring sets, production offices, and audition spaces fully accessible is essential for inclusivity. This means providing wheelchair access, adaptive equipment, and accessible restrooms, and considering all forms of disabilities (physical, sensory, and cognitive) in the design of workspaces, and if such spaces are hired, checking for these facilities before hiring.

Inclusive Hiring Practices: Employers in the screen industry should actively recruit and promote people with disabilities, both in front of and behind the camera. Mentorship programs, internships, and targeted outreach efforts can help break down barriers and create more opportunities for individuals living with disability.

Education and Awareness: Increasing awareness about disability inclusion among industry professionals is crucial. This can be achieved through mandatory diversity and sensitivity training, promoting the idea that people living with disabilities can and should be part of the creative process at all levels of production.

Government and Industry Support: Governments in the U.S., UK, and Australia can play a role by incentivising production companies that hire people living with disabilities, ensuring they comply with accessibility standards, and creating funding streams for disabled creators and storytellers. For example, the UK's Disability Confident scheme encourages employers to attract and retain disabled talent.

Supporting Creatives with Disabilities Behind the Camera: Developing programs that specifically support writers, directors, producers, and crew members with disabilities can help amplify authentic stories. By having more people with disabilities in key creative positions, the industry will benefit from more diverse and genuine portrayals of disability.

While progress has been made, there is still a long way to go in addressing the challenges faced by people living with disabilities in the screen industry. By improving representation, making production spaces accessible, and adopting more inclusive hiring practices, the industry can begin to reflect the full diversity of society. Only then will the screen industry truly embrace its role as a space for all stories, perspectives, and talents.

Company making a difference - Bus Stop Films

Bus Stop Films is a pioneering organisation based in Australia that uses filmmaking as a tool to raise awareness and provide education about people living with disabilities. The organisation offers accessible film studies programs specifically designed for people living with disabilities and other marginalised communities. These programs aim to make filmmaking inclusive, offering students the opportunity to learn about various aspects of film production in a supportive and accessible environment.

Bus Stop Films has produced numerous award-winning films that showcase the talents of people living with disabilities. These films have been recognised both nationally and internationally, highlighting the creative abilities of participants and challenging societal perceptions of disability. The program provides participants with practical skills in filmmaking, including screenwriting, directing, acting, and editing. Beyond technical skills, the program also promotes social inclusion, confidence, and creative expression among its participants. By engaging in the filmmaking process, students gain valuable life skills and increased self-esteem. The organisation's work has significantly increased visibility and representation of people with disabilities in the media. By focusing on stories that are often overlooked, Bus Stop Films plays a crucial role in promoting diversity and inclusion within the film industry.

People of Colour

People of colour face numerous challenges in the film industry, both in front of and behind the camera. Despite increasing awareness and initiatives for diversity and inclusion, systemic issues continue to affect the careers, opportunities, and representation of people of colour. Here are the key challenges:

Underrepresentation & Typecasting on Screen:

People of colour are often underrepresented in leading and significant roles. When they are cast, it is often in stereotypical roles that reinforce harmful or limited narratives, such as playing the criminal, the sidekick, or the "exotic" character. These roles don't allow actors to show their full range of talent or take on more complex, multifaceted characters. There is a tendency to depict people of colour as "exotic" or "other," reducing them to caricatures rather than authentic representations. This is particularly problematic in stories where their racial or ethnic identity is exaggerated for the sake of plotlines, while their true cultural experiences are ignored.

Many productions include one or two actors of colour as a token gesture toward diversity, without giving them substantial roles or opportunities for character development. This approach may meet diversity quotas but does not offer true representation or inclusion.

Statistics:

In the U.S., a 2022 study by UCLA found that while people of colour make up nearly 40% of the population, only 27% of lead roles in films were held by non-white actors.

In the UK, a report by the British Film Institute (BFI) revealed that people of colour are cast in 12% of lead roles, despite being 14% of the population. This is a better number than the US and Australia.

In Australia, Screen Australia's 2021 report showed that only 7% of lead roles in TV dramas were held by people of colour, far below their population proportion of 24%.

Lack of Behind-the-Camera Representation:

People of colour are significantly underrepresented in key creative roles such as directors, writers, and producers. This lack of diversity behind the camera means that stories about people of colour are often told by white creatives, which can result in inauthentic or biased portrayals.

Systemic racism within the industry makes it difficult for people of colour to break into key behind-the-scenes roles. There is a lack of mentorship, funding, and networking opportunities for emerging filmmakers of colour, which limits their access to resources and opportunities.

Statistics:

In the U.S., only 6% of film directors in the top-grossing films of 2021 were people of colour, according to the Directors Guild of America (DGA).

In the UK, the Creative Diversity Network's 2021 report found that only 3% of off-screen roles, including writers, producers, and directors, were held by people of colour.

In Australia, the Screen Diversity and Inclusion Network (SDIN) found that people of colour held less than 5% of key creative roles in film and television.

Pay Disparity:

Actors, writers, and directors of colour are often paid less than their white counterparts for similar roles. Even when they achieve similar levels of success or acclaim, people of colour often face wage gaps, which is a reflection of broader inequities in the industry.

Due to fewer opportunities and limited representation, people of colour often lack the negotiating power to secure better deals, resulting in lower pay and fewer benefits compared to their white colleagues.

Barriers to Entry for Emerging Talent:

People of colour often face more significant challenges in securing funding for their projects or being recognised in film festivals and awards. Many film grants, fellowships, and funding opportunities are less accessible to emerging creators of colour, particularly when the selection panels are not diverse.

The industry relies heavily on networks and connections, and people of colour often lack access to the same social and professional networks as their white counterparts. This leads to fewer opportunities for advancement, mentorship, and collaboration.

There are, however, in recent times, has been a shift in funding bodies and organisations with quotas and initiatives focussing on people of colour or Indigenous people. We look at these later in the book.

Racism and Microaggressions on Set:

People of colour in the film industry often report experiencing racism, whether overt or in the form of microaggressions. This could be anything from being dismissed or overlooked in decision-making to experiencing bias in casting or hiring decisions.

Many sets lack a cultural understanding of the experiences of people of colour. This can lead to insensitive handling of issues related to race, ethnicity, and identity, further marginalising those working on set.

Diversity Fatigue - Superficial Commitment to Diversity:

While diversity and inclusion have become popular buzzwords, many initiatives fail to make a meaningful impact. Companies may implement diversity policies without making real changes in hiring practices, resulting in frustration and "diversity fatigue" for those who see these efforts as performative.

Limited Opportunities for Authentic Storytelling:

People of colour often face obstacles when trying to tell authentic stories about their communities. White executives and producers frequently control which stories are deemed marketable, which can limit the range of narratives told by and about people of colour.

Independent filmmakers of colour often lack the same access to distribution, marketing, and festival exposure as their white counterparts, making it harder for their stories to reach wider audiences.

Potential Solutions:

More Inclusive Casting and Hiring Practices: Productions need to prioritise casting actors of colour in leading roles that reflect the diversity of their audience, not just as token characters. Similarly, behind-the-scenes hiring must actively seek out writers, directors, and producers of colour to create more authentic stories.

Mentorship and Networking Opportunities: Creating mentorship programs and networking opportunities specifically for people of colour can help break down the barriers to entry in the industry. This could involve partnering with industry veterans to provide guidance and connections for emerging talent.

Accessible Funding for Filmmakers of Colour: More funding and grants specifically aimed at filmmakers of colour can help ensure they have the resources needed to develop and produce their projects. Funders and festivals should also diversify their selection panels to ensure a broader range of voices are supported.

Pay Equity and Transparency: Addressing the wage gap between actors and creators of colour and their white counterparts is essential. Transparency in pay structures and more equitable compensation practices can help create a fairer industry.

Cultural Sensitivity Training: Production companies can implement mandatory cultural sensitivity training to prevent racism and microaggressions on set, ensuring that all actors and crew feel respected and valued in their work environment.

Authentic Storytelling and Control Over Narratives: It's important for creators of colour to have control over their narratives. Supporting filmmakers and writers of colour in telling their own stories with authenticity can diversify the range of content available and provide more meaningful representation on screen.

People of colour in the film industry face numerous challenges, from underrepresentation and stereotyping to pay disparity and limited access to opportunities behind the camera. While progress has been made, there is still much work to be done to ensure that the industry becomes truly inclusive. By addressing systemic barriers, supporting emerging talent, and promoting authentic storytelling, the film industry can create a more equitable space for all creators and performers.

THE LGBTQIA+ Community

The LGBTQIA+ community faces significant challenges within the screen industry, both in terms of on-screen representation and behind-the-scenes opportunities. While there have been improvements in recent years, many barriers still exist, and the industry remains a difficult space for LGBTQIA+ individuals to thrive and express their identities authentically. Below are some of the most prominent challenges faced by the LGBTQIA+ community in the film and television industry:

Underrepresentation and Misrepresentation on Screen:

Limited LGBTQIA+ Characters: Although LGBTQIA+ representation on screen has improved, it remains far below reflecting the actual population. In 2021, GLAAD's "Where We Are on TV" report found that only 11.9% of regular characters in primetime television in the U.S. were LGBTQIA+, a figure that is still not fully reflective of the broader LGBTQIA+ community. In the UK and Australia, similar gaps in representation persist.

Misrepresentation and Stereotyping: When LGBTQIA+ characters are represented, they are often confined to harmful stereotypes—such as the promiscuous gay man, the tragic queer character, or the flamboyant comic relief. These portrayals often fail to capture the complexity of LGBTQIA+ identities and experiences, reducing them to one-dimensional characters.

Queer-baiting: Another common issue is "queer-baiting," where media teases the possibility of LGBTQIA+ characters or relationships without fully committing to their portrayal. This can frustrate LGBTQIA+ audiences, as it trivialises their identities for profit without offering genuine representation.

Straight Actors in Queer Roles: A significant issue in LGBTQIA+ representation is the casting of cisgender, heterosexual actors in queer or transgender roles. This practice, sometimes referred to as "queerface," not only takes away opportunities from LGBTQIA+ actors but also leads to inauthentic portrayals. Straight and cisgender actors may not fully understand the nuances of queer or trans experiences, leading to misrepresentations on screen.

Queer Narratives Told by Non-Queer Writers: LGBTQIA+ stories are often written by non-LGBTQIA+ creators, which can result in inaccurate or reductive narratives that fail to capture the lived experiences of the community. This is particularly common in Hollywood, where many queer stories are written through a heteronormative or cisnormative lens.

Lack of Intersectional Representation:

Limited Portrayals of LGBTQIA+ People of Colour and Disabled LGBTQIA+ Individuals: LGBTQIA+ characters of colour, disabled LGBTQIA+ people, and transgender characters are significantly underrepresented. When they are portrayed, it's often through narrow or stereotypical lenses, ignoring the intersectionality of race, gender identity, sexuality, and disability.

Transgender and Non-Binary Erasure: Although there has been progress in representing cisgender gay and lesbian characters, transgender, non-binary, and gender non-conforming individuals remain largely invisible in mainstream media. When trans characters do appear, they are often played by cisgender actors, which perpetuates a lack of authentic representation.

Lack of Opportunities for LGBTQIA+ Creatives Behind the Camera:

LGBTQIA+ individuals are often underrepresented in directing, writing, and producing roles, which limits the ability to tell authentic LGBTQIA+ stories. The lack of queer creatives behind the scenes results in fewer opportunities for genuine storytelling from LGBTQIA+ perspectives. Without LGBTQIA+

writers and directors, queer narratives are frequently filtered through non-LGBTQIA+ lenses, leading to inauthentic or misrepresented portrayals.

Discrimination and Hostility on Set:

Homophobia and Transphobia: LGBTQIA+ actors and crew members often face overt or covert homophobia and transphobia on set. This can range from inappropriate comments, exclusion, or lack of respect for pronouns and gender identities to outright harassment or discrimination. These hostile environments make it difficult for LGBTQIA+ individuals to work comfortably and safely.

Lack of Supportive Policies: Many production companies do not have strong anti-discrimination policies in place, leaving LGBTQIA+ individuals vulnerable to mistreatment. Without robust protections, reporting harassment or discrimination can be risky, and many individuals may fear retaliation or being blacklisted.

Fear of Being "Outed":

Many LGBTQIA+ actors still feel pressured to stay closeted to protect their careers. The fear of being "outed" or pigeonholed in the industry can prevent actors from taking on LGBTQIA+ roles or being authentic about their identities. For many, the industry remains a place where being openly queer or trans can result in fewer opportunities or being passed over for major roles.

Challenges in Distribution and Marketing:

Niche Marketing of LGBTQIA+ Stories: Many LGBTQIA+ films and TV shows are marketed as niche content, limiting their distribution to smaller platforms or festivals. This reduces their visibility to mainstream audiences and reinforces the idea that LGBTQIA+ stories are only for LGBTQIA+ viewers, rather than universal stories for all.

Lack of Studio Support: Major studios are often hesitant to back LGBTQIA+ projects, especially those that centre on transgender characters or narratives that do not fit the traditional mould of LGBTQIA+ stories. Independent filmmakers struggle to secure funding and distribution, often relying on small budgets or crowdfunding.

Solutions for Creating Change in the Industry:

More LGBTQIA+ Characters and Complex Storytelling: The industry needs to increase the quantity and quality of LGBTQIA+ characters on screen. Representation should include a wide range of LGBTQIA+ identities, with stories that go beyond stereotypes. Complex LGBTQIA+ characters should be featured in all genres and roles, not just in stories that revolve around their identity.

Hiring LGBTQIA+ Creatives in Key Roles: Hiring more LGBTQIA+ writers, directors, and producers is essential for authentic storytelling. Creators from within the LGBTQIA+ community can tell more nuanced and diverse stories, bringing greater accuracy and depth to LGBTQIA+ representation.

Creating Safe, Inclusive Work Environments: Production companies need to enforce strict anti-discrimination policies and provide training on LGBTQIA+ inclusion. Ensuring that sets are safe and welcoming for LGBTQIA+ actors and crew is critical for fostering creativity and comfort.

Ending the Casting of Straight, Cisgender Actors in LGBTQIA+ Roles: Whenever possible, LGBTQIA+ actors should be cast in LGBTQIA+ roles. This not only provides more opportunities for LGBTQIA+ performers but also ensures that portrayals are authentic and sensitive to the complexities of queer and trans identities.

Funding and Support for LGBTQIA+ Projects: Studios, festivals, and funding bodies should actively seek out and support LGBTQIA+ filmmakers and stories. Increasing the availability of financial resources for LGBTQIA+ creators will help level the playing field and bring more diverse stories to the screen.

Recognising Intersectional Identities: The industry needs to tell more stories about LGBTQIA+ people of colour, disabled LGBTQIA+ individuals, and transgender or non-binary people. Intersectional representation is key to reflecting the true diversity of the LGBTQIA+ community and its varied experiences.

The LGBTQIA+ community faces systemic challenges in the screen industry, from underrepresentation and typecasting to discrimination on set and limited opportunities behind the camera. However, through more inclusive casting, authentic storytelling, and better support for LGBTQIA+ creatives, the industry can take meaningful steps toward greater equality and representation. The path to real change involves not just increasing visibility but also ensuring that LGBTQIA+ people have control over their own narratives and the space to tell their stories authentically.

Cisgender White Males

You might be surprised to find this section in the book, but I believe that to build a more sustainable, happy, and healthy industry, we need to include everyone. After all, the last thing we want to do is fall into the trap of typecasting or exclusion.

Cisgender white males have long dominated the film and television industry, holding a significant share of both on-screen roles and behind-the-camera positions. This demographic has historically benefited from privilege and access to opportunities that have been less available to women, people of colour, and LGBTQIA+ individuals. However, despite these advantages, cisgender white males are not without challenges, particularly in a changing industry that is increasingly focused on diversity, inclusion, and the redefinition of traditional roles.

Here are some of the unique challenges faced by cisgender white males in the screen industry:

Increased Competition in a Changing Landscape:

Shifting Focus on Diversity and Inclusion: As the industry moves towards greater inclusivity, there has been a push to provide more opportunities for underrepresented groups, including women, people of colour, and LGBTQIA+ individuals. This shift has created increased competition for cisgender white males, especially in areas like casting and directing, where there is a growing emphasis on diversifying both the stories told and the people who tell them.

Perception of Privilege: Many cisgender white males may feel the effects of being perceived as the "default" or "privileged" group, which can lead to challenges in finding roles or positions that align with the industry's current focus on diversity. As more opportunities are intentionally given to underrepresented groups, some cisgender white males may feel a sense of displacement or uncertainty about their place in the evolving industry.

Typecasting and Stereotypical Roles:

While cisgender white male actors often have greater access to leading roles in the film industry compared to other groups, they also face the challenge of being typecast into traditional, one-dimensional characters. These roles frequently emphasise narrow and outdated concepts of masculinity—such as the "tough guy," "hero," or emotionally detached male figure. This typecasting limits the range of characters they can portray, often restricting them from exploring more complex, emotionally diverse roles. According to a study by USC's Annenberg Inclusion Initiative, **72% of leading roles in the top-grossing films from 2007 to 2019** were filled by white male actors, but many of these characters fit within conventional, stereotypical moulds of masculinity.

Cisgender white male actors also experience pressure to conform to these traditional expectations, leaving little room for vulnerability or the exploration of non-traditional male traits. This can restrict their artistic range and make it difficult to break out of the typical "masculine" roles they are offered. While these roles may bring visibility, they often lack the emotional depth or complexity that many actors seek to challenge themselves creatively.

Gender Expectations and Shifting Masculinity:

On the other side of the spectrum, as the film industry evolves, with more diverse and nuanced stories being told, cisgender white males are finding themselves navigating changing definitions of masculinity. The shift toward more complex portrayals of male identity presents both opportunities and challenges. On one hand, there is greater room for actors to explore characters who reflect a broader range of emotions and experiences. On the other hand, this shift can create tension for actors who have built their careers playing more conventional male archetypes. For many, adapting to these new expectations means redefining their artistic identity in an industry that is slowly moving away from rigid gender roles.

Challenging Toxic Masculinity:

One of the key areas where this shift is happening is the challenge to "toxic masculinity," which refers to harmful social expectations that pressure men to be dominant, aggressive, or emotionally distant. More films are addressing these issues, asking actors to play roles that confront or subvert these traditional notions of masculinity. While this can lead to more dynamic and compelling storytelling, it can also be difficult for actors who are used to roles rooted in conventional masculinity. This shift requires them to explore vulnerabilities and emotions that their earlier roles may not have allowed, which can be both a rewarding and challenging adjustment.

So for actors, while cisgender white males continue to have significant opportunities in leading roles, they often face the limitation of being typecast into traditional masculine characters. However, with the industry's evolving understanding of gender roles and masculinity, there are growing opportunities for more nuanced and emotionally rich portrayals, allowing actors to expand their range and break free from old stereotypes.

Increased Scrutiny and Accountability:

Pressure to Support Diversity: As leaders in an industry that has – rightfully so - long been criticised for its lack of diversity, cisgender white males, particularly those in positions of power (directors, producers, and studio executives), face heightened scrutiny to be active advocates for inclusion. There is a growing expectation for them to champion diverse voices, hire inclusively, and ensure equitable representation behind and in front of the camera. Failing to do so can lead to public criticism or a reputation for being out of touch with the industry's current values.

Accountability for Past Inequities: In the wake of movements such as #MeToo and Time's Up, cisgender white males in the screen industry are often subject to increased accountability for past behaviours and systemic issues that have marginalised others. They may be expected to engage in self-reflection, reform their practices, and actively support change, which can be a complex process to navigate.

Navigating Industry Changes as Established Professionals:

Challenges for Established Actors and Filmmakers: Cisgender white males who have built their careers over decades may face challenges adapting to an industry that is undergoing significant transformation. As younger, more diverse voices emerge and disrupt traditional power structures, older cisgender white males might feel their influence waning or struggle to remain relevant in a landscape that values new perspectives.

Balancing Experience with Modern Expectations: Long-established cisgender white male actors, directors, and producers may find it difficult to balance their years of experience with the modern industry's push for innovation and representation. They are often required to evolve their storytelling, leadership, and creative approaches in ways that align with modern values while still honouring their past work.

Perceived Decline in Opportunities:

Decreased Access to Certain Roles: As casting directors actively seek to diversify their rosters, some cisgender white males may experience a perceived decline in opportunities, particularly for roles traditionally held by men. While opportunities for cisgender white males remain abundant, there is a noticeable shift in which types of roles are prioritised, particularly as diverse casting becomes more normalised.

Potential Solutions and Adaptations:

Embracing Diverse Storytelling: Cisgender white male actors and filmmakers have the opportunity to contribute to a more inclusive industry by embracing diverse storytelling. Whether by taking on roles that challenge traditional gender norms or supporting underrepresented voices behind the camera, they can help shape the future of film and television in meaningful ways.

Exploring Vulnerability and Complex Masculinity: By moving away from stereotypical portrayals of masculinity, cisgender white male actors can push for roles that explore vulnerability, emotional depth, and the complexities of modern male identity. This shift not only expands their range as actors but also contributes to a broader understanding of masculinity on screen.

Advocating for Inclusion Behind the Camera: Cisgender white males in positions of influence—such as directors, producers, and studio executives—can play a pivotal role in fostering diversity by championing inclusive hiring practices and mentoring up-and-coming talent from underrepresented backgrounds.

Adapting to Industry Changes: As the industry continues to evolve, cisgender white males can adapt by staying open to change, collaborating with diverse creatives, and continuing to learn about the importance of inclusion in storytelling. By evolving with the industry, they can remain relevant and contribute positively to its growth.

While cisgender white males continue to occupy prominent positions in the screen industry, they are not immune to the challenges brought about by a shifting cultural and professional landscape. Increased competition for roles, pressure to support diversity, and the need to evolve traditional portrayals of masculinity present unique obstacles. However, these challenges also offer opportunities for growth, adaptation, and contributing to a more inclusive industry where all voices are represented authentically and meaningfully.

CHAPTER 12

Movements of Change

As awareness of the demanding conditions in the film industry has grown, so too have the efforts to address these issues. Various initiatives, advocacy groups, and legislative actions are working towards creating a more balanced and sustainable work environment. This chapter explores these efforts, highlighting success stories and the roles of industry leaders in driving change.

Initiatives and Advocacy Groups

Several organisations and advocacy groups have emerged with the specific goal of improving working conditions in the film industry. Groups like Time's Up, Women in Film (WIF) and Women In Film and Television (WIFT/I), have been at the forefront of advocating for gender equality, better working conditions, and support for underrepresented voices in the industry. These organisations provide resources, support networks, and advocacy for policies that promote fair treatment and work-life balance.

The Sustainable Production Alliance (SPA) is another key player, focusing on environmentally friendly and sustainable practices in filmmaking. While their primary goal is to reduce the environmental impact of productions, their efforts also include promoting practices that improve the well-being of cast and crew, such as reducing long hours and encouraging sustainable work practices.

Key Advocacy Groups and Their Achievements in Improving Equality and Working Conditions (Past and Current Initiatives)

UNITED STATES

Women in Film (WIF)

Achievements: Founded in 1973, WIF provides extensive support and resources for women in the film industry, including mentorship programs, scholarships, and research initiatives. They have consistently worked to address and highlight gender disparities within the industry. Notably, WIF has been influential in conducting and publishing annual reports that spotlight these issues and drive change.

Key Programs and Initiatives:

WIF Fellowship Program: Mentorship is a cornerstone of WIF's activities. Created in honour of our 50th Anniversary, this flagship program welcomes Fellows from all areas of the entertainment industry for a year of mentoring, master classes, network building, and one-on-one career strategy sessions.

- **ReFrame Initiative:** In partnership with the Sundance Institute, WIF co-founded the ReFrame Initiative to promote gender parity in Hollywood. The ReFrame project offers a certification called the ReFrame Stamp, which is awarded to films and television productions that demonstrate a commitment to hiring practices that are inclusive and equitable. The initiative works with major studios, production companies, and networks to encourage the adoption of gender-balanced hiring practices.

- **Sexual Harassment Help Line:** In response to the #MeToo movement, WIF launched a Sexual Harassment Help Line in 2018. It has since transferred its operations to The Hollywood Commission in 2024. This service provides a confidential resource for individuals in the industry who have experienced harassment or misconduct. The helpline offers access to legal services, counselling, and guidance on how to navigate these challenging situations, reflecting WIF's commitment to creating a safe working environment for all women in the industry.

- **Advocacy and Research:** WIF is heavily involved in advocacy and research efforts aimed at highlighting the systemic barriers faced by women in the screen industries. Through research reports, WIF sheds light on issues such as the gender pay gap, underrepresentation in key creative roles, and the prevalence of gender-based discrimination. These findings are used to advocate for industry-wide changes and to inform their initiatives.

- **Educational Programs and Workshops:** WIF offers a variety of educational programs and **workshops** designed to equip women with the skills they need to succeed in the industry. These programs cover a wide range of topics, including directing, producing, screenwriting, and digital media. WIF's educational efforts are geared toward helping women develop their craft, gain confidence, and navigate the business side of the industry.

- **Networking Events and Panels:** Networking is a critical component of WIF's strategy to empower women in the industry. WIF organises numerous networking events, panels, and screenings that provide women with opportunities to connect with industry professionals, share their work, and build their careers. These events are often centred around important industry topics, such as diversity and inclusion, and feature high-profile speakers and panelists.

- **Public Advocacy and Industry Influence:** WIF is a leading voice in advocating for gender equality in the screen industries. The organisation regularly engages in public advocacy campaigns to raise awareness about the challenges women face in Hollywood and to push for meaningful change. WIF collaborates with industry stakeholders, including studios, production companies, and guilds, to promote policies and practices that support gender equity.

- **Emerging Filmmakers Program:** The **Emerging Filmmakers Program** is designed to support new talent entering the industry. This program provides resources, mentorship, and opportunities for emerging female filmmakers to showcase their work. WIF aims to create a pipeline of talented women who are equipped to succeed in a competitive industry.

- **Film Finishing Fund:** Historically, WIF has administered WIF also administers the Film Finishing Fund, which provides grants to help women filmmakers complete their projects. This fund is particularly aimed at independent films that are directed by women, offering critical support at a stage when funding is often scarce. The Film Finishing Fund has supported numerous films that have gone on to screen at major film festivals and receive wide acclaim.

UNITED KINGDOM

Raising Films

Achievements: Founded in 2015, Raising Films has focused on providing resources, advocacy, and conducting research to improve working conditions for parents and carers. The organisation has been instrumental in raising awareness of the difficulties faced by this group and pushing for systemic change within the industry.

Key Programs and Initiatives:

Research and Advocacy: Raising Films conducts in-depth research to highlight the issues faced by parents and carers in the screen industries. One of their significant contributions is the "Raising Our Game" report, published in 2017. This report provided critical insights into the barriers faced by carers and parents, such as the lack of flexible working arrangements, job insecurity, and the stigma associated with caregiving responsibilities. The findings from this research have been used to advocate for policy changes and better support within the industry.

Raising Films Survey Reports: Raising Films has conducted several surveys, including the "Honey, I Hid the Kids!" report in 2018. These surveys gather data on the working conditions of parents and carers, providing evidence-based recommendations to improve industry practices. The organisation uses this data to influence stakeholders and push for more inclusive and supportive work environments.

Support and Resources: Raising Films offers a range of resources designed to help parents and carers navigate the challenges of working in the screen industry. These resources include practical guides on managing work-life balance, tips for negotiating flexible work arrangements, and advice on dealing with discrimination. The organisation also provides information on accessing financial support and legal advice, helping individuals protect their rights and maintain their careers while fulfilling their caregiving roles.

Collaborations and Partnerships: Raising Films collaborates with various industry bodies, unions, and organisations to amplify its impact. They work closely with groups like WIFT (Women in Film and Television) UK **and the** British Film Institute (BFI) to advocate for changes that benefit parents and carers. These partnerships help Raising Films influence broader industry practices and ensure that the voices of parents and carers are heard at the highest levels.

Events and Workshops: The organisation hosts events and workshops aimed at supporting parents and carers. These events provide networking opportunities, professional development, and a platform to share experiences and solutions. Workshops often focus on specific challenges, such as returning to work after a career break or managing mental health while balancing work and caregiving responsibilities.

Campaigns and Public Advocacy: Raising Films engages in public advocacy campaigns to raise awareness about the challenges faced by parents and carers in the industry. These campaigns often coincide with the release of their research reports and aim to influence public opinion and industry policies. By shining a light on these issues, Raising Films works to create a more equitable industry for all.

Impact and Recognition: Raising Films has been widely recognised for its work in advocating for parents and carers. Their research and advocacy have led to tangible changes in industry practices, including greater awareness of the need for flexible working arrangements and more supportive policies for caregivers. The organisation has been instrumental in sparking conversations around work-life balance in the screen industries, and its efforts continue to drive progress toward a more inclusive and supportive work environment.

Through these efforts, Raising Films is making significant strides in addressing the unique challenges faced by parents and carers in the screen industries, ensuring that they can thrive in their careers without sacrificing their caregiving responsibilities.

The Film and TV Charity

Achievements: Founded in 1924, the charity offers a broad range of services, including financial support, mental health services, and general advice for industry professionals. One of their significant initiatives is the Whole Picture Program, which was launched in response to a mental health crisis identified in the industry through their 2019 Looking Glass Survey. This program includes the Whole Picture Toolkit, designed to improve mental health practices across productions.

Key Programs and Initiatives:

Financial Support and Grants: The Film and TV Charity continues its original mission of providing financial support to industry workers in need. The charity offers grants and emergency financial assistance to those facing hardship, helping them cover essential living costs, unexpected medical expenses, or other urgent needs. This support is crucial for freelancers and those in precarious employment situations, which are common in the industry.

Mental Health Services: A significant focus of the charity in recent years has been on improving the mental health and wellbeing of industry workers. The Whole Picture Program, launched in response to findings from the 2019 Looking Glass Survey, is a comprehensive initiative aimed at tackling the mental health crisis in the film and TV industries. This program includes the development of the Whole Picture Toolkit, which provides resources and guidelines to help productions create mentally healthy working environments.

Additionally, the charity offers a 24/7 Support Line, a confidential service that provides mental health counselling, legal advice, and financial guidance. This support line has been a lifeline for many in the industry, particularly during the challenges posed by the COVID-19 pandemic.

The Looking Glass Survey and Advocacy: The Looking Glass Survey is one of the charity's landmark research efforts, providing in-depth insights into the mental health challenges faced by workers in the screen industries. The survey revealed alarming rates of mental health issues, including high levels of stress, anxiety, and depression among industry professionals. These findings have driven the charity's advocacy efforts, pushing for systemic changes to improve working conditions and support mental wellbeing across the industry.

Diversity, Equity, and Inclusion Initiatives: The Film and TV Charity is committed to promoting diversity, equity, and inclusion within the industry. It has launched initiatives aimed at supporting underrepresented groups, including women, people of **colour**, and those from marginalised communities. These initiatives include offering targeted grants, creating networking opportunities, and advocating for inclusive practices in the workplace.

Career Development and Training: The charity provides a range of career development resources, including workshops, mentoring programs, and online courses. These resources are designed to help industry professionals build their skills, navigate career challenges, and advance their careers in a competitive environment. The charity also offers legal advice and guidance on issues such as contracts, intellectual property, and employment rights.

Community Building and Networking: Building a supportive community is another key aspect of the charity's work. The organisation hosts events, forums, and networking opportunities that bring industry professionals together to share experiences, exchange ideas, and support one another. These events are particularly important for freelancers and others who may feel isolated in their work.

Public Advocacy and Industry Influence: The Film and TV Charity plays an influential role in advocating for better working conditions and mental health support in the screen industries. By collaborating with industry bodies, production companies, and policymakers, the charity works to ensure that the needs of workers are recognised and addressed at all levels of the industry.

Impact and Recognition: The Film and TV Charity has had a profound impact on the lives of those working behind the scenes in the UK's screen industries. Its efforts have been instrumental in raising awareness about the challenges faced by industry workers and in pushing for changes that promote wellbeing and inclusion. The charity's programs and initiatives have been widely recognised and supported by industry stakeholders, and its work continues to be essential in creating a healthier, more sustainable industry. Through its comprehensive support services, advocacy efforts, and commitment to improving the lives of industry professionals, The Film and TV Charity remains a vital resource for the UK's screen industries.

AUSTRALIA

Women in Film and Television (WIFT) Australia

Founded: WIFT New South Wales (WIFT NSW) was established in 1982, and WIFT Australia as a national organisation was officially launched in April 2018. The national organisation was formed to unify various state chapters under a broader mission to achieve gender equality across the Australian screen industry.

Achievements: WIFT Australia works to advance the status of women in the screen industries by providing professional development, networking opportunities, and advocacy for gender equality. They organise events, panels, and various programs aimed at career development for women in film and television.

Notable Actions: Women in Film and Television (WIFT) Australia is actively involved in numerous initiatives and programs designed to support and advance the careers of women in the screen industries. Here's an expanded look at some of their key activities:

MentorHer Program: MentorHer is one of WIFT Australia's flagship programs aimed at fostering the professional growth of women in the screen industries through mentorship. This program pairs emerging female talent with experienced industry professionals to provide guidance, support, and networking opportunities. The mentorships are tailored to the needs of participants, focusing on areas such as career development, leadership skills, and navigating the challenges of the industry. This program plays a critical role in helping women overcome barriers to advancement and in building a more equitable industry.

ScreenMATE Bystander Program: Launched in 2019, the ScreenMATE Bystander Program is a significant initiative designed to address gender-based violence and discrimination within the screen and games industries. This program provides workshops that teach participants how to recognise harmful behaviours and develop the confidence to intervene. It's particularly focused on the unique challenges faced in freelance-heavy environments where traditional HR support structures might be lacking. This program reflects WIFT's commitment to creating safer, more inclusive workspaces.

ElevateUs Program: The ElevateUs program is another notable initiative by WIFT Australia, in collaboration with Screen Australia, aimed at providing professional development opportunities for women in the screen industry. This program includes workshops, masterclasses, and networking events designed to elevate the skills and careers of women across various roles in film and television. It's part of WIFT's broader strategy to close the gender gap in leadership positions within the industry.

CinefestOZ WIFT Australia Writers Retreat: WIFT Australia also organises the CinefestOZ WIFT Australia Writers Retreat, which offers female writers a focused environment to develop their scripts and ideas with the guidance of experienced mentors. This retreat provides an invaluable opportunity for participants to hone their craft, receive feedback, and connect with industry professionals.

Advocacy and Research: WIFT Australia is deeply involved in advocacy efforts aimed at promoting gender equality in the screen industries. This includes conducting research to identify the challenges women face, such as their underrepresentation in key creative roles and the impact of workplace culture on their careers. WIFT uses this research to advocate for policy changes and to raise awareness within the industry about the need for more inclusive practices.

Networking and Community Building: Beyond structured programs, WIFT Australia is dedicated to building a strong community of women in the screen industries through regular networking events, panel discussions, and screenings. These events provide a platform for women to share their experiences, celebrate their achievements, and support each other's professional journeys.

Public Advocacy and Industry Influence: WIFT actively participates in public discourse and collaborates with industry stakeholders to influence policies and practices. For instance, WIFT has been vocal in advocating for better representation of women in leadership roles and for the implementation of industry-wide standards to prevent harassment and discrimination.

WIFT Australia's efforts are crucial in driving the cultural and structural changes needed to ensure that women can thrive in the screen industries. Through these programs and initiatives, WIFT continues to empower women and work towards a more equitable and inclusive industry.

WIFT Australia's efforts are crucial in driving the cultural and structural changes needed to ensure that women can thrive in the screen industries. Through these programs and initiatives, WIFT continues to empower women and work towards a more equitable and inclusive industry.

Screen Australia's Gender Matters Program

'Gender Matters' is the umbrella name of Screen Australia's efforts to address the underrepresentation of women, non-binary and gender diverse practitioners in the Australian screen industry.

Since 2015, Gender Matters has comprised of Screen Australia's targeted programs and initiatives to improve gender equity in the industry, supporting the Gender Matters Taskforce, and other measures including Screen Australia's Gender Matters KPI. The Gender Matters Taskforce is a volunteer-based advisory body for the agency, comprised of women and gender diverse screen practitioners working across the Australian screen sector. The Taskforce is proudly committed to supporting systemic change within the industry, by creating opportunities and empowering women and gender diverse practitioners.

Here is a summary of what the Taskforce does, its achievements, and the outcomes of these achievements:

What the Gender Matters Taskforce does:

Promotes Gender Equality: The Taskforce works to ensure greater participation of women, non-binary, and gender-diverse people in key creative roles within the Australian screen industry, such as writers, producers, and directors.

Implements Initiatives: It supports a variety of programs and initiatives designed to increase access and opportunities for women and gender-diverse individuals. These include mentorship programs, funding initiatives, industry events, partnerships and targeted support for female-led projects.

Additionally, Screen Australia reports gender data annually, which includes:

Gender Matters KPI: the agency sets a measurable goal in its Corporate Plan, known as the Gender Matters KPI, to track and ensure progress toward gender parity in the industry. The KPI has been expanded to include non-binary and gender-diverse key creatives.

Protagonist information: Screen Australia publishes the percentage of women protagonists in the dramas that receive development and production funding. Protagonist data is separate from the KPI and is the agency's measure of on-screen representation of women.

Industry-wide data: Screen Australia also publishes industry-wide gender data, which is also separate to the KPI. The industry-wide data includes gender information of key creative roles on drama and documentary titles entering production in Australia. While indicative only, the industry-wide data is a useful to monitor the representation of women in key creative roles across the broader Australian screen industry, in addition to Screen Australia-funded projects.

Achievements since Gender Matters launched:

Successful KPIs: Screen Australia has consistently met its gender parity targets. For the period from 2016/17 to 2018/19, 56% of funded projects had women in at least half of the key creative roles. From 2019/20 to 2022/23, 55% of the key creative roles across all projects that received Screen Australia development and production funding were women.

Innovative Programs:

Brilliant Stories and Brilliant Careers: These programs funded the development of female-led dramas and supported female-led businesses.

Attachments for Women: This initiative required certain funded projects to include paid positions for women, expanding in later years to become more inclusive.

Better Deals: This provided financial incentives for distributors to support female-led films.

Recent Initiatives: In recent years, Screen Australia and the Taskforce have launched programs like:

- **ElevateUs:** A mentorship program aimed at fostering the next generation of women and gender diverse screen professionals.

- **Credit Maker:** A program providing women with opportunities to gain credits on significant productions.

Outcomes of Achievements:

Increased Representation: The consistent achievement of Gender Matters KPIs indicates a significant increase in the representation of women in key creative roles across the industry.

Cultural Shift: These efforts have contributed to a broader cultural shift towards inclusivity within the Australian screen industry, ensuring that a more diverse range of voices are heard and represented in film and television.

Ongoing Commitment: The continuation of Gender Matters and the ongoing updates to KPIs and programs, including the expansion to include non-binary and gender-diverse creatives in the KPI and on the Taskforce, demonstrate a sustained commitment to achieving and maintaining gender equity in the industry.

In summary, the Gender Matters program has played a crucial role in promoting gender equity within the Australian screen industry through targeted initiatives and measurable goals. Its efforts have led to significant progress in increasing the representation of women and gender-diverse individuals in key creative roles, fostering a more inclusive and diverse industry.

Screen Australia's Diversity and Inclusion Programs

Overview: Screen Australia implements targeted initiatives aimed at promoting diversity and inclusion within the Australian screen industry. Notable programs and internal efforts include:

Gender Matters: As discussed in an earlier chapter.

First Nations Department: since 1993, the First Nations Department had led the way in promoting First Nations screen stories and storytellers. Entirely staffed by First Nations Australians, the Department drives change by providing significant funding for the creation and sharing of authentic First Nations screen stories for all platforms.

Other Screen Australia Items:

Seeing Ourselves - Screen Australia released a significant study of diversity called Seeing Ourselves in 2016. It looked at diversity on Australian screens since television began in 1956. The agency released a follow up report in 2023, Seeing Ourselves 2: Diversity, Equity and Inclusion in Australian TV Drama, which examined the diversity of the main characters in scripted Australian TV drama broadcast between 2016 and 2021.

Industry Development - Screen Australia has taken a number of positive steps in promoting a more equitable, accessible and inclusive screen industry, and is committed to working on a whole-of-sector response to address the current skills shortage and challenges as a result of increased production activity. In 2023, Screen Australia established a dedicated Industry Development business unit with a focus on developing and implementing national programs to support capacity building and skills development for the Australian screen sector. Initiatives launched by the

Industry Development team have included the *Below-the-Line (BTL) Next Step* program, the *Skills Development Fund*, the *Transferable Skills & Returning Crew Training Fund,* and the *Access Coordinator Training Program.*

- The agency's advocacy and capacity-building work directly align with the Federal Government's National Cultural Policy: *Revive*, which encourages creative talent to be nurtured through safe and inclusive work cultures.

- **Developing the Developer** - An intensive workshop aimed at increasing the pool of experts in the field of story development. With a focus on improving access for practitioners from diverse backgrounds, the workshop covers fiction development methodologies and tools as well as market context. Participants are also offered additional mentoring for career development, including placement funding in story development in the industry. This is one of Screen Australia's key talent identification and development initiatives.

- **Talent Camp -** another initiative that Screen Australia helmed was Talent Camp. The program, initiated by AFTRS and Screen Australia with the support of all state screen agencies, is a response to audience demand for rich and engaging stories and the industry's concern about the lack of diversity in the Australian screen sector.

  Talent Camp is an incredible opportunity for emerging creatives to get their ideas production ready and it plays an important part in getting more diverse and distinctive stories on our screens.

- **Emerging Writers' Incubator Initiative with SBS and the state agencies** - a nationwide initiative to support the development of diverse fiction writing talent in the Australian screen sector.

INTERNATIONAL

Women In Film and Television International (WIFTI) with WIFT chapters around the world.

Women In Film and Television International (WIFTI) is a global network of Women in Film and Television (WIFT) chapters, established to support and empower women working in the screen industries worldwide. The WIFT movement began with the founding of the first chapter in Los Angeles in 1973, and WIFTI itself was officially established in 1997 to unite these chapters and amplify their impact on a global scale.

Founding and Growth:

- **WIFT (1973)**: The original Women in Film chapter was founded in Los Angeles by Tichi Wilkerson Kassel, then publisher of *The Hollywood Reporter*. The aim was to support women working in film and television by providing them with networking opportunities, education, and advocacy. This chapter quickly became a model for similar organisations around the world.

- **WIFTI (1997)**: Recognising the growing number of WIFT chapters globally, Women in Film and Television International (WIFTI) was established to act as an umbrella organisation that connects these chapters. WIFTI helps coordinate international efforts, share resources, and advocate for gender equality across the screen industries on a global scale.

Key Programs and Initiatives:

- **Networking and Collaboration:** WIFTI serves as a global network, connecting over 50 WIFT chapters around the world. This network facilitates international collaboration, allowing members from different countries to share knowledge, resources, and opportunities. It also enables cross-border networking, which is essential in the increasingly globalised screen industries.

- **Advocacy for Gender Equality:** One of WIFTI's primary objectives is to advocate for gender equality in the film, television, and digital media industries. The organisation works to raise awareness about the challenges women face in these fields, including issues such as underrepresentation, pay disparity, and workplace discrimination. WIFTI actively campaigns for policy changes and promotes best practices to ensure that women have equal opportunities in the industry.

- **Education and Professional Development**: WIFTI, in collaboration with its member chapters, offers a variety of educational programs aimed at developing the skills and careers of women in the screen industries. These programs include workshops, seminars, and masterclasses on topics ranging from directing and producing to screenwriting and digital media. WIFTI also supports mentorship programs that pair emerging female talent with experienced industry professionals.

- **International Awards and Recognition:** To celebrate the achievements of women in the screen industries, WIFTI organises international awards and recognition programs. These awards highlight the contributions of women in various roles, from directors and producers to editors and cinematographers, promoting their work on a global stage.

- **Global Advocacy Campaigns:** WIFTI coordinates global campaigns to address specific issues affecting women in the industry. For example, the organisation has launched initiatives focused on increasing the representation of women in leadership roles, promoting diversity and inclusion, and addressing sexual harassment in the workplace. These campaigns often involve partnerships with other industry organisations and advocacy groups.
- **WIFTI Summit:** WIFTI regularly hosts international summits and conferences that bring together women from its member chapters to discuss key issues facing the industry. These events provide a platform for networking, learning, and advocacy, and often feature prominent speakers from the global film and television community.

Impact and Global Reach:

- **Global Chapters**: WIFTI represents a global network of over 50 chapters, with thousands of members worldwide. These chapters are active in regions including North America, Europe, Asia, Africa, and Oceania, each tailored to address the specific needs of women in their local industries.
- **Advancing Women in Global Cinema**: Through its various programs and initiatives, WIFTI has made significant strides in advancing the careers of women in the screen industries. The organisation has been instrumental in pushing for greater gender parity and has played a key role in supporting female filmmakers, producers, and other industry professionals across the globe.
- **Cultural Exchange and Diversity**: WIFTI's global network fosters cultural exchange and promotes diversity within the screen industries. By connecting women from different backgrounds and regions, WIFTI encourages the sharing of diverse perspectives and stories, enriching the global film and television landscape.

WIFTI continues to be a leading voice in the fight for gender equality in the screen industries, providing women with the resources, support, and advocacy needed to succeed in their careers (WIFT Australia) (ScreenHub Australia) (WIFT VIC).

Examples of Productions Implementing Work-Life Balance Policies and Their Impact

There are several notable success stories where productions have implemented practices that promote work-life balance. For example, the production of certain television series and films has adopted policies such as limiting shooting days to 10 hours, providing on-set childcare, and offering flexible scheduling options. These initiatives have shown that it is possible to produce high-quality content without compromising the well-being of those involved.

One prominent example is the TV show "The Good Place," which was known for its humane working hours and positive set environment. The show's leadership prioritised the health and well-being of its cast and crew, proving that a respectful and supportive work culture can coexist with creative success. Here are a few more examples:

BBC Studios

- **Initiatives**: Implementation of the "Flexible Working Policy" allowing for remote work options, flexible hours, and parental leave.
- **Impact**: Employees reported higher levels of job satisfaction and work-life balance. The flexible work arrangements helped retain talent and improved overall employee morale, setting an example for other studios in the UK film and television industry.

"Bluey" (Ludo Studio, Australia)

- **Initiatives**: Work-from-home options and flexible hours to accommodate parenting needs.
- **Impact:** They had a happier workforce, with parents able to balance their professional and personal lives effectively. The studio's approach has been beneficial in attracting and retaining talented employees, reinforcing the importance of flexibility in the modern workplace.

"Carmen & Bolude"

- **Initiatives**: Four-day work weeks, 10-hour days, job sharing, and working from home.
- **Impact**: These policies fostered a supportive work environment, reduced burnout, and improved work-life balance for the cast and crew. The innovative approach to scheduling demonstrated that it is possible to maintain productivity while prioritising employee well-being.

Legislative Efforts and Their Impact

In addition to industry-led initiatives, legislative efforts are also playing a role in driving change. Laws and regulations concerning working hours, overtime pay, and workplace safety are being reviewed and updated to better protect workers in the film industry. For example, recent changes in California labour laws have placed stricter limits on working hours and provided greater protections for workers, including those in entertainment.

Unions and guilds continue to be instrumental in negotiating these protections. The International Alliance of Theatrical Stage Employees (IATSE), for example, has been a strong advocate for better working conditions, pushing for limits on working hours and improved benefits for its members. The impact of these efforts is gradually being felt, with more productions adopting practices that prioritise the well-being of their workers.

The movement towards better work-life balance in the film industry is gaining momentum, driven by advocacy groups, industry leaders, and legislative efforts. While there is still much work to be done, these efforts are paving the way for a more sustainable and humane working environment. The next chapter will explore potential solutions and practical steps that can be taken to continue this positive trajectory.

CHAPTER 13

Production-Led Solutions

Addressing the challenges of work-life balance in the film industry requires a multifaceted approach, and much of the responsibility lies with producers, production companies, and executives. This chapter will focus on solutions that can and should be led by those in leadership positions, from implementing shorter work weeks to enhancing health and wellness programs. These strategies are not just theoretical but are grounded in real-world examples and case studies, both from within the film industry and beyond, showing how thoughtful leadership can create a healthier, more sustainable work environment.

Implementing 4-Day Work Weeks

One of the most promising solutions is the implementation of a 4-day workweek. This concept, which has gained traction in various industries, involves reducing the standard workweek from five days to four, without a reduction in pay. The idea is to increase productivity and job satisfaction by allowing employees more time to rest and recharge.

The benefits of a 4-day workweek are manifold. Studies have shown that shorter workweeks can lead to increased productivity, reduced stress, and improved overall well-being. In the film industry, where long hours are the norm, this change could significantly reduce burnout and turnover. Several companies have successfully implemented this model, demonstrating its feasibility and effectiveness.

Case Studies from Other Industries

For instance, a New Zealand-based company, Perpetual Guardian, conducted a trial of the 4-day workweek and found that employees were more productive, engaged, and satisfied with their work-life balance. These examples show that reducing the number of workdays does not necessarily lead to a decrease in productivity; instead, it can foster a more focused and motivated workforce. Here are some more examples:

Buffer's Experiment: Increase in Productivity: A 22% increase in productivity was observed during a three-year trial of a four-day work week. This experiment also saw a decrease in absenteeism by 66%, a reduction in stress levels, and higher job satisfaction among employees.

Henley Business School Study: Employee Reports: In a study by Henley Business School, 77% of workers reported increased productivity when working a four-day week. This indicates that employees are able to maintain or even enhance their output despite reduced working hours.

Microsoft Japan: Significant Boost: Microsoft Japan conducted a four-day workweek trial and reported a 40% boost in productivity compared to the previous year. This trial demonstrated the potential for substantial productivity gains when employees are given more rest and personal time.

Global Trends: General Improvements: Other trials and studies across different countries, including Spain and Iceland, have consistently shown productivity increases ranging from 20% to 40%. These studies highlight the effectiveness of the four-day workweek in various cultural and economic contexts.

4-Day Work Weeks – Opening Thoughts

Implementing a 4-day work week in film production requires careful planning and adjustment, but it is very possible to do this with minimal impact. Productions would need to optimise schedules and workflows and be efficient with planning, communication and prioritising tasks.

Additionally, clear guidelines and expectations would need to be established to ensure that the reduced hours are used effectively.

Ideally, you'd maintain the same number of working weeks but shift to a 4-day workweek instead of 5 during development, pre-production, and post-production. However, during principal photography, you'd likely need to extend the filming schedule weeks. Unlike other stages, production requires a fixed number of days to complete the shoot and capture all the necessary content, making it harder to reduce the number of days without adding extra weeks.

Steps for Transitioning to a 4-Day Work Week in Film Production – Outside of the Principal Photography period

Pilot Program:

This might not be practical for smaller productions, but if possible, begin with a pilot program to test the feasibility. Select a specific department or team to trial the four-day work week for a set period. Establish clear goals and metrics to measure the success of the program, such as productivity levels, employee engagement, and absenteeism rates. Collect data on productivity, employee satisfaction, and overall performance. Adjust the approach based on feedback and results.

Communication and Buy-In:

Some might welcome this change without questions while others might need some motivation. It is important to clearly communicate the reasons for the change, the expected benefits, and how the new schedule will work. Ensure all employees understand the objectives and have an opportunity to voice concerns and ask questions.

Secure buy-in from management and Heads of Departments. Their support is crucial for successful implementation and adherence to the new schedule.

Flexible Work Arrangements:

Offer flexibility within the four-day framework, such as staggered start times or options to choose the day off. This can help accommodate different roles and personal preferences.

Incorporate remote work opportunities to complement the four-day work week, which can further enhance flexibility and work-life balance.

Workload Management:

Focus on essential tasks and prioritise workload to ensure that productivity remains high despite the reduced hours.

Utilise productivity tools and automation to streamline processes and reduce manual tasks, allowing employees to focus on more critical activities.

Wellness:

Encourage employees to use their extra day off for rest, personal activities, or professional development.

Legal and Compliance Considerations:

Ensure compliance with labour laws and regulations regarding work hours, overtime, and employee rights.

If necessary, update employment contracts to reflect the new work schedule and any changes in terms and conditions.

Implementing 4-Day Work Weeks During Principal Photography

It's important to ensure the crew is on board with this decision, as some may not be keen on working an extra week for the same pay they'd receive in 4 weeks. While those who prioritise work-life balance will likely appreciate the shift, others—especially younger crew members without family commitments—might prefer the traditional 5-day workweek. It's best to discuss this with potential team members before they join to gauge their preferences. Fortunately, there are plenty of crew members who prefer a 4-day workweek, so it's ideal to hire those who are not only on board but excited about the change.

If working with unionised cast and crew, ensure that the new schedule complies with union regulations and agreements.

Practically it is not too difficult, it is simply a matter of adjusting your shooting schedule accordingly and creating a detailed schedule that maps out all scenes to be shot within the 4-day work weeks, the same as what you would if it were a 5-day week.

When we shot 4 days, and 5 weeks on Carmen & Bolude, we were not able to keep the 4 days to exactly the same days (eg. Mon to Thu) because of the consideration for locations and cast availabilities. However, it would be ideal and definitely something to strive towards.

Ideally, you'd stick to 10-hour workdays to keep that work-life balance in check. Going longer could defeat the purpose. But sometimes, you might need to stretch the day to 12 hours, even if it's just on a few occasions.

Budget Adjustments:

Cost Analysis: Conduct a thorough cost analysis to understand the financial implications of a 4-day workweek. This might include potential overtime costs, equipment rentals, and location fees.

In my experience, if you structure your schedule around a 4-day work week instead of 5, and increase the shooting days, there shouldn't be any need for additional overtime. Additionally, by setting a flat rate for all possible resources, we found that this approach eliminates or minimises any extra costs.

Monitoring and Evaluation:

Conduct regular check-ins to monitor the progress and address any issues that arise promptly. Create a feedback loop where cast and crew can voice their concerns or suggestions regarding the new work schedule. Be prepared to make adjustments to the schedule or processes based on feedback and observations to ensure the smooth running of the production.

By carefully planning and executing these steps, a 4-day work week can be successfully implemented during principal photography, enhancing work-life balance without compromising the production's efficiency and quality.

Shorter Workdays

Another approach is to implement shorter workdays. This involves reducing the number of hours worked each day while maintaining the same number of working days in a week but having more filming days (or not). Shorter workdays can help employees maintain better energy levels and reduce the likelihood of fatigue-related errors.

Impact on Productivity and Employee Well-being

Shorter workdays have been shown to improve productivity by allowing employees to maintain focus and energy throughout their shifts. For example, in Sweden, several companies experimented with six-hour workdays and found that employees were not only more productive but also happier and healthier. This approach could be particularly beneficial in the film industry, where long hours often lead to physical and mental exhaustion. In the film industry, shorter workdays would generally be 8-hour days though and no differentiation between the stages of production would be required here.

Productivity Increase with Shorter Workdays in the Film Industry - Key Findings:

Timewise and Bectu Vision – Case Study:

- **Increase in Productivity**: Implementing an 8-hour workday in the film and TV industry can lead to a significant increase in productivity. The study found that shorter workdays contribute to improved employee well-being and job satisfaction, which directly enhances productivity.

- **Employee Well-being**: By reducing the standard workday from 10 hours to 8 hours, employees experienced less fatigue and stress, resulting in better focus and efficiency during working hours.

- **Financial Viability**: The study highlighted that while extending the production schedule might increase costs by an estimated 4%, the benefits of increased productivity and improved employee retention outweigh these costs.

Global Comparisons:

The feasibility study referenced international models from countries like France, Sweden, and Spain, where shorter workdays in the film and TV industry have shown positive results in productivity and employee satisfaction.

The research indicated that shorter working hours promote a healthier work-life balance, leading to enhanced creativity and efficiency among film industry professionals.

Practical Steps for Implementation:

A with 4-day work weeks, and where possible, start with pilot projects or teams to test the effectiveness of shorter workdays. Monitor productivity, employee satisfaction, and overall project outcomes to gather data and make informed decisions.

Allow for flexible start and end times in development, pre- and post-production, within the 8-hour workday framework to accommodate different roles and personal preferences.

Identify and eliminate unnecessary tasks and streamline workflows to ensure essential tasks are completed efficiently within the reduced hours.

Collect regular feedback from employees to continuously improve the implementation process and address any challenges promptly.

By adopting these strategies, film productions can successfully implement shorter workdays, leading to increased productivity, better employee well-being, and overall improved project outcomes.

As with 4-day work weeks, negotiate flat-rate deals with vendors to avoid additional costs associated with overtime or extended use and offer offer incentives for cast and crew to stay on schedule and avoid delays that could lead to additional costs.

I have spoken with Joanna Beveridge from *Shippers* who successfully implemented 8-hour workdays on her production. As an independent project with a total duration of 84 minutes, she had nothing but praise for this method.

Joanna Beveridge, Writer & Producer - *As a producer, I've always noticed a troubling trend on sets that I work on—people were constantly tired, exhausted, and, frankly, burnt out. It was affecting not only their well-being but also the overall atmosphere on set and work efficiency. That's when I realised something needed to change, not just for the sake of the crew but for the success of the production as well.*

For my next project, Shippers, I decided to take a different approach. Instead of the standard 10-hour shoot days, I opted for 8-hour days. I wasn't sure how the crew would react initially, but to my surprise, most people were on board. There were a few people who had some doubts, but once we got into the rhythm, even they embraced the change.

With the change, the crew wasn't going home completely drained. They came back the next day feeling refreshed and ready to give their best, which had a noticeable impact on both productivity and morale. The shorter days allowed for a better work-life balance, and people had more time to recharge, spend with loved ones, or simply rest.

To accommodate the shorter days, we extended the shoot schedule by about 1/5. Some crew members felt like they were working more days for the same pay, which was a valid concern. It required a mindset shift to understand that while the number of days increased, they had far more free time during those days to relax or handle personal matters. We made sure to explain this approach when interviewing for the roles on the production. If anyone wasn't comfortable with the model, we encouraged them to pass on the opportunity, as we knew many others would jump at the chance to work under these conditions.

Interestingly, the few who pushed back were newer to the industry. They hadn't yet experienced the long-term toll that extended hours take on someone's physical and mental health, and many of them didn't have families. On the other hand, the more experienced crew, especially those with families, were incredibly supportive. They valued the healthier work-life balance and appreciated the change. The overall impact on crew morale and performance was incredibly positive.

We also introduced a small but impactful perk: cast and crew were given the choice between having breakfast on set or receiving a travel allowance and a slightly later start to their day. Surprisingly, most people chose the travel allowance, which, from a producer's perspective, was fantastic. Breakfast usually cost about $20 per person, but we offered $10 for petrol, which was enough to cover their travel costs. It saved us money and gave people more flexibility in starting their day.

After seeing how well this model worked on Shippers, I'm committed to adapting it in future projects wherever possible. It's about creating a sustainable, balanced work environment that benefits both the production, and the people involved. This experience has shown me that there's a better way to work, and I plan to make it a priority moving forward.

Job Sharing

Job sharing involves two people splitting the responsibilities of a single role, allowing both to work part-time while ensuring the role is fully covered. This can be structured in various ways to accommodate both the needs of the production and the schedules of the individuals involved. For instance:

- **Alternate days:** One person works on Mondays and Wednesdays, while the other works on Tuesdays and Thursdays, ensuring full-week coverage.

- **Half-days:** One employee covers the morning shift, and the other works in the afternoon, allowing continuous coverage throughout the day without overburdening either individual.

- **Alternating weeks:** Each person works full-time for one week and then has the next week off, providing flexibility while maintaining a consistent presence in the role.

- **Task-based sharing:** In some cases, responsibilities can be split based on specific tasks, such as one person handling pre-production work while the other manages post-production tasks.

This type of arrangement can provide much-needed flexibility, prevent burnout, and boost productivity by allowing individuals to focus on their strengths while sharing the workload.

Who Might Benefit from Job Sharing:

- **Parents:** Job sharing offers flexibility for parents juggling work and childcare, enabling them to maintain a career without sacrificing family time.

- **Carers:** Those caring for elderly or ill relatives can benefit from a more manageable schedule.

- **People re-entering the workforce:** Individuals returning to work after a break, whether for health or personal reasons, can ease back into their careers without the overwhelming pressure of full-time hours.

- **Students:** Job sharing allows students to gain valuable industry experience while balancing their studies.

- **Health concerns:** For those with health issues that make full-time work challenging, job sharing offers a way to stay engaged without risking well-being.

- **Side projects:** Professionals with other commitments, such as freelancing or personal projects, can balance both by job sharing.

- **General work-life balance:** Even those simply seeking a better work-life balance can find job sharing a sustainable solution.

Making Job Sharing Work

To ensure job sharing is effective, employees need to adopt several strategies:

- **Come as a team:** Present a job-sharing arrangement as a team, outlining how tasks will be split and who will be responsible for what, ensuring clarity and accountability.

- **Clear guidelines:** Define roles and responsibilities upfront to avoid confusion, ensuring that both individuals know exactly what tasks they are responsible for.

- **Effective communication:** Use shared documents and platforms to leave detailed notes and ensure both parties are updated. Daily updates and regular check-ins can help both employees stay aligned.

- **Task management tools:** Platforms like Trello or Asana can help track shared tasks, and a shared inbox ensures both parties have access to relevant correspondence. Even Google Drive, Docs and Sheets or Dropbox can be used.

- **Regular feedback:** Job sharers should regularly provide and receive feedback to continuously improve the arrangement and address any issues.

Benefits of Job Sharing:

- **Enhanced work-life balance:** Employees can better manage personal and professional commitments, leading to reduced burnout and greater satisfaction.

- **Retention of talent:** Job sharing allows talented individuals to remain in the industry even if they can't commit to full-time roles.

- **Professional growth:** Job sharers provide each other with support, feedback, and development opportunities, making it a mutually beneficial arrangement.

I have spoken with Racheal Rauch after becoming familiar with her and her advocacy for job-sharing, and found what she said very inspiring and hopeful:

Racheal Rauch, Development Consltant - *"Chronic Fatigue Syndrome (CFS) hit me when I was living and working in London and led me to move home to Australia. For several years after, I was mostly bedridden. I couldn't work or live the life I wanted. When I finally started to recover, getting back to work in the film and television industry was daunting. Our industry is known for its long hours and intense demands, and I knew that jumping back into that full swing physically wasn't possible for me.*

I started looking for part-time work, hoping to find a way to work in and contribute to the industry, without compromising the progress I'd made on my health. I recalled an organisation in the UK that I was familiar with called Share My Telly Job. They promote job-sharing as a way to maintain a career, while still having time for other important aspects of life. Job sharing as a path to re-enter the industry, as well as work sustainably, seemed ideal for my situation and a solid answer to the sector-wide problems of access and inclusion. I wondered why this isn't more mainstream in Australia. There didn't seem to be anyone doing targeted advocacy work to achieve this.

That question sparked something in me and because I'm a person of action, I started agitating in this space. I researched job sharing worldwide and quickly realised how beneficial it could be for so many people, including myself. It can help broad swathes of film/TV practitioners: creating opportunities for parents who need to balance work with childcare, caregivers who have family or friends to look after, people dealing with chronic illnesses, those with other projects or passions, and even students who need flexibility to manage their studies. But also, people who want a better work/life balance – which is a great deal of us!

The more I researched, the more convinced I became that job sharing could really take off in Australia's screen industry. First, I consulted for a recruitment company and delivered a report on the potential for job-sharing in our industry. I reached out to Screen Australia to share what I had found and discuss how we could bring this concept to life. I was a guest speaker on the Screen Vixens podcast, at Crew Con 2023 and at SXSW Sydney 2023.

As part of my advocacy in this space, I reached out to Screen Well to see if we could work together on advancing the job-sharing frontier. This aligns with Screen Well's work in the mental health and wellbeing space of our industry. We applied to Screen Australia and secured funding to undertake Australia's first ever job-sharing pilot program on a Matchbox Pictures production. We launched our report "Breaking Down the Barriers to Job-Sharing" in conjunction with Crew HQ and provided a free webinar on our findings. It's incredibly exciting to see this idea start to take shape, and I'm hopeful that it will lead to broader adoption of job sharing across our industry.

As I write this, I'm about to give birth, which has made the idea of work-life balance even more personal for me. When I first started exploring job *sharing, it was about managing my health and finding a way to work that didn't compromise my recovery. But now, it's about creating a balance that allows me to be there for my family, while still doing the work I love and to maintain longevity in the industry.*

This journey has been about more than finding a way to work that suits my needs. It's been about advocating for a better way of working for everyone. Time and time again I've heard how crew on production have "no life." It doesn't have to be this way. We can be passionate about our careers and good at our jobs, while not sacrificing other areas of our lives which are important to us. I believe that job sharing is a key solution for so many of us who are trying to juggle the high demands of our industry, with the equally important demands of our personal lives. My continued work in this space isn't about making job-sharing mandatory, it's about having the option on the table for those of us that need it in order to access and be included in the workplace, and to work sustainably. In the screen industry we problem solve on a daily basis, so finding ways to work flexibly is something we can absolutely do – where there's a will, there's a way! I'm proud of what I've accomplished so far, and I'm excited to see how job sharing can help reshape the landscape of work-life balance in our industry."

Flexible Scheduling

Flexible scheduling allows employees to choose their working hours within certain parameters, offering flexibility that accommodates their personal lives without disrupting production schedules. This approach can be particularly useful for parents, caregivers, or professionals with other commitments.

Implementing Flexible Scheduling on Set:

Staggered start/end times: Productions can offer staggered start or end times, giving employees the flexibility to begin or end their day at times that work best for them.

Remote work options: For certain roles, such as pre-production tasks, remote work can provide flexibility while still meeting project deadlines.

Examples of Flexible Scheduling in Film Productions:

"The Mandalorian" (Disney+): This production used virtual technology to allow for flexible shooting schedules, reducing the need for extensive on-location shoots and enabling more manageable hours for the crew.

"Game of Thrones" (HBO): By using multiple units filming simultaneously across various locations, the show was able to accommodate the complex schedules of its cast and crew, providing more flexibility.

"Carmen & Bolude": This production implemented a four-day workweek, job sharing, and remote work options, showing that flexible scheduling could lead to reduced burnout while maintaining high productivity.

Practical Tips for Implementing Flexible Scheduling:

Assess feasibility: Not every role can accommodate flexible scheduling, so it's important to assess which positions can offer flexibility without compromising quality.

Use technology: Collaboration tools like Slack, Asana, and remote access systems enable seamless communication and project management, even when employees are working flexible hours.

Trust-based culture: Flexible scheduling works best when employees are trusted to manage their time effectively, focusing on outcomes rather than hours worked.

Benefits of Flexible Scheduling:

Improved employee well-being: Flexible hours allow employees to better manage personal responsibilities, reducing stress and promoting better work-life balance.

Increased productivity: Employees who have more control over their schedules are often more productive and focused when they are working.

Higher job satisfaction: The ability to work flexible hours often leads to higher job satisfaction, which can result in better retention and a more motivated workforce.

📄 See Template: Flexible Scheduling Implementation Guide

Implementing Paid Family Leave

Paid family leave is crucial for supporting work-life balance, particularly for parents and caregivers. Providing paid time off for new parents, for example, can help them adjust to their new responsibilities without the added stress of financial concerns.

Key Health Benefits of Paid Family Leave:

Maternal and Infant Health:

Paid leave plays a crucial role in improving both maternal and infant health, and the benefits extend far beyond the immediate post-birth recovery period. One of the most significant impacts is the reduction in rehospitalisation rates. Studies show that paid leave reduces the likelihood of mothers and infants being rehospitalised by more than 50%. This is likely due to the extra time mothers have to properly recover, attend follow-up appointments, and care for their infants, which helps prevent complications that could lead to hospitalisation.

Paid leave also has a profound effect on mental health. Each additional week of paid leave decreases the likelihood of mothers reporting poor mental well-being by 2%. This time allows mothers to adjust to the demands of parenthood without the stress of returning to work too soon, which can exacerbate feelings of anxiety or depression. Mental health support during this period is essential for the overall well-being of both the mother and the infant, as a mother's mental health can directly influence her ability to care for her child.

Breastfeeding duration is another area where paid leave makes a significant difference. Longer paid leave is associated with higher rates of breastfeeding, which has well-documented benefits for both maternal and infant health. Breastfeeding helps protect infants from infections and illnesses while also reducing the mother's risk of developing certain cancers and chronic conditions like heart disease and diabetes. In fact, mothers who are able to take extended paid leave are more likely to breastfeed for the recommended duration, ensuring both they and their babies receive these important health benefits.

Additionally, paid leave can positively affect infant immunisation rates. When mothers are granted more than 12 weeks of paid leave, infant immunisation rates tend to rise. This is likely because mothers have more time to attend paediatric appointments and follow through on their child's immunisation schedule, which is critical for preventing diseases during early childhood. By allowing mothers the time and flexibility to focus on their own and their child's health, paid leave fosters a healthier start for both mother and infant, reducing long-term healthcare costs and promoting overall well-being.

These statistics highlight just how important paid leave is, not only for ensuring better health outcomes in the short term but also for supporting long-term physical and mental health for mothers and their children.

Child Development:

Paid leave for fathers has been shown to significantly increase their engagement with their children, which in turn leads to better developmental outcomes. When fathers are given the opportunity to take time off work, they become more involved in day-to-day caregiving, which fosters stronger emotional bonds and contributes to the child's social, emotional, and cognitive development. Studies have shown that children with highly engaged fathers are more likely to perform better in school, have stronger social skills, and experience fewer behavioural issues as they grow older. In fact, research by the OECD found that children whose fathers take paid leave in their early years tend to have better language and academic performance by the time they reach school age.

Additionally, paid leave helps reduce parental stress, which can play a crucial role in preventing serious issues like child abuse. Lower stress levels in parents, particularly during the critical early years of a child's life, are linked to a decrease in incidents of physical harm. Studies show that one of the most common causes of severe physical head trauma in children under 2 is abuse related to parental stress or frustration. When parents, especially fathers, are able to take paid leave, it reduces the overall stress in the household by sharing caregiving responsibilities more equally. This, in turn, lowers the risk of physical harm and abuse.

Moreover, paid paternal leave helps normalise the involvement of fathers in caregiving, which has a positive ripple effect in the long run. Fathers who take leave are more likely to stay engaged in their children's lives as they grow, contributing to better family dynamics and stronger, healthier parent-child relationships. As a result, both parents and children benefit from the emotional, psychological, and developmental advantages that come with more balanced caregiving responsibilities.

Long-Term Benefits:

Paid leave significantly reduces the risk of chronic conditions like breast cancer, ovarian cancer, diabetes, and obesity for mothers by allowing them the necessary time to recover physically and mentally after giving birth. With this time, mothers can prioritise self-care, including maintaining a healthy diet, staying active, and attending regular checkups, which are crucial in lowering the risk of these conditions. Additionally, paid leave helps manage stress, a key factor in preventing chronic health issues, such as diabetes. Without the pressure to rush back to work, mothers can focus on their well-being, leading to better long-term health outcomes—particularly important for managing conditions like PCOS and diabetes, where diet and self-care play a crucial role.

Examples of Countries and Companies with Effective Family Leave Policies:

COUNTRIES

- **Sweden**

    Policy: 480 days of paid parental leave per child; 240 days per parent, with 90 days reserved for each.

    Impact: High parental engagement and improved family health outcomes.

- **Canada**

    Policy: In Canada, parents can share up to 40 weeks of parental leave. However, if both parents share the leave, they can receive an additional 5 weeks, bringing the total to 45 weeks. This is under the Extended Parental Benefit option, which provides benefits at 33% of average weekly earnings for up to 61 weeks. Alternatively, under the Standard Parental Benefit option, parents can share 35 weeks of leave, with the additional 5 weeks bringing the total to 40 weeks, with benefits at 55% of average weekly earnings.

    Impact: The policy is designed to promote gender equality in caregiving by encouraging both parents to participate in childcare. The non-transferable weeks incentivise fathers to take leave, contributing to a more balanced distribution of caregiving responsibilities.

    Better child development outcomes are associated with the ability of both parents to be more involved during the early years, which is supported by various studies linking parental leave to improved child well-being.

- **Norway**

    Policy: Norway offers 49 weeks of parental leave at 100% pay or 59 weeks at 80% pay. The policy reserves a minimum of 15 weeks for each parent (often referred to as the "father's quota" and "mother's quota"), which is non-transferable. This ensures that both parents are involved in childcare.

    Impact: The policy is designed to promote high parental involvement by encouraging fathers to take leave, which has been successful in Norway. This involvement is linked to better child development outcomes, as children benefit from the active participation of both parents during early childhood.

- **Germany**

    Policy: In Germany, parents can take up to 14 months of parental leave combined. This leave is shared between the parents, with each parent entitled to at least two months. The leave can be taken by one parent or shared between both, but a single parent can only take up to 12 months. The remaining two months are reserved for the other parent to encourage both parents' participation in childcare. During this period, parents receive Elterngeld (parental allowance), which covers 67% of their income, up to a certain maximum amount.

    Impact: The policy has led to increased parental bonding by allowing parents to spend more time with their children during the crucial early stages of development. It also promotes balanced gender roles in caregiving, as the policy design encourages both parents to take leave.

OTHER COUNTRIES' FAMILY LEAVE POLICIES

- **Australia**

    Policy: Starting from July 1, 2023, parents in Australia are entitled to 20 weeks of paid parental leave, which can be shared between both parents. This leave is designed to be flexible, allowing parents to decide how they want to split the leave. The policy is structured to gradually increase, with the leave extending to 26 weeks by July 2026.

Impact: The policy aims to improve gender equality in caregiving by encouraging both parents to participate in childcare. It also provides better support for families, allowing more time for parents to bond with their children during the critical early years without the financial strain of returning to work prematurely.

- **United Kingdom**

    Policy: In the UK, parents can indeed share up to 50 weeks of leave, with 37 weeks paid at the statutory rate. SPL allows parents to share leave following the birth or adoption of a child. The statutory rate is currently set at £172.48 per week or 90% of the parent's average weekly earnings, whichever is lower. Mothers in the UK are entitled to up to 52 weeks of maternity leave. Of these, 39 weeks are paid: the first 6 weeks at 90% of their average weekly earnings (with no cap), and the remaining 33 weeks at the statutory rate.

    Impact: These policies aim to promote better family bonding by allowing both parents to spend significant time with their new child. The flexibility in sharing leave also supports a more equitable distribution of childcare responsibilities between parents. Extended time off for mothers, particularly during the initial weeks post-birth, contributes to better health outcomes for both mothers and children. This time allows for physical recovery and supports breastfeeding, which has numerous health benefits for the child.

- **United States**

    Policy: Family and Medical Leave Act (FMLA) is a federal law that provides eligible employees with up to 12 weeks of unpaid, job-protected leave per year for specific family and medical reasons, including the birth or adoption of a child. However, this leave is unpaid, and not all employees are eligible, as eligibility depends on factors like the size of the employer and the length of time the employee has worked there. Some U.S. states have implemented their own paid family leave programs. For example, California offers up to 8 weeks of paid family leave to eligible employees. Other states with similar programs include New York, New Jersey, Rhode Island, Washington, and Massachusetts, among others.

Impact: The impact of parental leave policies in the U.S. indeed varies significantly by state. In states that offer paid leave, studies have shown better health outcomes for mothers and children and higher job retention rates among parents. These benefits are particularly pronounced in states with comprehensive paid leave programs, as they allow parents to take time off without the financial burden of unpaid leave.

COMPANIES

- **Netflix**

    Policy: Up to one year of paid parental leave for both mothers and fathers: Netflix is known for its generous parental leave policy, especially in the United States. The policy allows new parents, including both mothers and fathers, to take up to one year (12 months) of paid parental leave following the birth or adoption of a child. Employees have the flexibility to return to work part-time, full-time, or take their leave in intervals as needed.

    Impact: This policy has been associated with improved employee retention and satisfaction. Netflix's approach to parental leave is part of its broader emphasis on a supportive and flexible work environment, which helps attract and retain talent. The generous leave policy allows parents to bond with their children without the financial pressure to return to work prematurely, contributing to higher job satisfaction and loyalty.

- **Google**

    Policy: Google offers birth mothers up to 18 weeks of paid maternity leave. This can be extended if there are complications. Other parents, including fathers and adoptive parents, are eligible for 12 weeks of paid parental leave. This leave is designed to be flexible, allowing parents to take time off to bond with their new child.

Impact: Enhanced employee well-being and productivity: Google's parental leave policy is part of its broader commitment to employee well-being. Providing generous paid leave helps reduce stress for new parents, allowing them to focus on their family without financial worries. This support contributes to higher employee satisfaction, retention, and overall productivity, as employees are more likely to return to work motivated and engaged after taking the necessary time to bond with their new child.

- **Microsoft**

    Policy: Microsoft offers birth mothers up to 20 weeks of paid maternity leave. This policy is designed to give mothers ample time to recover and bond with their newborns. Other parents, including fathers, adoptive parents, and partners, are eligible for 12 weeks of paid parental leave. This is part of Microsoft's broader commitment to supporting families.

    Impact: This generous parental leave policy contributes to higher levels of employee satisfaction and retention. By supporting employees during significant life events, Microsoft enhances its reputation as a family-friendly employer, which helps attract and retain top talent. Employees benefit from being able to take sufficient time off to care for their new child without worrying about their job security or financial stability.

Enhanced Health and Wellness Programs

Health and wellness programs tailored to the specific needs of film industry professionals can also play a significant role in improving work-life balance and general wellbeing. These programs can include on-set health services, mental health support, stress reduction programs, and fitness facilities.

Larger companies and studios are able to, and do implement their own programs, but independent productions and smaller companies have the support of industry-wide support companies such as *Screen Well*, *Film in Mind* and the *Whole Picture Program*.

Effective Health and Wellness Programs in the Film Industry:

SCREENWELL

Screen Well was born following Ben Steel's transformative experience of writing and directing the 2019 documentary *The Show Must Go On*. Alongside the release of the film, Ben and the team at Film Art Media created and delivered a series of wellbeing events designed specifically for screen workers. This journey led Ben to the conclusion that the industry required specialised mental health and wellbeing support, which was the driving force behind Screen Well's founding in 2021.

Screen Well began by delivering Mental Health First Aid (MHFA) training to screen workers and with the support of our advisory group, founding supporters and partners, we have become the go-to organisation for mental health and wellbeing training, advocacy, and insight for the screen industry.

In addition to continuing to support individuals with subsidised MHFA training and a range of free resources, Screen Well also supports:

- Screen businesses with training, resources, and services designed to improve the wellbeing of teams, as well as creativity and productivity.

- Educators with training and workshops designed to support the next generation of screen workers.

- The broader industry with research, resources, advocacy, and initiatives designed to improve the mental health and wellbeing outcomes of the industry.

Everything we do at Screen Well is about creating a more sustainable and mentally healthy screen industry.

Wellbeing Awareness & Skills Program

Wellbeing Awareness and Skills Program (WASP) has specifically been created to better prepare the next generation of emerging screen talent. Specifically, this program is for tertiary Film and TV students studying creative or technical skills and want to pursue a career in the Australian screen industry. Over five modules, participants will develop the knowledge and skills they need to more effectively manage their wellbeing and thrive in the screen industry.

Navigating A Creative Life

A unique 60-minute keynote presentation that spans the life-long creative pursuit of one creative individual: actor and filmmaker, Ben Steel. From the spark of an adolescent dream and the heights of celebrity and fame, to the depths of depression and suicide ideation, before finding a path to recovery and redemption. Like life, this presentation is an emotional rollercoaster, filled with vulnerability and honestly that will inspire, encourage reflection and provide an overwhelming message of hope.

For Screen Businesses - Screen Well helps businesses create safer and more supportive workplaces, so that they can achieve the best possible outcomes. They support screen businesses and organisations to improve their wellbeing outcomes, which can also improve business outcomes.

Mental Health Essentials

Mental Health Essentials is a one or two-hour screen industry-specific presentation and workshop designed to provide essential workplace wellbeing information; introduce basic interventions that help reduce wellbeing risks in screen workplaces; and help increase peer-to-peer support.

Mental Health Essentials can be presented by any of our team and features a selection of relevant screen-based research, short clips, scenarios and interactive elements designed to engage teams.

Mental Health First Aid

They deliver Mental Health First Aid (MHFA) training directly to screen businesses and organisations, either online or face-to-face over 12-hours. MHFA is the help provided to a person who is developing a mental health problem; is experiencing the worsening of a mental health problem; and/or is in a mental health crisis.

These are essentials skills to have embedded in your teams to create safer and more inclusive workplaces for all.

Safeguarding productions

They can help safeguard screen productions by reviewing shooting scripts and assessing all potential wellbeing risks. They do this from the perspective of the content, as well as the production, such as assessing shooting schedules, production environments, as well as the existing resources and processes in place. The result of our risk assessments are recommendations to mitigate the risks identified and we can also support productions to make our recommendations happen.

They remind productions that are fully aware of budget-related constraints and pressures and that for them, this is not about adding to those pressures, it's about helping productions to improve to their wellbeing outcomes in a realistic and practical way, which we know can also improve the creative and commercial outcomes of productions.

Leadership Matters Workshops

They run workshops for leaders and creative teams based on the *Leadership Matters* report, designed to bring to life how leaders can improve the creative and wellbeing outcomes of their screen projects.

They offer a one-hour presentation, with interactive elements, followed by a Q&A designed to unpack the culture of the screen industry and how leaders can increase their impact.

They also offer a two-hour learning experience. The additional time allows for more interactivity, discussion and opportunities for participants to reflect on their own leadership style and practices.

Research Projects:

Through research, Screen Well better understand the mental health challenges the screen industry faces, so they can design effective programs and initiatives to address them.

Screen Well collaborates with universities, independent consultants and industry stakeholders on a range of research initiatives.

Screen Industry alcohol consumption study:

Screen Well has partnered with researchers from the School of Psychological Sciences at the University of Melbourne to explore the extent and impact of alcohol use in the screen industry. More than a research project, the study has an in-built intervention to help reduce alcohol consumption.

Leadership Matters Report

Bullying, discrimination, harassment, and destructive work conditions have all emerged as central themes of recent screen industry reports, leading to calls for cultural change. While the impacts on mental health and well-being have been reported in the past, this new report Leadership Matters goes a step further by examining the impact on creative and commercial outcomes, as well as detailing how leaders can play a pivotal role in improving these outcomes and the long-term sustainability of the industry.

MPTF (MOTION PICTURE & TELEVISION FUND) WELLNESS PROGRAM

Overview: MPTF is a well-established organisation that provides a range of health and social services to entertainment industry workers, including wellness programs, mental health support, and retirement services. The organisation has been a cornerstone of support for the Hollywood community for over a century, offering various services tailored to the unique needs of industry professionals.

Services:

Regular Health Screenings, Fitness Classes, and Support Groups: MPTF offers these services as part of its wellness initiatives. The organisation provides regular health screenings to ensure that industry workers maintain good health. Fitness classes and support groups are also available, helping individuals stay physically active and mentally resilient.

Mobile Clinic: MPTF operates a mobile clinic that reaches workers on set, making healthcare more accessible to those who might not otherwise have time to visit a healthcare facility.

Impact: services have significantly improved access to healthcare for industry workers, which is particularly important given the demanding nature of the entertainment industry. By providing on-set services and a wide range of wellness resources, MPTF helps reduce health-related absenteeism and improves overall well-being among industry professionals.

SAG-AFTRA HEALTH PLAN

Overview: The SAG-AFTRA Health Plan indeed provides comprehensive health insurance coverage to members of the Screen Actors Guild-American Federation of Television and Radio Artists (SAG-AFTRA). This plan is designed to cater specifically to the needs of entertainment industry professionals, offering various benefits tailored to their unique work environment.

Services: The plan covers a wide range of health services, including preventive care, mental health services, and substance abuse treatment. These are essential components of the coverage, given the demanding nature of the entertainment industry.

Impact: The plan contributes to enhanced mental and physical health support for union members. By providing access to comprehensive healthcare services, the SAG-AFTRA Health Plan helps maintain a healthier and more productive workforce, which is critical in the entertainment industry where health issues can directly impact career opportunities.

FILM IN MIND

Overview: Film in Mind is an organisation that provides therapeutic support specifically tailored for the filmmaking community, with a particular focus on independent documentary filmmakers. The organisation recognises the unique challenges faced by those in the film industry, especially in high-pressure and emotionally demanding roles.

Services:
- Film in Mind offers various forms of therapy to help filmmakers address mental health issues and manage stress. This includes one-on-one sessions, group therapy, and even team-focused therapy to support entire film crews.
- The organisation provides consultations to assess the emotional risks associated with film projects, helping filmmakers to anticipate and manage potential mental health challenges.
- This service is aimed at helping filmmakers manage the ongoing stress and mental health issues that can arise from their work,

ensuring they have the support they need throughout their projects.

Impact: Film in Mind fosters a supportive environment that enhances overall well-being and productivity within the filmmaking community. Their services are designed to help filmmakers navigate the emotional complexities of their work, leading to better mental health outcomes and more sustainable careers.

THE WHOLE PICTURE PROGRAM

Overview: The Whole Picture Program is a comprehensive mental health initiative specifically aimed at addressing the mental health crisis in the film, TV, and cinema industries. It was initiated by The Film and TV Charity in response to concerning findings about the mental health of industry professionals.

Services:

- A dedicated 24/7 helpline offering immediate mental health support for those in the industry.
- These networks connect industry professionals to share experiences and provide mutual support.
- The program offers training to help industry members recognise and address mental health issues.
- The initiative includes campaigns aimed at destigmatising mental health issues within the film and television industry.

Impact: The Whole Picture Program aims to promote a healthier work environment by providing resources and support to film and TV professionals. This includes improving mental health outcomes and reducing incidents of harassment and bullying through increased awareness and better support structures.

NETFLIX WELLNESS INITIATIVES

Overview: Netflix offers a range of wellness programs and benefits designed to support employee health and work-life balance. This commitment aligns with the company's broader philosophy of fostering a flexible and supportive work environment.

Services:
- Netflix provides on-site fitness facilities at some of its major offices, allowing employees to engage in physical fitness conveniently.
- Netflix offers mental health support, including access to counselling services, which are part of their broader commitment to employee well-being.
- Netflix is well-known for its generous parental leave policy, which allows new parents to take up to a year of paid leave, offering significant support during the early stages of parenting.
- Flexibility is a key component of Netflix's work culture, allowing employees to manage their schedules in a way that best suits their personal and professional needs.
- Netflix provides wellness reimbursements that employees can use for fitness classes, gym memberships, and other health-related expenses, enhancing their ability to maintain a healthy lifestyle.

Impact: These initiatives have contributed to improved employee satisfaction and retention at Netflix. The company's focus on wellness and flexibility has been praised for helping to reduce stress levels and enhance overall wellness among its workforce.

DISNEY'S "HEALTHY LIVING" PROGRAM

Overview: Disney's wellness program, often referred to as "Healthy Living," is focused on promoting a healthy lifestyle among its employees. This program is part of Disney's broader commitment to employee well-being, aiming to create a supportive environment that encourages physical and mental health.

Services:
- Disney provides access to fitness centres for employees, particularly at larger locations like their corporate offices and theme parks.
- Regular health screenings are offered to employees to help them monitor and maintain their health.
- Disney offers wellness coaching and nutrition programs as part of its efforts to support healthy living. These services help employees make informed health decisions and develop sustainable wellness habits.
- Disney promotes mental health through employee assistance programs (EAPs) that offer counselling services, as well as mindfulness workshops and other mental health resources.

Impact: The program has led to increased employee engagement and reduced healthcare costs, fostering a culture of health and wellness within the company. By providing these resources, Disney helps its employees maintain better overall health, which can lead to lower absenteeism and higher productivity.

WARNER BROS. WELLNESS PROGRAM

Overview: Warner Bros. offers a comprehensive wellness program aimed at supporting the health and well-being of its employees. The program is part of the broader benefits package provided by Warner Bros. Discovery, which includes a range of health and wellness resources.

Services:
- Warner Bros. provides on-site fitness centres at several of its locations, allowing employees to maintain their physical health conveniently.
- The company offers wellness workshops that cover various aspects of health and well-being, including stress management and mental health.
- Regular health screenings are available to help employees monitor and maintain their health.

- Warner Bros. offers access to mental health resources, including counselling services and support through their Employee Assistance Program.
- The company also provides ergonomic assessments to ensure that employees have a healthy and safe work environment, which is particularly important for preventing workplace-related injuries.

Impact: The program has led to enhanced employee morale and productivity, reduced absenteeism, and the fostering of a supportive work culture. By prioritising employee health and well-being, Warner Bros. helps create a positive workplace environment that benefits both the employees and the company as a whole.

SONY PICTURES WELLNESS PROGRAM

Overview: Sony Pictures has developed a comprehensive wellness program focused on the physical, mental, and financial well-being of its employees. This program is part of the company's broader commitment to supporting its workforce through various health and wellness initiatives.

Services:
- Sony Pictures provides access to on-site fitness facilities, allowing employees to maintain their physical health conveniently.
- The company offers wellness activities such as yoga and meditation classes to help employees manage stress and improve mental health.
- Sony Pictures provides mental health resources, including counselling services and support through their Employee Assistance Program (EAP).
- Financial well-being is also a focus, with workshops aimed at helping employees manage their finances effectively.
- The company promotes healthy eating through various initiatives, which may include access to healthy food options on-site or programs aimed at encouraging better nutrition.

Impact: These wellness services have contributed to enhanced employee well-being, increased engagement, and a supportive work environment that prioritises health. By offering a range of wellness options, Sony

Pictures fosters a culture where employees can thrive both personally and professionally.

NBCUniversal WELLNESS PROGRAM

Overview: NBCUniversal offers a comprehensive wellness program designed to improve the overall health and wellness of its employees. This aligns with the company's commitment to creating a supportive work environment.

Services:

- NBCUniversal provides access to on-site health centres where employees can receive medical care and wellness services.
- The company offers on-site fitness facilities to encourage physical activity and help employees maintain a healthy lifestyle.
- NBCUniversal supports mental health through various resources, including counselling services and access to Employee Assistance Programs (EAP).
- The company provides ergonomic assessments to ensure that workstations are set up to promote comfort and prevent injury.
- NBCUniversal organises wellness challenges to engage employees in healthy behaviours and foster a culture of well-being.

Impact: These initiatives have led to reduced healthcare costs, improved employee morale, and higher productivity levels. By investing in employee health, NBCUniversal helps to create a more engaged and productive workforce, while also fostering a supportive work culture.

UNIVERSAL MUSIC GROUP (UMG) WELLNESS PROGRAM

Overview: UMG's wellness program focuses on holistic well-being, offering various resources and activities designed to promote a healthy lifestyle among its employees.

Services:
- UMG offers access to fitness facilities for its employees, which is a common feature in corporate wellness programs.
- The company provides workshops focused on various aspects of wellness, including physical, mental, and financial well-being.
- UMG has initiatives aimed at supporting the mental health of its employees, including counselling services and Employee Assistance Programs (EAPs).
- The company includes financial wellness as part of its overall well-being strategy, helping employees manage their financial health.
- UMG encourages employees to engage in community service, which is an integral part of its holistic approach to wellness.

Impact: The program has led to enhanced overall well-being, increased employee satisfaction, and a positive organisational culture. By addressing various aspects of employee health, UMG fosters a supportive work environment that benefits both the employees and the company.

On-Set Health Services and Wellness Facilities

Providing access to healthcare professionals on set is a great way to ensure the well-being of everyone involved in a production. Having a nurse or first-aid professional available can help address any immediate health concerns, from minor injuries to more serious medical issues, which is particularly important given the physically demanding and sometimes unpredictable nature of film production. This kind of support can also prevent small issues from escalating, ensuring that crew members and cast stay healthy and productive throughout the shoot.

In addition to healthcare access, wellness facilities like gyms or relaxation spaces can make a huge difference, especially during long and intense workdays. A simple area for crew and cast to take a break, stretch, or even meditate can help people recharge, both physically and mentally. This can reduce burnout, improve focus, and ultimately boost productivity. Even small production companies can create low-cost wellness spaces—

whether it's a quiet room with some comfortable chairs or an outdoor area where people can unwind for a few minutes.

Mental health support is equally important. Offering access to counselling services, whether on set or through external programs, can give individuals a much-needed outlet to deal with stress, anxiety, or other pressures they may be facing. Additionally, organising stress management workshops or seminars can provide the tools and strategies needed to manage the high-pressure environment that's often part of film production. This not only helps individuals cope with the challenges of the industry but also fosters a healthier, more supportive workplace culture.

For independent productions and smaller companies that may not have the budget for full-scale wellness programs, there are still practical steps that can make a big impact:

Partner with Local Healthcare Providers: You don't need a full-time doctor on set. Partnering with local clinics or healthcare professionals to provide on-call services can ensure timely access to care when needed.

Create Simple Relaxation Areas: Even a designated quiet space or a small relaxation room with basic amenities like comfortable seating, water, and low lighting can help crew members take a breather during long shoots.

Provide Access to Mental Health Resources: While hiring a full-time counsellor may be costly, offering access to telehealth services or affordable counselling programs can give your team support when they need it. You can also consider organising virtual mental health sessions or workshops.

Encourage Breaks and Downtime: Independent productions can prioritise scheduling regular breaks, even if the budget is tight. This shows that you value the well-being of your team and can help prevent burnout, especially during long shoot days.

Promote Physical Activity: If building a gym isn't feasible, encourage movement and physical activity with simple initiatives like stretching sessions or group walks during lunch breaks. This can help alleviate physical strain and mental fatigue during the workday.

By implementing these accessible strategies, smaller productions can still prioritise health and well-being without the need for a large budget. It's about creating an environment where everyone feels supported and valued, which can lead to better morale, productivity, and overall success on set.

On-Site Daycare and Family-Friendly Policies

One of the most effective ways to support parents in the industry is by providing on-set and production-office daycare (I will call it 'on-site' daycare) and implementing family-friendly policies. This chapter explores the benefits of these measures, provides examples of successful implementations, and offers practical advice for creating a supportive environment for parents.

The Importance of Providing Daycare on Set

Having a safe, regulated childcare facility staffed by qualified professionals allows parents to focus on their work knowing their children are in good hands. This is particularly helpful in the film industry, where long hours and unpredictable schedules can make traditional childcare options difficult to manage. Offering on-site daycare not only reduces stress for parents but also boosts morale and productivity, as employees are able to concentrate more fully on their work without worrying about their children's care.

Having on-site daycare also encourages a more inclusive work environment by enabling more parents, particularly mothers (especially those who are still breastfeeding), to participate in film projects. It addresses one of the significant barriers that prevent carer parents from taking on certain roles or projects—concerns about managing childcare. By providing a practical solution, productions can attract and retain talented professionals who might otherwise be unable to participate due to family responsibilities.

Studies show that on-site daycare facilities significantly increase employee productivity and improve overall work satisfaction. Here are some key findings:

The Bright Horizons Survey showed that 90% of parents using full-service on-site daycare reported increased concentration and productivity at work. Employees can focus better on their tasks knowing their children are well cared for nearby, leading to higher efficiency and reduced stress.

JLL Analysis found that companies offering on-site childcare experienced higher employee engagement and reduced absenteeism. On-site childcare facilities help attract and retain skilled talent, particularly working mothers who might otherwise leave the workforce due to childcare challenges. This directly supports employee engagement and productivity.

The Wellable Study showed that providing on-site childcare is seen as a highly valuable benefit by employees, ranking above other popular perks such as gym memberships and mental well-being programs. This benefit enhances employee morale, increases focus, and supports a better work-life balance, which collectively boosts productivity.

Creating a supportive environment for parents requires thoughtful policies and a commitment from leadership. Here are some guidelines for establishing family-friendly policies:

Creating a family-friendly environment on site starts with understanding the specific needs of your cast and crew. Every production is different, so it's important to assess the resources available and determine how best to implement measures that support work-life balance.

Setting up on-site daycare on a small budget

For independent productions and smaller production companies, implementing on-site childcare might seem like a big challenge, but there are practical and budget-friendly ways to make it work. Here's a list of steps you can take to create a supportive childcare situation on set:

Partner with Local Childcare Providers: Instead of setting up a permanent childcare facility, consider partnering with local daycare centres or qualified childcare providers. You can arrange for them to be available on-site during shooting and working hours or have a nearby facility where parents can drop off their children.

Hire Qualified Caregivers for the Set: Bring in certified childcare professionals on a temporary basis. This could be a single caregiver or a small team, depending on the size of your crew. They can set up a designated area for childcare during production hours, ensuring the children are in safe hands while their parents work.

Create a Child-Friendly Space: Set aside a quiet, safe space on site where children can stay during the day. You don't need a fully equipped daycare centre—just a comfortable area with toys, books, and space for naps. Make sure the space is child-proof and meets safety standards.

Check Insurance and Legal Requirements: Before offering on-site childcare, make sure you're covered. Check local regulations, liability insurance policies, and any legal requirements for providing childcare. This ensures that you're in compliance with safety standards and protects both the company and the parents.

Coordinate with Parents: Communicate with the parents on your team ahead of time to understand their childcare needs. Find out how many children will be present, their ages, and any specific requirements they may have. This will help you tailor the childcare setup to suit everyone's needs.

Flexible Hours for Childcare Services: Since filming schedules can be unpredictable, offering flexible childcare hours is essential. Whether it's starting early or staying late, making sure childcare is available during shooting times will ease the burden on parents.

Cost Sharing with Crew Members: If the production budget is tight, consider a cost-sharing model. Some productions work with crew members to split the cost of on-site childcare. This way, the production absorbs some of the expense, and parents contribute a smaller, affordable fee for the service.

Provide Childcare Grants or Stipends: If setting up on-site childcare isn't feasible, offer childcare stipends to parents. This can help cover the cost of off-site daycare or a nanny while they're working on set, making it easier for parents to manage both their work and family responsibilities.

Rotate Childcare Among Parents or Crew (if appropriate): For smaller productions, if hiring childcare professionals isn't in the budget, parents or crew members could take turns watching the children in a designated area during breaks or less busy times. This would require clear scheduling and coordination but could be a budget-friendly solution.

By being creative and flexible, even smaller productions can provide meaningful childcare solutions. Offering support like this not only helps parents feel valued and focused on their work but also contributes to a more inclusive, family-friendly work environment—something that can attract and retain talent in the long run.

I realise that the mobility of film sets on a daily basis adds some extra challenges when setting up this plan and this area/s, so I recommend thorough planning and keeping this in mind when choosing locations and your unit bases for the days of filming. If budget permits, maybe a dedicated person could be helpful in charge of the planning and execution of the daycare strategy and managing logistics.

Setting up on-site daycare on a larger budget

For larger productions and bigger production companies, implementing a comprehensive childcare solution on set is not only feasible but also a valuable way to support working parents and attract top talent. Here's a list of things you can do to establish a well-rounded childcare program for your team:

Create a Full-Service On-Set Daycare: With the resources available in bigger productions, setting up a dedicated, fully equipped childcare facility on set is a practical option. This facility can be staffed with certified childcare professionals and designed to accommodate children of different ages, with areas for play, naps, and educational activities. A full-service daycare provides parents with peace of mind and allows them to focus fully on their work.

Hire Certified Childcare Providers: Ensure that the childcare facility is staffed by qualified and certified caregivers who can handle a variety of needs, including infants, toddlers, and older children. This professional staff should be equipped to provide not just basic care, but also engaging, age-appropriate activities that keep the children happy and occupied throughout the day.

Provide Flexible Hours: Film production schedules can be unpredictable, so offering flexible childcare hours is crucial. The daycare should be available before and after typical working hours to accommodate early call times or late shoots. This flexibility ensures parents don't have to worry about finding additional care when their workday stretches beyond the typical 9 to 5.

Create Child-Friendly Zones: Designate specific areas on set where children can spend time safely if daycare isn't an option for the entire day. These zones could include play areas or quiet spaces where children can relax or play while their parents work. This can be particularly useful during shorter workdays or when children are only on set for part of the time.

Offer On-Site Childcare for Night Shoots or Extended Filming Hours: During long or overnight shoots, provide on-site childcare options to accommodate parents working these hours. You can rotate caregivers or offer additional shifts for childcare professionals to ensure there's always coverage for late-night or extended hours. This flexibility will help parents who need childcare beyond the standard schedule.

Coordinate Childcare Programs During Location Shoots: For productions that require travel or location shoots, organise temporary childcare arrangements at or near the shooting location. Partner with local childcare centres or bring along a team of certified caregivers to ensure continuity of care for crew members traveling with their families.

Partner with Local Schools or Daycare Centres If building an on-set facility is impractical for a specific project, consider partnering with nearby schools or daycare centres to offer discounted rates or reserved spaces for crew members. This gives parents access to reliable care close to the set while maintaining flexibility based on the production's location.

Provide Childcare Stipends or Reimbursements: For productions where on-set childcare isn't feasible, offer childcare stipends or reimbursements. This allows parents to arrange for off-site childcare while still receiving financial support from the company. It's a practical solution that ensures all parents are supported, even when on-set care isn't available.

Set Up Parenting Lounges or Family-Friendly Areas: Establish family-friendly lounges where parents can bring their children during breaks or downtime. These areas can be equipped with comfortable seating, toys, books, and snacks, creating a space for families to relax together while still being close to set.

Include Childcare as Part of Employee Benefits For larger production companies, incorporating childcare services into employee benefits packages is an excellent way to support parents. Offering benefits like childcare discounts, stipends, or on-site daycare access shows that the company is committed to providing long-term support for families.

Offer Back-Up Care Programs: Establish a back-up care program for when regular childcare arrangements fall through, such as when a nanny is unavailable or a daycare is closed. By providing access to temporary care providers or emergency childcare services, parents can work without last-minute stress when their usual arrangements aren't available.

Host Family-Friendly Events: Organise occasional family-friendly events where crew members can bring their children to set for a behind-the-scenes experience. These events foster a sense of community and allow parents to share their work with their families in a relaxed and fun setting.

Invest in Childcare Certification for Staff: Invest in certifying a small group of staff in childcare basics or first aid. This can be particularly helpful during unexpected situations where immediate care is needed and a professional caregiver isn't available. It ensures there's always someone nearby who can provide initial support if necessary.

Communicate Childcare Policies Clearly: Make sure that all childcare policies and options are clearly communicated to the entire cast and crew. Have a designated contact person or department to handle childcare-related questions, ensuring that everyone knows how to access these resources.

Offer Childcare as a Retention Tool: Use childcare support as a way to attract and retain talent. By promoting your family-friendly policies and emphasising the availability of on-set childcare, you can stand out as an employer that values the work-life balance of its team, making your production company an attractive place to work.

By taking these steps, larger production companies can offer meaningful childcare solutions that reduce stress for parents, improve morale, and increase productivity. Providing childcare on set not only makes life easier for working parents but also enhances the overall working environment, leading to a more inclusive, supportive, and efficient production team.

Childcare Subsidies and Support Programs

In addition to on-set daycare, productions can offer childcare subsidies or financial assistance to help parents cover the costs of off-site childcare. This can be particularly beneficial for productions that are unable to provide on-site facilities. Subsidies can be offered as part of a benefits package or through partnerships with local childcare providers.

Productions can also establish support programs, such as flexible spending accounts or tax benefits for childcare expenses. These programs can help parents manage the costs associated with childcare, making it easier for them to participate in demanding film projects.

Flexibility and Remote Work in Film

The film industry, traditionally reliant on physical presence, has seen a shift towards more flexible and remote work arrangements, especially in recent years. This chapter explores the potential for remote work in various film industry roles, the technologies that facilitate this shift, and strategies for balancing the need for on-set presence with the benefits of remote flexibility.

Buffer's 2023 State of Remote Work: According to Buffer's report, a significant portion of respondents prefer remote work. In the 2023 report, 71% of respondents indicated that they preferred fully remote work. This preference highlights the value of remote work flexibility in enhancing job satisfaction.

Regarding career growth, 36% of remote workers did report finding career growth easier in recent years. This shift is often attributed to a focus on performance-based evaluations rather than traditional measures like time spent in the office, which tends to benefit those who work remotely.

The report suggests that the ability to work remotely has indeed contributed to higher productivity and better work-life balance. Employees have more control over their schedules, allowing them to manage work and personal responsibilities more effectively, which can lead to enhanced job satisfaction and productivity.

RemoteJobs.org Study: Companies that offer remote work options have reported higher retention rates and better talent attraction. The flexibility provided by remote work allows employees to pursue nontraditional work arrangements, making these companies more appealing to top talent. Organisations that embrace remote work can reduce turnover and attract a broader pool of skilled professionals.

Opportunities for Remote Work in Various Roles

While the hands-on nature of many film industry roles has historically limited remote work opportunities, advancements in technology have opened up new possibilities. Several roles, particularly in pre-production and post-production, are well-suited to remote work. For example:

In today's digital world, much of the film and TV development work, as well as pre-production tasks, post-production and beyond can now be done remotely, thanks to the rise of collaborative technologies and cloud-based solutions. With the right tools and communication strategies in place, everything from script development to casting, budgeting, scheduling, and even creative discussions can happen efficiently without needing to gather in a physical space. Apart from the occasional need to inspect locations or physical resources, most of the early stages of filmmaking no longer require everyone to be on set or in an office.

Script Development and Writing: Screenwriting is a natural fit for remote work, as it's typically a solo task or a collaborative process that can happen via video calls, email, and shared documents. Tools like Final Draft and Google Docs allow writers to collaborate in real-time, making changes, adding notes, and exchanging ideas with the entire writing team without ever needing to be in the same room. Writing teams can meet virtually to brainstorm and workshop scripts, keeping the development phase moving efficiently.

Casting: Casting has also moved into the digital age. Self-taped auditions are now a standard practice, where actors record their performances and send them to casting directors for review. This eliminates the need for in-person auditions during early stages. Callbacks and chemistry reads can easily be conducted over video conferencing platforms like Zoom or Skype, allowing casting decisions to move forward without scheduling conflicts or travel expenses. This not only streamlines the casting process but also widens the talent pool, as actors can audition from anywhere in the world.

Creative and Production Meetings: Pre-production meetings involving producers, directors, department heads, and other key stakeholders can happen remotely with ease. Video conferencing platforms allow for real-time discussions, screen-sharing capabilities, and even virtual whiteboards for planning and brainstorming sessions. Creative decisions around costume design, makeup, special effects, and set design can be shared through digital portfolios, concept art, and mockups, enabling feedback from all key players without needing physical proximity.

Scheduling and Budgeting: Software like Movie Magic Scheduling and Movie Magic Budgeting allow production teams to work collaboratively on detailed plans remotely. These tools enable producers, line producers, and production managers to build schedules, create breakdowns, and plan budgets, all while receiving real-time feedback from department heads and key team members, wherever they are located. Changes can be updated instantly, and documents can be shared across teams via cloud platforms like Dropbox, Google Drive, or dedicated film production management tools like StudioBinder.

Remote Collaboration for Design Departments: Art departments, costume designers, and even set builders can work remotely during pre-production. Digital tools allow them to share design concepts, sketches, 3D models, and material ideas. Platforms like Adobe Creative Cloud, Blender, or other 3D rendering software make it possible for these teams to work together from afar, while frequent virtual meetings ensure the production's visual style and direction are aligned.

Location Scouting (with Remote Options): While in-person visits to locations are often necessary for final decisions, initial location scouting can also be done remotely. Many location scouts now use virtual tours, Google Earth, and high-resolution photographs to give directors and producers a strong sense of what a location offers before an in-person visit is scheduled. This approach saves time and money during early pre-production and narrows down location options before committing to on-site inspections.

Post-Production Planning: Even some elements of post-production planning can start in the pre-production phase, and many of these tasks can be handled remotely. Editors, visual effects teams, and sound designers can be brought into the planning process through virtual meetings and remote collaboration software. This early collaboration ensures everyone is on the same page before the actual shooting begins and allows the post-production team to prepare workflows, understand creative goals, and get set up for when footage begins to come in.

With the exception of physical location scouting and checking physical resources, nearly all aspects of film and TV development and pre-production can be done remotely. From script development and casting to production meetings, design collaborations, and scheduling, digital tools and remote communication allow productions to move forward smoothly. This flexibility gives production teams the ability to work more efficiently, save on overhead costs, and reduce the stress of coordinating schedules and travel—while keeping the creative momentum going.

Post-production has become one of the most adaptable phases of filmmaking, with the vast majority of tasks now able to be done remotely. Thanks to advancements in technology, from cloud-based editing software to high-speed internet and virtual collaboration tools, nearly every aspect of post-production can be handled from anywhere in the world. Whether it's editing, sound design, visual effects, or colour grading, remote work has transformed how post-production teams collaborate and deliver final projects.

Remote Editing: Editing is one of the most important parts of post-production, and it has fully embraced remote workflows. With tools like Adobe Premiere Pro, Avid Media Composer, and Final Cut Pro, editors can now access, share, and edit footage in real-time from anywhere. Cloud-based platforms like Frame.io allow editors to upload rough cuts and share them with directors, producers, or clients for feedback without needing to meet in person. Real-time notes and revisions can be made through these platforms, streamlining the editing process.

For productions with large files or teams spread across multiple locations, high-speed file-sharing systems like Dropbox or Google Drive ensure that everyone can access the latest footage and project files. This system has made it possible for editing teams to remain productive, regardless of where they are in the world.

Sound Design and Mixing: Sound design and mixing can also be done remotely, using software such as Pro Tools, Logic Pro X, or Adobe Audition. Sound designers and audio engineers can collaborate with directors and editors through shared sessions, exchanging sound effects, music, and dialogue mixes remotely. Audio files are easily shared online, and real-time collaboration tools enable teams to make live adjustments as needed.

Remote sound mixing sessions have become a common practice, where directors can listen in and give feedback while sound engineers adjust levels from another location. Many teams also rely on video conferencing platforms to discuss changes, ensuring that communication is seamless during the creative process.

Visual Effects (VFX): The visual effects industry has been at the forefront of remote work for years. VFX artists can work from any location using powerful remote computers and cloud rendering platforms. Software such as Autodesk Maya, Blender, and Adobe After Effects allow artists to create complex CGI, compositing, and digital effects from home studios or anywhere with an internet connection.

Studios like Weta Digital and ILM have long integrated remote workflows, where VFX artists across the globe collaborate on blockbuster films and TV shows. These teams can work asynchronously, with assets shared via cloud platforms, ensuring that large-scale visual effects projects stay on track without the need for everyone to be in the same physical space.

Colour Grading: Colour grading, traditionally done in a studio environment, has also shifted to remote workflows. Professional colourists can work remotely using software like DaVinci Resolve, which enables high-quality grading from home or remote studios. Directors and DPs (Directors of Photography) can review graded footage in real-time via remote collaboration tools, providing feedback instantly.

Streaming solutions like Streambox allow directors to view the colourist's work in full quality, maintaining the precision required for grading while working from different locations. This remote setup ensures that the look and feel of the film are preserved while keeping the post-production team spread across various locations.

Remote Collaboration and Project Management: To keep post-production running smoothly, communication and project management are crucial. Tools like Slack, Zoom, and Microsoft Teams have made it easy for post-production teams to stay connected, hold review sessions, and ensure that everyone is aligned on the creative vision. File-sharing services like WeTransfer, Dropbox, and Google Drive allow teams to exchange large files without delay, ensuring that editors, sound designers, and VFX teams have access to the latest versions of the project.

Platforms like Frame.io and Wipster are designed specifically for remote collaboration in the film industry. These platforms allow team members to leave time-coded notes on video files, facilitating clear feedback loops between directors, editors, sound designers, and VFX artists. This real-time communication ensures that changes can be made quickly and accurately, no matter where team members are located.

Remote Review and Final Delivery: Final review and delivery of projects can be done entirely remotely as well. Once a project reaches the final stages, producers and clients can review the completed film via secure online platforms. These platforms allow for final approval without needing in-person meetings or screenings.

Final delivery of the project can be done via cloud-based platforms, making it easy to send finished films to distributors, broadcasters, or streaming platforms. The entire process, from editing to final delivery, can be managed remotely, ensuring a smooth transition from production to release.

Many productions are now finding that remote workflows can increase productivity, as teams are able to collaborate across different time zones, effectively working around the clock. This asynchronous model allows for more flexibility in scheduling, making it easier to accommodate creative changes without delaying the project.

Marketing and Distribution: Public relations, social media management, and distribution planning are roles that naturally lend themselves to remote work. Teams can manage campaigns, interact with audiences, and coordinate releases from different locations.

Challenges & Solutions of Remote Work

While remote work has opened up significant opportunities for flexibility and efficiency, it also presents challenges that need to be addressed to ensure long-term success. Harvard Business Review (HBR) has highlighted several of these challenges, including feelings of isolation and difficulty in maintaining work-life boundaries, which are common across many industries. However, these challenges can be mitigated with the right strategies. Below are some of the key challenges associated with remote work and practical solutions to address them.

Challenge 1: Isolation and Lack of Social Interaction

One of the most well-documented issues with remote work is the feeling of isolation that can come from working away from a physical team environment. This isolation can lead to decreased morale, engagement, and even mental health challenges like anxiety and depression. For creative industries like film and TV production, which rely heavily on collaboration, the lack of in-person interactions can hinder creative brainstorming and team cohesion.

Solution 1: Foster Virtual Connections and Support Networks

To combat isolation, companies should actively foster virtual social interactions and support networks. Regular team check-ins, virtual coffee breaks, or informal hangouts can create opportunities for employees to connect on a personal level. Additionally, virtual brainstorming sessions or creative workshops can simulate the collaborative atmosphere of being in the same room, helping to keep creative teams engaged and connected.

Another important approach is encouraging mental health support. Providing access to counselling services, virtual mental health workshops, or stress management resources can offer employees much-needed support. Making it clear that mental health is a priority can create a more supportive work environment, even when working remotely.

Challenge 2: Difficulty in Setting Boundaries Between Work and Personal Life

Remote workers often struggle with setting clear boundaries between work and home life. The lack of a physical office can lead to overworking, blurred boundaries, and burnout. This is especially challenging in industries like film, where deadlines and creative processes can require long hours and intense focus.

Solution 2: Implement Structured Schedules and Clear Boundaries

Encouraging employees to create structured work schedules can help separate their professional and personal lives. Setting clear expectations around working hours and providing guidelines for taking regular breaks ensures that employees aren't constantly "on." Managers should emphasise the importance of unplugging at the end of the workday to prevent burnout.

Offering flexible schedules that allow employees to manage their time better can also help. For example, allowing workers to take a break for family obligations or personal time and make up the hours later in the day can create a more balanced work-life dynamic. Companies can also encourage the use of task management tools like Trello or Asana, which help employees organise their workloads efficiently, ensuring they stay focused during work hours and can disconnect afterward.

Challenge 3: Communication Gaps and Misunderstandings

In a remote setting, communication can easily become fragmented or unclear, leading to misunderstandings, missed deadlines, or frustration. Without the casual face-to-face interactions of an office environment, it can be harder to ensure everyone is aligned and up to date on key project details.

Solution 3: Establish Clear Communication Protocols

To address communication challenges, it's important to establish clear communication protocols from the start. Define which tools should be used for different types of communication—whether it's Slack for quick team updates, Zoom for meetings, or email for formal documentation. Standardising communication channels ensures that everyone knows where to go for information and how to collaborate effectively.

Setting regular check-ins with teams or departments can also ensure alignment. Weekly meetings or daily stand-ups provide opportunities to clarify any concerns and keep everyone on the same page. Additionally, using collaborative tools like Google Docs, Notion, or Frame.io for document sharing, feedback, and updates can help streamline workflows, making it easier for remote teams to collaborate in real-time.

Challenge 4: Access to Technology and Resources

Remote work environments can present challenges when employees don't have access to the necessary tools or technology. This can be particularly problematic in technical fields like post-production in film and TV, where specialised software, powerful computers, or high-speed internet are essential for performing key tasks.

Solution 4: Invest in Technology Resources and Remote Infrastructure

To overcome technology challenges, companies need to ensure that all employees have access to the necessary resources to work effectively from home. This could include providing employees with laptops, high-speed internet stipends, or remote access to specialised software via cloud-based platforms. In industries like film production, where large files and complex programs are the norm, investing in cloud storage solutions and remote editing tools ensures that teams can continue working without technical disruptions.

Companies should also offer IT support for remote employees to help troubleshoot issues quickly, ensuring minimal downtime. Making sure employees are trained to use remote collaboration tools effectively can also reduce tech-related frustrations and help maintain productivity.

Challenge 5: Maintaining Team Morale and Engagement

Remote work environments can sometimes make it harder to maintain team morale and engagement. Without the energy and camaraderie of working together in person, teams may start to feel disconnected from the company's mission or disengaged from their roles, which can affect both performance and creativity.

Solution 5: Regular Recognition and Virtual Team Building

To keep morale high, it's important to actively recognise and celebrate employee achievements, even in a virtual setting. Offering praise for good work, sharing team successes in virtual meetings, and rewarding accomplishments with digital incentives can boost motivation and foster a sense of accomplishment.

Virtual team-building activities are also crucial for keeping teams engaged. Organising virtual happy hours, trivia nights, or creative competitions can help teams bond and build relationships beyond work tasks. Keeping these activities fun and inclusive will enhance team spirit, even in a remote environment.

Conclusion:

Remote work has proven to be highly effective, but it comes with its own set of challenges, such as isolation, communication gaps, and difficulty setting boundaries. However, by proactively addressing these issues with strategies like fostering virtual connections, implementing structured schedules, standardising communication protocols, and providing access to technology, companies can create a positive remote work environment. By doing so, businesses not only maintain productivity but also ensure the well-being and engagement of their teams.

SUMMARY: Technologies Enabling Remote Collaboration

The shift towards remote work in the film industry has been significantly aided by advancements in technology. Key tools and platforms include:

Video Conferencing Tools: Platforms like Zoom, Microsoft Teams, and Google Meet enable real-time communication and collaboration. They are essential for virtual meetings, table reads, and creative discussions.

Cloud-Based Collaboration: Services like Google Workspace, Slack, and Trello allow teams to share documents, manage projects, and track progress. These tools are invaluable for coordinating efforts across different locations.

Editing and VFX Software: Programs like Adobe Premiere Pro, Avid Media Composer, Frame.io and DaVinci Resolve have remote collaboration features that enable editors and VFX artists to work together seamlessly, even when geographically dispersed.

Digital Asset Management (DAM) Systems: DAM systems help organise and store digital assets like footage, sound effects, and graphics, making them accessible to all team members, regardless of location.

Video Conferencing and Communication Tools

Zoom
- **Description:** Widely used for video conferencing, virtual meetings, and webinars.
- **Features:** High-quality video and audio, screen sharing, breakout rooms, and recording options.

Slack
- **Description:** A messaging app for teams that allows for real-time communication and collaboration.
- **Features:** Channels for different projects, direct messaging, file sharing, integrations with other tools.

Microsoft Teams
- **Description:** A collaboration platform that combines chat, video meetings, file storage, and app integration.
- **Features:** Video calls, team chat, file sharing, integration with Microsoft Office 365.

Project Management and Collaboration Tools

Trello
- **Description:** A visual project management tool that uses boards, lists, and cards to organise tasks.
- **Features:** Task assignments, due dates, checklists, file attachments, integrations.

Asana
- **Description:** A task and project management tool designed to help teams organise, track, and manage their work.
- **Features:** Task assignments, project timelines, milestones, integrations.

Monday.com
- **Description:** A work operating system that powers teams to run projects and workflows with confidence.
- **Features:** Customisable workflows, task tracking, automation, integrations.

File Sharing and Storage

Google Drive
- **Description:** A cloud storage service that allows for file storage, sharing, and collaboration.
- **Features:** Real-time collaboration on documents, spreadsheets, presentations, 15GB of free storage.

Dropbox
- **Description:** A cloud storage service for storing and sharing files and collaborating on projects.
- **Features:** File syncing, sharing, collaborative editing, 2GB of free storage.

Box
- **Description**: A cloud content management and file sharing service for businesses.
- **Features:** Secure file sharing, collaboration tools, workflow automation, integrations.

Video Editing and Review Platforms

Frame.io
- **Description:** A video review and collaboration platform designed for creative teams.
- **Features:** Real-time video review, commenting, version control, integrations with editing software.

Wipster
- **Description:** A video collaboration and review platform that simplifies the feedback process.
- **Features**: Frame-accurate commenting, version control, approvals, integrations with editing tools.

Shotgun
- **Description**: A project management and collaboration platform for creative teams in the media and entertainment industry.

- **Features**: Production tracking, review and approval, asset management, integration with creative tools.

Screenwriting and Storyboarding

Final Draft
- **Description:** Industry-standard screenwriting software used by professionals.
- **Features:** Script formatting, collaboration, revision tracking, story mapping.

Celtx
- **Description**: A pre-production suite for film, video, and media production.
- **Features**: Scriptwriting, storyboarding, shot lists, scheduling, budgeting.

WriterDuet
- **Description**: A collaborative screenwriting software for writing and editing scripts.
- **Features**: Real-time collaboration, version history, script formatting, cloud storage.

NVIDIA's Hybrid Work Solutions for Media & Entertainment

NVIDIA has developed hybrid work solutions tailored for the media and entertainment industry. These solutions integrate high-performance computing, collaboration tools, and secure remote access, allowing creative professionals to work from both studio and home.

This hybrid model has enabled film production teams to maintain high productivity and creativity, ensuring that projects stay on track even when team members are working remotely.

Minim's Industry-Wide Insights

Many film studios have adopted hybrid work models where employees split their time between on-site and remote work. This approach has been particularly effective in areas like post-production and visual effects, where high-speed internet and advanced software tools facilitate remote collaboration.

The hybrid model has led to increased flexibility, allowing film professionals to manage their work-life balance better while maintaining high levels of productivity and creativity.

Technicolour's Remote Collaboration Tools

Technicolour has implemented a hybrid work model that includes the use of remote collaboration tools such as cloud-based workflows and virtual production environments. This allows teams to work seamlessly from different locations.

This model has enhanced the efficiency of film production processes, reducing the need for physical presence on set and enabling real-time collaboration across various geographies.

Warner Bros. Animation

Warner Bros. Animation has adopted a hybrid work model where animators and other staff can work both remotely and in the studio. The use of secure VPNs, cloud storage, and collaborative platforms has facilitated this transition.

The flexibility provided by this hybrid approach has improved employee satisfaction and allowed for continued production without significant interruptions.

Pixar's Hybrid Work Environment

Pixar has embraced a hybrid work model that leverages advanced digital tools and cloud-based technologies to enable remote work for animators, editors, and other creative professionals.

This model has maintained the high quality of Pixar's productions while offering employees the flexibility to work from various locations, fostering a more adaptable and resilient workforce.

"The Mandalorian" (Disney+)

During the production of "The Mandalorian", they utilised advanced virtual production techniques, including the use of Stagecraft, which combines physical sets with virtual backgrounds rendered in real-time.

Key collaborators, including directors and visual effects teams, worked remotely to create and adjust virtual environments. This allowed for creative input from various locations while maintaining a high-quality production standard.

The innovative use of technology not only ensured continuity during challenging times but also set a new standard for efficient and flexible filmmaking practices.

"The Batman" (Warner Bros.)

"The Batman" employed a hybrid work model that combined on-set shooting with extensive remote work for post-production processes. This included key areas such as editing, visual effects, and sound design. Given the restrictions and challenges during the pandemic, this approach was essential to keeping the production on track.

The post-production teams utilised collaborative tools such as Frame.io and Evercast. These tools allow professionals to work together in real-time, even when physically apart, facilitating the review and approval processes for editing, VFX, and other post-production tasks. This technology was crucial in maintaining the high standards required for a major film like The Batman while enabling team members to work from different locations.

The hybrid work model and use of remote collaboration tools allowed The Batman's production to continue smoothly despite pandemic restrictions. This approach ensured that high-quality post-production work could be completed on schedule, helping the film maintain its planned release timeline and meet the high expectations of both the studio and the audience.

"Dune" (Legendary Entertainment/Warner Bros.)

"Dune" implemented a mix of on-location shooting and remote post-production work. The film's visual effects were handled by teams distributed globally, coordinating remotely.

Used platforms like Slack, Zoom, and specialised VFX collaboration tools to manage the workflow across different continents.

Ensured that the production stayed on track and maintained high visual standards, demonstrating the feasibility of remote collaboration in high-budget films.

"Soul" (Pixar Animation Studios)

Pixar moved to a fully remote work model during the final stages of production, including editing, sound design, and animation adjustments.

Employed tools like Zoom for meetings, Slack for communication, and proprietary animation software for real-time collaboration.

Demonstrated that even complex animation projects could be completed remotely without sacrificing quality, setting a precedent for future animated films.

"Depart"

An independent film titled "Depart" was produced with a blend of on set and remote work.

The production used a minimal on-set crew, with only one person present on the set while the rest of the team coordinated remotely. They utilised the Blackmagic Pocket Cinema Camera 6K and relied heavily on tools like Microsoft Teams for real-time communication, camera setup, and troubleshooting. Remote collaboration was facilitated through extensive pre-production planning, virtual camera tests, and using 4K capture cards to integrate camera feeds into their remote setups.

This hybrid model allowed the production to maintain high production values while adapting to the constraints of remote collaboration, showcasing the feasibility and effectiveness of combining on-set and remote work in filmmaking.

"Searching"

"Searching" is an independent film directed by Aneesh Chaganty. It is a notable example of a film that integrates digital interfaces as a core part of its narrative. The film is unique in that it unfolds entirely on computer screens and smartphones, which naturally facilitated a more digital and remote production process.

The film's narrative required extensive use of digital interfaces, such as social media, video chats, and other online tools, which played directly into the film's story. This setup lent itself well to remote collaboration among the production team.

Remote editing tools, cloud-based storage, and video conferencing were indeed used to coordinate production efficiently, particularly during post-production. The digital nature of the film allowed for significant portions of the work to be done remotely, especially in post-production, where editing, visual effects, and sound design could be managed without requiring the physical presence of the entire team.

While the principal photography involved some on-set shooting, the nature of the film's content, focusing on screen-based interactions, allowed for a streamlined production process that minimised the need for extensive on-location shooting.

The success of "Searching" demonstrated that remote collaboration could be effectively integrated into the production process without compromising quality or creative vision. The film was critically acclaimed and commercially successful, proving that innovative approaches to filmmaking—especially those involving remote work—could yield high-quality results.

Remote Learning and Training Opportunities

The rise of remote work has also expanded opportunities for learning and training in the film industry. Online courses, workshops, and mentorship programs have become more accessible, allowing professionals to develop new skills and advance their careers.

Online Courses and Workshops: Platforms like MasterClass, Coursera, and Udemy offer courses on various aspects of filmmaking, from screenwriting to cinematography. These courses are often taught by industry experts and provide valuable insights and techniques.

Virtual Mentorship and Coaching: Remote mentorship programs connect emerging talent with experienced professionals, providing guidance and support. These programs can be particularly beneficial for underrepresented groups in the industry.

Access to Industry Conferences and Events: Many industry conferences and events have moved online, or are running hybrid models, making them more accessible to a global audience. These virtual events provide opportunities for networking, learning, and staying up to date with industry trends.

The shift towards remote work in the film industry offers significant benefits, including greater flexibility, cost savings, and access to a broader talent pool. By leveraging technology and adopting hybrid work models, the industry can continue to innovate and adapt to changing conditions. As we move forward, it's essential to balance the advantages of remote work with the unique demands of on-set production, ensuring that all aspects of filmmaking can thrive.

Flexible Workspaces

Creating flexible workspaces that cater to various working styles is essential for boosting productivity and employee satisfaction. Offering a variety of options—such as quiet zones for focused work, collaborative spaces for team projects, and ergonomic furniture for comfort—ensures that employees can choose the environment that best supports their tasks.

To make these workspaces truly effective, it's important to involve employees in the design process. By gathering input and allowing them to have a say in selecting workspace options, you create a more tailored and supportive environment.

Regularly updating these spaces based on feedback and evolving needs is also key. As the way people work changes, adapting workspaces ensures that the environment continues to promote both well-being and efficiency for everyone on the team.

Flexible workspaces offer several benefits that positively impact both employees and productivity. These environments cater to various tasks and preferences, boosting productivity by 32%, according to a study by Steelcase. Allowing employees to choose workspaces that best suit their needs enhances comfort, while promoting spontaneous interactions and teamwork fosters collaboration. Research by Gensler shows that 90% of employees are more satisfied with their work environment when they have access to flexible workspaces. Additionally, data from the American Journal of Preventive Medicine indicates that ergonomic furniture, such as standing desks, can reduce the risk of musculoskeletal issues, leading to health improvements.

Promoting Work-Life Balance through Company Culture

Company culture plays a significant role in promoting work-life balance. A culture that values and supports work-life balance can help prevent burnout, improve job satisfaction, and enhance overall productivity.

Leadership commitment is crucial in establishing a culture that prioritises work-life balance. This commitment can be demonstrated through policies such as flexible working hours, limits on overtime, and support for taking time off. Recognising and rewarding efforts to maintain work-life balance can also reinforce these values within the company.

A respectful and empathetic culture is essential for supporting all team members, particularly in an industry as demanding as film. This culture can be fostered through open communication, active listening, and addressing issues such as harassment and discrimination promptly and effectively.

Implementing work-life balance through company culture requires a proactive approach, focusing on policies, practices, and behaviours that encourage employees to prioritise their well-being alongside their work responsibilities. Here are some key ways to achieve this:

Lead by Example: Leadership plays a critical role in establishing a culture of work-life balance. Managers and executives should model healthy work-life habits, such as leaving work on time, taking breaks, and not sending emails outside of business hours. When leaders set the tone, it shows employees that it's acceptable to maintain boundaries between work and personal time.

Encourage Flexibility: Offering flexible working hours or remote work options helps employees manage their time more effectively. Flexibility allows employees to balance personal responsibilities, like childcare or medical appointments, without feeling pressured to sacrifice work performance. This trust-based approach empowers employees to take control of their schedules, leading to increased satisfaction and productivity.

Promote Time Off: Encourage employees to take their allotted vacation days and personal time off. A company culture that values time off helps employees recharge and prevents burnout. Offering "mental health days" or ensuring that employees do not feel guilty for taking leave is also crucial for creating a healthy environment.

Limit After-Hours Work: One of the easiest ways to promote work-life balance is by setting clear expectations regarding after-hours communication. Ensure that employees are not expected to respond to emails or work calls outside of business hours unless it's urgent. Establishing this boundary helps employees fully disconnect during their personal time, which is essential for mental and emotional well-being.

Encourage Regular Breaks: Promote the idea that taking short, regular breaks during the workday is important for maintaining productivity and focus. Whether it's a lunch break, a walk, or a short pause to refresh, creating a culture where employees feel comfortable taking breaks can prevent fatigue and enhance overall job satisfaction.

Offer Wellness Programs: Integrating wellness initiatives into the workplace can help employees manage stress and maintain a healthy work-life balance. This could include offering gym memberships, providing access to counselling services, organising meditation or yoga sessions, or even hosting workshops on stress management and healthy living.

Set Realistic Expectations: Avoid setting unrealistic deadlines or creating an environment where employees feel they need to constantly overperform. Encouraging realistic workloads and understanding that employees need time to rest fosters a healthier, more sustainable approach to work. Open communication about workload and capacity helps avoid unnecessary pressure.

Foster Open Communication: Creating a culture of open dialogue is crucial for maintaining work-life balance. Employees should feel comfortable discussing their workload or personal challenges with their managers without fear of judgment. Regular check-ins between employees and supervisors can help identify potential issues before they lead to burnout.

Encourage Team Bonding and Social Interaction: While work is important, fostering relationships within the team can improve the work environment and reduce stress. Organise team-building activities, social events, or informal gatherings to promote camaraderie. A supportive team atmosphere contributes to better mental well-being and makes it easier for employees to manage their work-life balance.

Recognise and Reward Balanced Behaviour: Rewarding employees for maintaining a healthy work-life balance can reinforce this cultural value. Instead of only rewarding employees for working long hours, recognise those who manage their time effectively, maintain high productivity, and make time for personal well-being. Public recognition of these behaviours helps shift the focus from working hard to working smart.

Provide Resources for Working Parents:
Supporting employees with families is a key part of fostering work-life balance. Offering resources like on-site childcare, parental leave, or flexible working schedules for parents can help them manage their family commitments without compromising their professional responsibilities.

Regularly Assess and Improve Policies: Finally, it's important to regularly review the effectiveness of work-life balance initiatives. Collect feedback from employees through surveys or open discussions to understand what's working and what could be improved. Adapting policies based on employee needs helps create a culture that continuously values work-life balance.

By embedding work-life balance into company culture, businesses can create a healthier, more engaged, and productive workforce. From flexible schedules and leadership examples to wellness programs and open communication, fostering a work environment where employees feel supported in balancing their professional and personal lives leads to better morale, reduced burnout, and overall higher performance.

Creating Safe and Inclusive Work Environments

Ensuring that all work environments are safe and inclusive is a fundamental responsibility of every production company. This includes addressing workplace harassment and discrimination and providing safe reporting mechanisms.

Productions must take a zero-tolerance approach to harassment and discrimination, implementing clear policies and procedures for reporting and addressing issues. Training on these policies, along with regular reviews and updates, can help ensure that they are effective and that all team members are aware of their rights and responsibilities.

Data and Statistics

Hollywood Commission Survey on Harassment and Discrimination (2020): According to a survey by the Hollywood Commission on Eliminating Sexual Harassment and Advancing Equality, 65% of women and 35% of men reported experiencing some form of harassment or misconduct in the entertainment industry.

The same survey found that 94% of respondents believed that having clear and confidential reporting mechanisms is critical for creating a safer work environment, yet many expressed concerns about the effectiveness and accessibility of these mechanisms in their workplaces.

USA Today Survey on Sexual Harassment in Hollywood (2018): The survey reported that 94% of women in the entertainment industry had experienced some form of sexual harassment or assault during their careers.

The survey also highlighted that fear of retaliation was a significant barrier to reporting, with 51% of respondents stating that they feared negative repercussions if they reported harassment.

Equal Employment Opportunity Commission (EEOC) Statistics: The EEOC reports that harassment charges account for nearly a third of all charges filed with the agency. In fiscal year 2020, the EEOC received 11,497 charges of sex-based harassment, indicating the ongoing prevalence of these issues across industries.

Studies supported by the EEOC show that regular training on anti-harassment policies can significantly reduce the incidence of workplace harassment and increase the likelihood of reporting incidents.

McKinsey & Company's "Women in the Workplace" Report (2020): This report highlights the importance of creating inclusive work environments. Companies with gender-diverse leadership teams were 21% more likely to experience above-average profitability. However, the report also noted that many women, particularly women of colour, still face significant barriers to advancement and are more likely to experience microaggressions and harassment.

This report emphasises that training programs on diversity, equity, and inclusion (DEI), when combined with clear policies and strong leadership commitment, are effective in reducing incidents of harassment and discrimination.

Time's Up Foundation "What Works" Guide (2019): The guide outlines best practices for creating safe and inclusive workplaces, emphasising the importance of zero-tolerance policies, regular training, and strong, transparent reporting mechanisms. It suggests that implementing these practices can lead to a significant reduction in workplace harassment and create a more supportive environment for all employees.

The Centre for Talent Innovation (2020): Their research shows that employees who feel psychologically safe at work—meaning they feel comfortable reporting issues without fear of retaliation—are more engaged and productive. Creating a culture of psychological safety is linked to lower turnover rates and higher overall job satisfaction.

Summary of Best Practices for Creating Safe and Inclusive Work Environments:

Zero-Tolerance Policies: Establishing and enforcing a zero-tolerance policy for harassment and discrimination is essential. This should include clear guidelines on what constitutes unacceptable behaviour and the consequences for violations. Zero-tolerance policies demonstrate a commitment to maintaining a respectful and safe workplace for everyone.

Regular Training: Providing regular, mandatory training for all employees on harassment, discrimination, and reporting procedures helps ensure that everyone understands their rights and responsibilities. Training should also cover unconscious bias, cultural competency, and how to be an active bystander in situations of harassment.

Confidential Reporting Mechanisms: Implementing confidential, accessible reporting mechanisms is crucial for encouraging victims to come forward without fear of retaliation. These mechanisms should be well-publicised and include multiple avenues for reporting, such as anonymous hotlines, online platforms, and direct access to human resources or a designated ombudsperson.

Support Systems for Victims: Providing robust support systems for victims is critical. This includes access to counselling services, legal support, and assistance in navigating the reporting process. Employers should ensure that victims receive the necessary emotional and professional support without facing retaliation or career setbacks.

Union and Guild Support: Collaborating with industry unions and guilds is essential in ensuring that workplace policies and practices align with broader industry standards for safety and inclusivity. Unions and guilds often provide additional resources, support, and advocacy for workers, including legal assistance, training, and mechanisms for reporting and addressing grievances. They play a critical role in protecting workers' rights and promoting a fair and equitable working environment.

Continuous Review and Improvement: Regularly reviewing and updating policies, procedures, and training programs is essential to ensure they remain effective and relevant. Organisations should conduct periodic audits to assess the effectiveness of their initiatives and make adjustments as needed. This process should involve feedback from employees at all levels to identify areas for improvement and to address emerging challenges.

Diverse Leadership: Promoting diverse leadership at all levels of the organisation is a key factor in creating an inclusive work environment.

Leadership that reflects the diversity of the workforce is more likely to understand and address the unique challenges faced by underrepresented groups. Diverse leadership teams are also more effective in fostering a culture of respect and inclusion, which is critical for creating a workplace where everyone feels valued and safe.

By implementing these best practices, productions can create a safer, more inclusive work environment that not only protects employees but also promotes a positive and productive culture. Ensuring that all team members are aware of their rights and have access to the necessary resources and support systems is fundamental to achieving these goals.

The ILO found that effective reporting systems contribute to a more inclusive and positive organisational culture, encouraging employees to speak up not only about harassment but also about other forms of discrimination and bias.

They also found that organisations with effective reporting mechanisms experience better overall performance and lower turnover rates, as employees feel safer, more supported, and more committed to the workplace.

An inclusive culture goes beyond policies; it involves creating an environment where diversity is valued, and everyone feels welcome. This includes celebrating diverse perspectives, providing equal opportunities for all team members, and actively working to eliminate barriers to inclusion.

Impact of Inclusive Culture on Employee Satisfaction: Data and Statistics

Overall Satisfaction: According to a Deloitte survey, employees who perceive their organisation as committed to diversity and inclusion report 83% higher levels of satisfaction compared to those in less inclusive environments. This demonstrates that fostering an inclusive culture directly contributes to higher overall job satisfaction.

Employee Engagement: The same Deloitte survey found that employees who feel included are 83% more engaged in their work. This level of engagement is crucial for productivity, as engaged employees are more likely to contribute positively to the organisation and invest in their work.

Reduction in Turnover: According to research by the Harvard Business Review, employees in inclusive workplaces are 42% less likely to leave their jobs. This reduction in turnover not only saves costs associated with recruitment and training but also contributes to a more stable and experienced workforce.

Mental Health Benefits: A study by the World Health Organisation (WHO) highlighted that inclusive workplaces that actively support diversity and mental health see a 67% reduction in work-related stress among employees. This improvement in mental well-being leads to higher productivity and reduces absenteeism.

Fostering Innovation and Creativity: According to McKinsey & Company, organisations with diverse and inclusive cultures are 35% more likely to outperform their competitors in terms of innovation. Diverse teams bring a variety of perspectives and ideas, which fosters creativity and drives innovative solutions to business challenges.

Team Effectiveness: Research by Catalyst found that teams working in inclusive environments are 70% more likely to report higher effectiveness. Inclusive leadership practices, such as involving team members in decision-making and valuing diverse perspectives, contribute to stronger team dynamics and better overall performance.

Company Image & Reputation: An inclusive culture also enhances a company's image, both internally and externally. According to a Glassdoor survey, 76% of job seekers consider a company's commitment to diversity and inclusion an important factor when evaluating potential employers. A positive image in this regard not only attracts top talent but also strengthens relationships with customers and stakeholders who value corporate responsibility.

Cultural Safety Officers

A new role I have recently learnt about is that of the Cultural Liaison, Cultural Safety Officer, or sometimes called a Diversity and Inclusion Officer. Their role is to ensure that individuals from diverse nationalities, ethnicities, and cultural backgrounds feel safe, respected, and supported throughout the production process. They serve as a point of contact for cast and crew members who may have concerns, feel mistreated, or need guidance on cultural matters.

What Cultural Safety Officers Do

Addressing Concerns and Complaints: Cultural liaisons are the point of contact for cast and crew members who feel they have been mistreated or discriminated against based on their nationality, culture, ethnicity, or religion. They listen to concerns, investigate issues, and mediate solutions to resolve conflicts fairly.

Promoting Cultural Safety: They ensure the set is a culturally safe space, free from discrimination or cultural insensitivity. This includes addressing and preventing microaggressions, stereotyping, and inappropriate behaviours while working closely with production leadership to maintain a respectful environment.

Cultural Awareness and Training: In some cases, cultural liaisons provide training to the crew and cast on cultural sensitivity, helping everyone understand and respect the cultural norms and values of diverse backgrounds. This helps reduce misunderstandings and promotes inclusivity on set.

Mediation and Conflict Resolution: When cultural or interpersonal conflicts arise, they serve as mediators, facilitating open dialogue and ensuring concerns are addressed respectfully, which helps maintain harmony on set, especially in multicultural teams.

Guidance on Cultural Practices: Cultural liaisons offer on-set guidance about customs, rituals, or sensitivities from various cultures. For instance, they ensure that cultural practices are respected during scenes involving specific traditions and that all participants feel comfortable.

Liaison with HR or Production Management: They often work with Human Resources or production management teams to escalate serious issues, ensuring complaints are handled appropriately and that the necessary actions are taken.

Providing Emotional Support: Beyond addressing formal complaints, cultural liaisons offer emotional support to individuals from diverse backgrounds, creating a safe space for them to voice their concerns and providing advocacy and reassurance.

Ensuring Compliance with Policies: They help ensure the production complies with diversity and anti-discrimination policies, whether they are local laws, union regulations, or internal guidelines, safeguarding the company from legal risks.

Creating a Bridge Between Cultures: Cultural liaisons foster better understanding and communication between people from different nationalities and backgrounds, helping to break down cultural barriers and ensuring everyone feels valued and included.

Benefits to Production Companies:

Improved Cultural Sensitivity and Accuracy: Cultural liaisons help ensure that portrayals of different cultures in the film are accurate and respectful, reducing the risk of misrepresentation and potential backlash. This can enhance the film's credibility and widen its audience appeal.

Prevention of Harmful Stereotypes: By addressing issues of stereotyping or cultural appropriation early in production, companies can avoid negative media attention and protect their brand's reputation.

Enhanced On-Set Inclusion: A cultural liaison creates a more inclusive environment where individuals from different cultural backgrounds feel supported. This improves morale, reduces conflicts, and enhances collaboration among cast and crew members.

Reduced Legal Risks: Cultural liaisons help prevent discriminatory practices or harassment, reducing the risk of lawsuits and formal complaints. Their proactive approach can save companies from costly legal challenges and reputational damage.

Compliance with Industry Standards: Many production companies must meet diversity and inclusion mandates. Having a cultural coordinator helps meet these standards, which is important for securing funding, awards, and distribution deals.

Increased Talent Pool: A commitment to inclusivity and cultural sensitivity makes companies more attractive to diverse talent. This can lead to more creative and innovative storytelling as actors, directors, writers, and crew from underrepresented backgrounds feel valued.

Positive Audience Engagement: Films that authentically represent diverse cultures resonate more deeply with global audiences, leading to better box office performance and stronger streaming numbers.

Better Workplace Environment: By mediating issues related to discrimination or misunderstandings, cultural liaisons create a healthier, more productive work environment, leading to higher job satisfaction and reduced turnover.

Fostering Creative Innovation: The diverse perspectives encouraged by cultural liaisons can lead to more authentic, compelling, and innovative storytelling, helping productions stand out in a competitive market.

Benefits to Employees:

Safe Reporting of Concerns: Employees can report concerns about discrimination or mistreatment to a cultural liaison, knowing that their issues will be heard, addressed, and resolved fairly and without fear of retaliation.

Emotional and Cultural Support: Cultural liaisons provide emotional support for cast and crew members who may feel isolated or misunderstood due to their background. This helps them feel more comfortable and confident in their work environment.

Promotion of Inclusivity: By addressing cultural sensitivities and fostering an inclusive environment, employees from diverse backgrounds feel more valued and respected, enhancing their work experience and job satisfaction.

Conflict Resolution: If conflicts arise on set, employees benefit from having a neutral mediator who can help resolve these issues in a respectful and culturally sensitive manner, preventing escalation and maintaining harmony.

Professional Growth and Confidence: By ensuring that cultural practices are respected and that individuals feel supported, cultural liaisons help employees from diverse backgrounds succeed in their roles, allowing them to grow professionally and contribute more fully to the project.

In summary, cultural liaisons serve as vital advocates for diversity and inclusion on set, improving the working environment for everyone involved. Their role ensures that production companies benefit from enhanced collaboration, legal protection, and access to a wider talent pool, while employees experience a more inclusive, respectful, and supportive workplace.

Access Coordinators

In recent years, the role of Access Coordinators has become increasingly important on film sets, as the industry moves towards inclusivity and accessibility for all workers, including those living with disabilities. Access Coordinators work to ensure that people living with disabilities—whether cast, crew, or extras—can fully participate in the production process. Their role is vital for creating a more equitable working environment, benefiting both individuals and production companies.

What Access Coordinators Do:

An Access Coordinator's primary responsibility is to identify and remove barriers that may prevent individuals living with disabilities from performing their roles effectively. They work closely with the production team to create an inclusive environment that accommodates the physical, sensory, and communication needs of professionals living with a disability. Here are some of the key tasks they perform:

Assessing Accessibility Needs: Before filming begins, Access Coordinators evaluate the set and location to identify any accessibility challenges. This might involve ensuring that there are ramps for wheelchair users, accessible toilets, or quiet spaces for people with sensory sensitivities. They also assess the need for assistive technologies, such as hearing loops or captioning services, depending on the individual's needs.

Adapting Workspaces and Equipment: Access Coordinators work to modify workspaces or equipment to ensure cast and crew living with disabilities can perform their duties without hindrance. This could involve adjusting camera setups, ensuring scripts are available in accessible formats (e.g., braille or large print), or providing alternative communication methods such as sign language interpreters.

Coordinating with Departments: The Access Coordinator liaises with various departments—including costume, set design, and transportation—to make sure that every aspect of the production is accessible. For example, they might collaborate with the costume department to ensure that clothing is easy to put on for those with mobility issues, or work with transportation teams to provide accessible transport to and from set.

Providing On-Set Support: During filming, Access Coordinators remain on hand to provide real-time support for individuals living with disabilities. They help to manage any issues that arise, whether that's an unexpected barrier or a need for additional accommodations. They also assist in facilitating communication between workers living with disabilities and other team members, ensuring that everyone's needs are met without disrupting the production schedule.

Training and Education: Access Coordinators often provide disability awareness training for crew members to foster a more inclusive environment. This training helps the wider team understand the challenges faced by colleagues living with disabilities and educates them on best practices for creating an accessible and supportive workspace. This kind of education reduces stigma, promotes understanding, and ensures everyone on set is aligned with the goal of inclusivity.

Benefits to Production Companies:

Hiring Access Coordinators isn't just about fulfilling a legal or ethical obligation—it can also be highly beneficial for production companies. Some of the key advantages include:

Diverse Talent Pool: By ensuring that film sets are accessible, production companies can tap into a broader talent pool. Individuals living with disabilities bring unique perspectives and skills to the table, and making the industry more inclusive allows production companies to hire the best talent, regardless of ability. This can also lead to richer storytelling, with authentic representation of disabled characters on screen.

Increased Productivity: When accommodations are made, cast and crew living with disabilities can perform their roles to the best of their ability. An Access Coordinator ensures that everything runs smoothly by preventing barriers from slowing down or derailing production. This means that any potential delays related to accessibility issues are minimised, leading to a more efficient and productive set.

Positive Reputation: By employing Access Coordinators and prioritising accessibility, production companies can enhance their reputation for inclusivity. This not only attracts a wider range of professionals to work on future projects but also appeals to audiences who value diversity and representation on screen. In an industry where public perception matters, being known as an inclusive and progressive company can provide a competitive advantage.

Legal Compliance: In many countries, there are legal requirements to provide reasonable accommodations for workers living with disabilities. Hiring an Access Coordinator ensures that the production company complies with these laws and avoids potential legal issues related to discrimination or failure to accommodate. By being proactive in making the set accessible, companies can avoid costly fines and reputational damage.

Benefits to Employees:

For individuals living with a disability and working in the film industry, the presence of an Access Coordinator can make all the difference in ensuring they have the support they need to succeed. Here's how:

Equal Opportunities: Access Coordinators help ensure that cast and crew living with disabilities have the same opportunities as their peers. By removing physical and communication barriers, these coordinators allow professionals living with disabilities to focus on their work, rather than the challenges of navigating an inaccessible environment.

Improved Well-Being: Having an Access Coordinator ensures that workers living with disabilities feel supported and understood. This reduces anxiety and stress, allowing individuals to fully immerse themselves in their roles without constantly worrying about their access needs. In turn, this leads to better mental and physical health outcomes, and greater job satisfaction.

Empowerment and Independence: With an Access Coordinator in place, individuals living with disabilities can take on roles they might otherwise have felt were unattainable. This sense of empowerment and independence is crucial for building confidence in the workplace and encouraging more disabled professionals to pursue careers in the film industry.

A Safer Workplace: Safety is always a top priority on a film set, and Access Coordinators ensure that individuals living with disabilities can navigate the workspace safely. Whether it's ensuring that pathways are clear for a wheelchair user or making sure that safety instructions are provided in accessible formats, Access Coordinators play a critical role in minimising risk and creating a safer environment for all.

In conclusion, Access Coordinators are becoming an essential part of film productions, ensuring that people living with disabilities can fully participate in the industry. Their role in identifying and removing barriers, providing on-set support, and fostering an inclusive culture benefits both production companies and employees. For production companies, Access Coordinators open up a diverse talent pool, increase productivity, and enhance the company's reputation. For employees, they provide crucial support, equal opportunities, and a safer, more empowering work environment. Ultimately, Access Coordinators are helping to create a more inclusive and accessible film industry for everyone.

Intimacy Coordination

Before I get into this section, I just need to say Intimacy Coordination deserves an entire book on its own. What I mention here is just top-layer introductory information. If you want to learn more about this, please feel free to do further research.

The Importance of Intimacy Coordination for the Actor's Wellbeing

A few years ago, I was introduced to the concept of intimacy coordination while working with two amazing intimacy coordinators, Steph Power of Intimacy Coordinators Australia, and Michela Carattini of Key Intimate Scenes, on completely separate and unrelated matters. Both of them are so passionate about the well-being of actors and everyone involved in our industry. Once I heard about the concept and realised how important it is for the well-being of actors, I couldn't believe it was such a recent concept. Then again, given how the industry has historically overlooked the well-being of its members, I guess I shouldn't have been too surprised.

Now that I know about it, I can't unlearn it. I honestly can't see myself ever working on a set where an intimacy coordinator might be needed and not have one there. I was lucky enough to produce a film with Michela, and she was incredible in teaching me even more about how vital intimacy coordination is.

Here's what I've learned about intimacy coordination and how it relates to general well-being:

Intimacy coordination is a growing practice within the film and television industry, aimed at supporting the safety, and dignity of actors when performing intimate scenes. Intimate scenes include nudity, semi-nudity or intimate physical contact, for example, due to kissing, simulated sex, general sensual touching, medical scenes, and even scenes where an actor might be subject to a high level of psychological vulnerability, for example playing a serial killer, rapist, etc.

This role has become increasingly important in recent years, as the industry recognises the physical, mental and emotional toll that performing these types of scenes can have on actors. Having an intimacy coordinator on set is crucial not only for protecting the well-being of the performers but also for creating a healthier and more respectful working environment overall.

The Role of Intimacy Coordination in Actor Well-being:

Creating a Safer Workplace: One of the primary responsibilities of an intimacy coordinator is to establish clear processes, boundaries and communication between actors and directors, whilst interrupting the power dynamic inherent in this working relationship. Intimate scenes can often be emotionally charged and physically vulnerable, and without qualified risk management, actors can feel pushed or pressured to perform things they don't want to. An intimacy coordinator maximises the likelihood that everyone feels safe, supported, and respected, which helps reduce anxiety, conflict and stress surrounding these performances. Often, just the presence of an intimacy coordinator changes on set behaviour and interactions for the better.

Consent and Boundaries: Intimacy coordinators work closely with actors to establish context-specific boundaries, checking consent at every stage of the process. This practice not only protects actors from potential harm but also empowers them by giving them agency over their bodies and performances. Knowing that their boundaries will be respected allows actors to focus on their craft, play, and take artistic risks without the added burden of fear or consequences for their career and working relationships.

Psychological Well-being: What actors do in the pretend space can affect their physical, biological and emotional selves, for example, whether they can access parts of their functioning, and their hormone and neurotransmitter production. Intimate scenes can activate complex emotions, especially when they evoke an individual's personal or community trauma. Intimacy coordinators provide evidenced-based strategies and support for, navigating emotional or psychological challenges that may arise. By creating an environment where actors feel more emotionally and culturally protected, intimacy coordination helps to minimise the potential harm of performing these scenes.

Improved Sense of Creativity & Communication: Having an intimacy coordinator fosters a clearer focus on storytelling and communication between actors and directors, ensuring that everyone is on the same page about the scene's requirements and limitations, and providing expert language, movement direction and choreography specific to intimate scenes. This reduces misunderstandings and helps actors lean into character without having to expose their private lives. When communication is clear and documented, actors are less likely to experience feelings of obligation or exploitation.

Benefits for Production Companies:

While intimacy coordination primarily focuses on the well-being of actors, there are also significant benefits for production companies:

Reduced Risk of Legal Issues: Intimacy coordinators help protect production companies from potential legal issues arising from misconduct or inappropriate behaviour during intimate scenes. By facilitating and documenting adherence to industry occupational health and safety, and providing for informed consent and alternative options at every stage, intimacy coordination reduces the risk of coercion, assault, harassment or other claims that could harm the production and its reputation.

Increased Efficiency: With an intimacy coordinator present, intimate scenes are often filmed more smoothly and efficiently, with less conflict. Because actors, directors and crew feel more mentally secure and understand the boundaries of the scene, they can focus on their jobs and performances, reducing the need for retakes, breaks and long discussions on set. This can save time and resources for the production.

Enhanced Performance: When actors feel safe and supported, their performances are often more authentic, interesting and emotionally compelling. Production companies benefit from the higher quality of performances, which can lead to a better overall product, stronger reviews, and more positive reception.

The Flow-On Effect of Positive Change:

The introduction of intimacy coordination is having a transformative impact on the industry, creating ripple effects of positive change:

Cultural Shift in Industry Practices: The presence of intimacy coordinators is both the result and driver of a cultural shift in how productions approach not only intimate scenes but also other aspects of actor welfare. This shift promotes greater awareness of consent, respect, and mental health on set, leading to a more humane and inclusive working environment.

Improved Relationships and Trust: With the implementation of intimacy coordination, trust between actors, directors, and production teams improves. Actors know they are in a safer space, fostering stronger, more collaborative relationships on set. This trust translates into more positive working conditions and a more harmonious creative process.

Increased Diversity and Inclusion: Because intimacy is often a more varied point of difference between cultures and communities, intimacy coordination also encourages a broader understanding of cultural competence and diverse perspectives, particularly when it comes to gender, sexuality, access, Indigenous and multicultural sensitivities. By respecting personal boundaries and creating an inclusive environment, productions can more accurately reflect the diversity of human experiences, leading to richer, more authentic healing and storytelling.

Normalisation of Well-being Practices: The introduction of intimacy coordinators is part of a larger trend toward normalising mental health and well-being practices in the industry. This positive shift is encouraging more productions to invest in the well-being of their cast and crew, recognising that a mentally and emotionally healthy team leads to better outcomes for everyone involved.

Example Scenarios Requiring Intimacy Coordination:

Sex Scenes: Any scene involving sexual activity—whether explicit or implied—requires careful planning to ensure actors feel safe and supported. Intimacy coordinators assess and manage risk for these moments, making sure that boundaries are respected and that consent is ongoing throughout the scene.

Nudity or Partial Nudity: Scenes involving nudity can leave actors feeling vulnerable. An intimacy coordinator ensures that actors are fully aware of what's required in the scene and that proper procedures, such as closed sets, modesty garments and barriers are in place. They also help ensure a scene meets the director's vision within the actors' consent boundaries.

Kissing and Physical Affection: Even simple acts of physical affection, like kissing, can cause risk, such as exchanging bodily fluids. Intimacy coordinators minimise risks for these moments so that both actors know exactly what will happen, take precautions as needed and are given clear communication about individual boundaries.

Simulated Sexual Violence: Scenes involving sexual violence are especially delicate and can be emotionally traumatic. Intimacy coordinators ensure that these scenes are handled with extreme care, checking in with actors regularly and offering emotional support to help them navigate the psychological challenges of the material.

Disturbing or Psychologically Intense Roles, Portrayal of Historical Violence: When actors play characters who are disturbed, violent, or engage in dark behaviours (such as portraying an abuser, serial killer, or psychologically troubled person), intimacy coordinators help them maintain emotional and psychological boundaries. This is crucial to protecting the actor's mental health while allowing them to fully immerse in the role without lingering emotional distress, or the retraumatising of an individual's personal or community history

Scenes Depicting Domestic Abuse or Assault: Scenes involving domestic violence or physical assault need careful handling, as these situations can trigger emotional responses in actors. Intimacy coordinators work closely with actors to establish consent and ensure that they feel safe both during and after filming.

Medical Scenes: Scenes including portraying dead bodies, childbirth, CPR, hospitalisations and medical procedures often involve intimate touching and exposure, with similar risks and vulnerabilities to other types of intimate scenes.

Scenes involving Children & Young People: Parenting scenes often involve intimate touching and exposure, such as changing a nappy, bathing, dressing or spanking. Psychologically difficult scenes involving children and young people need additional care and risk management in conjunction with the relevant child employment authority.

Conclusion: Intimacy coordination has become an essential practice in the film and TV industry, offering significant benefits to the well-being of actors and crew while also providing advantages for production companies. By fostering a culture of consent, open communication, and psychological safety, intimacy coordinators maximise the potential for actors to perform intimate scenes with confidence and security. The flow-on effect of this positive change is creating a healthier, more respectful, and inclusive industry, benefiting all stakeholders involved.

Companies Leading The Way

Understanding how successful companies have implemented policies that promote work-life balance and equal opportunities can provide valuable insights and serve as a blueprint for others in the film industry. In this chapter, we will explore the strategies of several companies that have made significant strides in these areas.

Case Study 1: Netflix

Netflix, a leading streaming service and production company, has earned a reputation for creating a supportive and inclusive work environment. Their progressive approach to work-life balance and equal opportunities has set a high standard in the industry.

Strategies Implemented:

Unlimited Parental Leave: Netflix offers a generous parental leave policy that allows parents to take up to one year of paid leave during the first year after a child's birth or adoption. This policy is designed to support parents in balancing their family responsibilities without the pressure of rushing back to work.

Flexible Work Hours: Netflix promotes a culture of flexibility, enabling employees to generally set their own work hours. This approach allows individuals to manage their personal and professional commitments effectively, while still being responsible for meeting key work objectives.

Inclusive Hiring Practices: Netflix actively focuses on recruiting talent from diverse backgrounds and has committed to increasing representation across all levels of the organisation. These efforts include setting goals for diversity in leadership roles and fostering an inclusive workplace culture.

Comprehensive Health Benefits: Netflix provides extensive health benefits, including mental health support. These benefits are a crucial part of their commitment to employee well-being, ensuring that employees have access to the resources they need to stay healthy and productive.

Impact: These policies have made Netflix an attractive employer, contributing to high levels of employee satisfaction and retention. By prioritising work-life balance, flexibility, and inclusive hiring practices, Netflix has created a work environment that fosters motivation, innovation, and loyalty among its workforce. This commitment to a supportive and inclusive culture not only benefits employees but also enhances Netflix's reputation as a leading company in the industry, setting a benchmark for others to follow.

Case Study 2: Google

Google, known for its innovative culture, has also been recognised for its efforts to promote work-life balance and equal opportunities. The company's policies reflect a strong commitment to employee well-being and diversity.

Strategies Implemented:

On-Site Childcare: Google does provide on-site childcare facilities at some of its campuses, such as the Mountain View headquarters. This service supports working parents by making it easier for them to balance their professional and personal lives, knowing that their children are being cared for nearby.

Generous Parental Leave: Google offers up to 18 weeks of paid parental leave for birth mothers and 12 weeks for other parents, including fathers and adoptive parents. This policy ensures that all parents have the opportunity to spend time with their newborns or newly adopted children without financial strain.

Diversity and Inclusion Programs: Google has implemented a wide range of programs aimed at increasing diversity and inclusion within the company. These include unconscious bias training, employee resource groups (ERGs) for various underrepresented communities, and initiatives to support women, people of colour, LGBTQ+ individuals, and other marginalised groups in the tech industry.

Workplace Flexibility: Google promotes flexible working arrangements, including remote work options and flexible hours. This flexibility helps employees manage their work and personal responsibilities more effectively. Google has particularly emphasised remote work options in response to the COVID-19 pandemic, with plans to continue offering flexible work arrangements in the future.

Impact: Google's commitment to work-life balance and equal opportunities has led to a diverse and inclusive workforce. The company's policies have not only improved employee satisfaction but have also contributed to its reputation as one of the best places to work. By fostering an environment that values diversity, flexibility, and employee well-being, Google has maintained a highly motivated and innovative workforce.

Case Study 3: Patagonia

Patagonia, an outdoor apparel company, is renowned for its progressive policies that support work-life balance and equal opportunities. The company's approach to employee well-being is deeply embedded in its culture.

Strategies Implemented:

Flexible Working Hours: Patagonia offers flexible working hours, allowing employees to manage their schedules in a way that suits their personal and professional needs. This flexibility is particularly important for employees with caregiving responsibilities, ensuring they can balance work with their family and personal lives.

On-Site Childcare: Patagonia provides on-site childcare at its headquarters in Ventura, California. This service makes it easier for parents to work without the stress of managing external childcare arrangements, contributing to a family-friendly work environment. The company is known for its strong support of working parents, which includes extended parental leave and other family-focused benefits.

Environmental and Social Responsibility: Patagonia encourages employees to engage in environmental and social activism, offering paid time off for volunteering and participation in environmental campaigns. This policy reflects the company's commitment to environmental stewardship and fosters a sense of purpose and community among employees, aligning personal values with corporate goals.

Inclusive Hiring Practices: Patagonia actively recruits from diverse talent pools and focuses on creating an inclusive workplace. The company's commitment to diversity is evident in its hiring practices and in its company culture, which emphasises respect, equality, and the value of different perspectives.

Impact: Patagonia's progressive policies have resulted in high levels of employee engagement and loyalty. The company's focus on work-life balance, environmental responsibility, and equal opportunities has made it a model employer in the outdoor industry and beyond. Patagonia's commitment to these values not only enhances employee satisfaction but also strengthens the company's brand as a leader in corporate social responsibility.

Case Study 4: Sony Pictures Entertainment

Sony Pictures Entertainment (SPE) has implemented a variety of policies to support work-life balance and promote equal opportunities within the film industry. Their efforts have been recognised as leading practices in the entertainment sector.

Strategies Implemented:

Flexible Work Arrangements: SPE offers flexible work arrangements, including telecommuting options and flexible hours. This flexibility allows employees to better balance the demands of their work and personal lives, contributing to higher job satisfaction and productivity.

Parental Leave and Family Support: SPE provides generous parental leave policies for new parents, along with resources such as lactation rooms and parenting workshops. These initiatives ensure that parents feel supported and valued in the workplace, helping them manage their family responsibilities while maintaining their careers.

Diversity and Inclusion Initiatives: SPE has established diversity and inclusion councils and employee resource groups (ERGs) to promote a culture of inclusion. These groups provide support, advocacy, and networking opportunities for underrepresented employees, fostering a more diverse and inclusive workplace.

Health and Wellness Programs: SPE offers comprehensive health and wellness programs, including mental health resources, fitness classes, and stress management workshops. These programs contribute to the overall well-being of employees, helping them maintain a healthy work-life balance and manage stress effectively.

Impact: SPE's commitment to work-life balance and equal opportunities has resulted in a positive and inclusive work environment. The company's policies have helped attract and retain top talent, contributing to its ongoing success in the competitive entertainment industry. By prioritising employee well-being and fostering a culture of diversity and inclusion, SPE continues to set a high standard within the sector.

The strategies implemented by Netflix, Google, Patagonia, and Sony Pictures Entertainment provide valuable insights into how companies can promote work-life balance and equal opportunities. By adopting similar policies, the film industry can create a more supportive and inclusive environment for all employees. These case studies demonstrate that prioritising employee well-being and diversity not only benefits individuals but also leads to greater organisational success.

See Worksheet: Documenting your team's accounts of working conditions

See Worksheet: Documenting your personal accounts of working conditions

CHAPTER 14

Personal Solutions

Job-Sharing (from the employee's side)

Please read the section on job-sharing in the above chapter. I feel that the employee and employer sections cannot be separated as both parties best see the full scope.

Taking Your Child to Meetings and Events

Bringing your child to work meetings and industry events can help balance professional and personal responsibilities, fostering a family-friendly environment that allows parents to stay engaged with their work without sacrificing time with their children.

This approach strengthens family bonds, encourages inclusivity by demonstrating a commitment to family-friendly practices, and reduces the stress of finding childcare during work hours. A study by the American Psychological Association shows that 60% of parents experienced reduced stress when they were able to integrate family responsibilities with work.

While ringing your child to a meeting can be a great way to balance work and family life, it's important to approach it thoughtfully. First, set clear expectations by ensuring the presence of your child is appropriate for the specific meeting or event. Consider the tone of the meeting and the people involved. Some professional settings may be more accommodating to a child's presence, while others might require a more formal approach.

Next, carefully choose where to meet. Opt for locations that offer child-friendly amenities, such as quiet rooms, playgrounds, or activities that can keep your child entertained if the meeting runs long. This helps minimise distractions and allows you to focus on the discussion, knowing your child is comfortably occupied.

Lastly, always communicate openly with colleagues or clients in advance. Let them know that you'll be bringing your child to the meeting, ensuring everyone is comfortable with the arrangement. Open communication helps avoid surprises and creates a more relaxed and understanding environment, where everyone is on the same page. When done thoughtfully, bringing your child to a meeting can showcase your ability to balance work and family, while maintaining professionalism.

Encouraging Walking Meetings

Walking meetings offer a great way to combine physical activity with work discussions, particularly for one-on-one or small group meetings. This approach not only boosts productivity but also promotes health by reducing the risks associated with a sedentary lifestyle. Research from the Mayo Clinic shows that walking can burn an additional 100 calories per hour compared to sitting, making walking meetings a simple way to incorporate movement into the workday. Moreover, walking has been shown to boost creativity, with fresh air and movement helping to enhance focus and stimulate creative problem-solving. A study from Stanford University even found that walking can increase creative output by an average of 60%.

In addition to these benefits, walking meetings can improve employee satisfaction. According to a survey by Inc. Magazine, 67% of employees feel more satisfied and engaged when they participate in walking meetings, as the relaxed atmosphere encourages open dialogue and a sense of well-being.

To implement walking meetings effectively, it's important to choose the right location—select safe and pleasant walking routes that allow for easy conversation. Keep the meetings informal to create a comfortable environment for discussion, and be mindful of time, keeping the meeting to a manageable 20-30 minutes.

By incorporating walking meetings into your routine, you can improve both the physical health and creativity of your team while enhancing overall engagement.

Being Outdoors

One of the simplest yet most effective remedies for improving mental well-being is spending time outdoors. I often take my laptop and do my work in a park or green area overlooking the ocean.

Research consistently shows that being in nature reduces stress, eases anxiety, and enhances overall mental health. Time in nature has been shown to lower cortisol levels, the hormone associated with stress, as the calming effects of green spaces, fresh air, and natural light help relax both mind and body.

Exposure to nature also improves mood and reduces anxiety symptoms by providing a mental reset, away from daily pressures. Being outdoors enhances cognitive function and creativity, offering mental clarity that aids focus and problem-solving. Physical activity, which often increases when outdoors, releases endorphins that combat stress and depression.

Additionally, exposure to natural light helps regulate sleep patterns, leading to better sleep, which is linked to lower stress and anxiety. Finally, being outside fosters a connection with nature, encouraging mindfulness and present-moment awareness, which can ground us and provide relief from the constant stream of thoughts and worries.

Outdoor Ideas:

Take Short Outdoor Breaks: Step outside for a few minutes during your workday. A short walk around the block, a visit to a nearby park, or even standing on your balcony can provide a quick mental refresh. These mini breaks can significantly reduce stress and help you return to work with a clearer mind.

Schedule Outdoor Time Daily: Make a habit of scheduling time outdoors each day. This could be a morning walk, an evening jog, or simply sitting in your garden or local park. Treat this time as an essential part of your routine, just like any other appointment.

Incorporate Nature into Your Work Environment: If possible, bring nature into your workspace. Set up your desk near a window with a view of the outdoors or add plants to your office to create a more natural atmosphere. Studies have shown that even a view of greenery or having plants around can reduce stress and enhance productivity.

Combine Exercise with Outdoor Activities: Take your workouts outside. Whether it's yoga in the park, a run on a nature trail, or cycling around your neighbourhood, exercising outdoors provides the dual benefit of physical activity and nature exposure.

Plan Outdoor Activities with Friends or Family: Make social plans that involve outdoor activities. Whether it's a picnic, a hike, or a casual stroll, spending time outdoors with loved ones can enhance your mood and provide social support, which is vital for mental health.

Use Lunchtime for Fresh Air: Instead of eating at your desk, take your lunch outside. Even if it's just for 20 minutes, this break can help you disconnect from work stress and enjoy a change of scenery.

Practice Mindfulness Outdoors: Use your time outdoors to practice mindfulness. Focus on the sights, sounds, and smells around you. Pay attention to the rustling of leaves, the chirping of birds, or the feel of the breeze on your skin. This mindful presence in nature can have a calming effect and help reduce anxiety.

Weekend Nature Getaways: Plan occasional weekend trips to natural settings like beaches, mountains, or countryside locations. A change of environment and immersion in nature can act as a powerful reset button, leaving you feeling refreshed and recharged.

Incorporate Outdoor Meetings: If you have the flexibility, suggest walking meetings or outdoor brainstorming sessions. The change of environment can stimulate creativity and reduce the formality of indoor meetings, leading to more productive and enjoyable interactions.

Set a Nature-Based Goal: Challenge yourself with a nature-based goal, such as visiting a new park each week, hiking a local trail, or starting a garden. These goals can provide motivation to spend more time outdoors and enjoy the associated mental health benefits.

Incorporating outdoor time into your daily routine doesn't require a significant amount of effort or a drastic lifestyle change. Small, consistent actions can make a substantial difference in reducing stress, alleviating anxiety, and enhancing mental health. Whether it's a quick walk outside, a nature-themed lunch break, or a weekend hike, finding ways to connect with the outdoors can lead to a healthier, happier, and more balanced life. So, step outside, breathe in the fresh air, and let nature work its magic on your mind and soul.

Separating Work and Family Time

Maintaining a clear boundary between work and family time is crucial for a healthy work-life balance. This means being fully present in each aspect of your life, without the constant distraction of work-related tasks.

People often say to me, "You're always so busy, when do you find time for yourself and your family?" What they don't realise is that I'm only "that busy" during my work hours. I make sure to block out time for my family, sleep and fitness first, and then allocate the rest to work. This way, I ensure a balance that allows me to be as busy as I need to be during work hours, without it affecting my personal life. By prioritising my family and well-being, I can dive into my work with full focus, knowing that I've already made time for what matters most.

During family time, make a conscious effort to put away phones, computers, and other devices that might draw you back to work. This creates a space where you can be fully present with your loved ones. And visa versa, when you are working, don't be distracted by anything else.

This helps in building stronger family bonds and ensures that your family gets your undivided attention, making the time spent together more meaningful while maximising your work time.

Dedicated Family Days

Having fixed, non-negotiable family days can ensure that you consistently make time for your loved ones, regardless of work demands.

Choose one day each week that is strictly for family activities. These days should be planned in advance and treated as sacred, non-workdays.

Mark these days on your calendar and communicate to your team that you will be unavailable for work-related activities. Use these days to engage in activities that everyone in the family enjoys.

This practice helps in creating family memories and provides a regular break from the stress of work, allowing you to recharge.

Compartmentalisation of the Mind

Compartmentalisation is a mental strategy that involves separating different aspects of life into distinct categories or "compartments," allowing you to focus on one area without being overwhelmed by concerns from another. In the demanding and often unpredictable screen industry, where the lines between work and personal life can easily blur, compartmentalisation can be a powerful tool for maintaining balance, well-being, and overall productivity.

Benefits of Compartmentalisation

Reduced Stress and Anxiety: By consciously separating work-related thoughts from personal matters, you can prevent the stress of one area from impacting another. This separation helps to avoid constant worry about work when you are at home or vice versa, leading to a more relaxed and peaceful state of mind.

Improved Focus and Productivity: Compartmentalisation enables you to fully concentrate on the task at hand, whether it's a demanding project or a personal commitment. This targeted focus enhances your productivity and allows you to complete tasks more efficiently without the mental distraction of unrelated issues.

Better Emotional Health: Keeping work and personal life separate can help manage emotions more effectively. You're less likely to bring work frustrations into your personal interactions or let personal problems affect your professional performance. This emotional balance contributes to overall mental well-being.

Enhanced Relationships: Compartmentalising allows you to be fully present when spending time with family and friends, leading to deeper, more meaningful connections. This presence strengthens relationships, providing a solid support system that is crucial for emotional health.

Increased Job Satisfaction: By clearly defining work time and personal time, you create a sense of structure and control over your life, which can increase job satisfaction. Knowing that personal time is protected can make work feel less intrusive and overwhelming.

Better Decision-Making: When you compartmentalise effectively, your mind is less cluttered, allowing you to think more clearly and make better decisions. This clarity can be particularly valuable in high-pressure environments like the screen industry, where quick, effective decision-making is often required.

How to Practice Compartmentalisation

Set Clear Boundaries: Establish specific boundaries between work and personal life. This might include fixed working hours, dedicated break times, and specific personal time in the evenings or weekends. Clearly communicate these boundaries to colleagues, family members, and yourself to ensure they are respected and adhered to.

Create Physical Separation: Whenever possible, designate separate spaces for work and personal activities. If you work from home, use a specific room or area for work tasks and a different area for relaxation and personal time. This physical separation reinforces mental boundaries and helps switch off from work when you're outside of that space.

Utilise Time Management Techniques: Plan your day using time management methods such as the Pomodoro Technique (work in focused intervals, followed by short breaks), time blocking (dedicating specific times to particular tasks), or task prioritisation (focusing on high-priority tasks first). These techniques help in organising your day and ensuring time is allocated effectively to both work and personal life.

Practice Mindfulness and Transition Rituals: Before transitioning from work to personal time, engage in mindfulness exercises or set rituals. Simple actions like deep breathing, stretching, a brief walk, or even a short meditation session can help signal your brain to switch from work mode to personal mode, easing the transition.

Set Digital Boundaries: Establish limits on checking work emails, messages, or notifications outside of work hours. Consider using tools that block or filter work-related communication after certain times. This practice helps to maintain mental space for personal life, free from work intrusions.

Develop a Support System: Rely on a network of colleagues, friends, and family members who respect and support your need to compartmentalise. Discuss your boundaries and the importance of work-life balance with them, so they understand and help reinforce your efforts.

Regular Self-Check-Ins: Make it a habit to regularly reflect on how well you are managing your work and personal life compartments. Self-check-ins help you identify areas where boundaries might be slipping and allow you to make adjustments. This reflection can be part of a weekly or monthly review of your personal and professional goals.

Use Technology Wisely: Leverage apps and tools designed to help with focus and organisation, such as calendar apps, task managers, and digital reminders. These tools can keep you on track, ensuring that you dedicate specific times to work tasks and personal activities without overlap.

Embrace Flexibility When Needed: While compartmentalisation is about setting boundaries, it's also essential to recognise when flexibility is necessary. Life is unpredictable, especially in the screen industry, so being adaptable and allowing some overlap when absolutely needed can reduce stress in the long run.

Engage in Reflective Journaling: Keeping a journal where you document your thoughts and feelings about work and personal life can be beneficial. Writing things down allows you to express emotions without letting them spill over into other compartments. It also helps in identifying patterns and triggers that disrupt balance.

Applying Compartmentalisation in the Screen Industry

Prioritise and Plan: Given the unpredictable nature of the screen industry, prioritise tasks and plan as much as possible. Identify critical work deadlines and personal commitments in advance, ensuring both are respected. This planning can help manage sudden changes or emergencies without overwhelming your personal life.

End-of-Day Routines: Establish a clear routine for ending the workday. This could involve shutting down your computer, organising your workspace, and engaging in a relaxing activity such as reading or listening to music. A consistent end-of-day routine can signal to your mind that it's time to shift from work to personal time.

Optimise Downtime: In the screen industry, downtime between projects or shoots can be unpredictable. Use this time wisely by engaging in personal activities, hobbies, or relaxation. Taking advantage of downtime helps reinforce the compartmentalisation process and reduces burnout.

Effective Communication: Be transparent with colleagues about your boundaries. If you're working during intense project phases, communicate your availability and when you need personal time. This transparency helps set expectations and prevents work from encroaching on personal life.

Leverage Professional Support: If you find compartmentalisation challenging, especially during high-stress periods, consider seeking professional support. Counsellors or life coaches specialising in the entertainment industry can provide valuable guidance and strategies tailored to your specific needs.

Adjusting Working Hours & Micromanaging Your Time

Flexibility in working hours can help parents align their work schedules with their children's routines, ensuring they are available during critical times.

It might sound a bit unconventional, but you can always adjust your working hours to fit around your children's schedules, working when they are at school or asleep. This has been key to how I manage my time.

Micromanaging your time can be highly beneficial in ensuring tasks are completed efficiently while also maintaining a healthy work-life balance. By breaking down your day into specific, manageable segments and assigning time slots to each task, you create a clear roadmap that keeps you focused and minimises distractions. This approach not only helps you prioritise important tasks but also prevents work from spilling over into personal time.

By managing your schedule closely, you can ensure that work gets done within designated hours, leaving more time for family and personal activities. Ultimately, micromanaging your time allows you to be more productive and maintain a balanced, fulfilling life.

I will give an example of how I micromanage my time a bit later on.

Using Communication Platforms Efficiently

Effective use of communication platforms can significantly reduce the time spent in unnecessary meetings and calls, freeing up more time for productive work, exercise and family.

Use platforms like WhatsApp to communicate with your team via voice messages instead of long meetings.

Encourage your team to send voice messages for non-urgent updates and quick discussions, this allows them to communicate at a time that is convenient for them, and in turn, this allows you to listen and respond at your convenience, minimising the disruptions to everyone's time.

This can streamline communication, save time, and reduce the need for lengthy meetings, allowing you to focus on more important things.

Enhancing Efficiency and Eliminating Distractions

One of the significant barriers to productivity and well-being is the presence of unnecessary clutter in our lives. This chapter explores the various forms of clutter, such as excessive social media use and other time-wasting activities and provides practical methods to enhance efficiency in both personal and professional settings.

Identifying Unnecessary Clutter

Digital Distractions:

Social Media: Platforms like Facebook, Instagram, Twitter, and TikTok can consume hours of your day without you realising it. The constant need to check updates and notifications disrupts focus and reduces productivity.

Emails and Notifications: An overwhelming number of emails and app notifications can interrupt your workflow, making it hard to concentrate on tasks that require deep focus.

Browsing the Web: Aimless surfing on the internet can lead to significant time wastage. It's easy to start with a quick search and end up spending hours reading unrelated articles.

Digital Detox:

Set Time Limits: Use apps like Screen Time (iOS) or Digital Wellbeing (Android) to monitor and set limits on your social media usage.

Scheduled Social Media Time: Allocate specific times during the day for checking social media, rather than sporadically throughout the day.

Unsubscribe and Filter: Regularly unsubscribe from unnecessary email lists and use filters to prioritise important emails.

Audit Your Apps: Review all the apps on your phone and computer. Uninstall those that are not essential or productive.

Notification Management: Turn off non-essential notifications. Only keep alerts for important communications.

Physical Clutter:

Disorganised Workspaces: A cluttered desk or office can create a chaotic environment that hinders productivity. Searching for documents or tools in a disorganised space takes time and adds to stress.

Excessive Possessions: Owning too many items can lead to clutter in your living and working spaces, making it hard to find what you need and creating a sense of overwhelm.

Physical Decluttering:

Organise Your Workspace: Dedicate time each week to organise your desk and office. Use storage solutions like shelves, drawers, and organisers to keep everything in its place.

Minimalism: Adopt a minimalist approach by regularly decluttering your possessions. Keep only what you need and use it frequently.

Daily Cleaning Habits: Incorporate a daily habit of tidying up your workspace before you end your day.

Workspace Makeover: Spend a weekend reorganising your workspace. Label storage items and create designated areas for different types of work materials.

Regular Upkeep: Schedule a monthly review to keep your workspace organised and clutter-free.

Mental Clutter:

Overthinking: Spending too much time worrying about future tasks or regretting past actions can prevent you from focusing on the present.

Multitasking: Trying to juggle multiple tasks at once can reduce efficiency and increase the likelihood of errors. However, multitasking isn't always detrimental. When done correctly, such as pairing a primary task with a routine, low-cognitive one (like listening to a podcast while exercising), it can be an efficient use of time.

Mental Clutter Management:

Mindfulness and Meditation: Practice mindfulness or meditation to calm your mind and reduce overthinking. Apps like Headspace and Calm can guide you through these practices.

Task Management: Use tools like to-do lists or apps like Trello and Asana to organise tasks. Break down larger tasks into smaller, manageable steps.

Daily Journaling: Start or end your day with journaling to clear your mind. Write down tasks, thoughts, and reflections to reduce mental clutter.

Enhancing Efficiency

Time Management Techniques:

Pomodoro Technique: Work for 25 minutes, then take a 5-minute break. After four cycles, take a longer break. This method helps maintain focus and prevent burnout.

Time Blocking: Allocate specific blocks of time for different tasks throughout the day. This can prevent tasks from overrunning and ensure a balanced workload.

Prioritisation: Use the Eisenhower Priority Matrix to prioritise tasks based on urgency and importance. Focus on important tasks that need immediate attention and delegate or eliminate less critical ones.

PRIORITY MATRIX

Date: ____/____/____

IMPORTANT & URGENT

IMPORTANT & NOT URGENT

NOT IMPORTANT & URGENT

NOT IMPORTANT & NOT URGENT

Optimising Work Processes

Batch Processing: Group similar tasks together and complete them in one go. For example, respond to all emails at once rather than sporadically throughout the day.

Automation: Use automation tools for repetitive tasks. For example, use tools like Zapier to automate data entry or email responses.

Streamlining Communication: Use communication tools like Slack or Microsoft Teams to centralise and streamline team communication, reducing the time spent on back-and-forth emails.

Adopt a New Time Management Tool: Experiment with a new time management tool or technique each month. See what works best for you and your workflow.

Review and Adjust: Regularly review your productivity methods. Adjust and refine them based on what you find most effective.

By identifying and eliminating unnecessary clutter from your life, you can significantly improve your productivity and well-being. Implementing these strategies will not only help you become more efficient in your work but also allow you to enjoy a more balanced and fulfilling personal life.

Staying Fit and Eating Healthy

Amidst the hustle and bustle of set life, maintaining physical fitness and healthy eating habits can often fall by the wayside. However, staying fit and eating well is crucial for ensuring sustained energy, mental clarity, and overall well-being, all of which are essential for peak performance in this challenging field.

Physical Fitness:

Working in film often requires long hours of intense physical activity, whether it's setting up equipment, performing stunts, or simply enduring the extended periods on set. Regular exercise helps build stamina and resilience, allowing individuals to meet these physical demands without succumbing to fatigue. A consistent fitness routine improves cardiovascular health, increases muscle strength, and enhances overall endurance, making it easier to navigate the rigours of a typical production day.

Exercise is not only beneficial for physical health but also for mental well-being. Regular physical activity releases endorphins, the body's natural mood elevators, which can help reduce stress and anxiety. Exercise also promotes better sleep, which is vital for cognitive function and emotional stability. With clearer minds and reduced stress levels, film professionals can maintain better focus and creativity, which are critical for problem-solving and innovative thinking on set.

The physical demands of the film industry can lead to burnout if not managed properly. Incorporating regular physical activity into daily routines helps to mitigate this risk by enhancing resilience and reducing the impact of stress. Exercise also fosters a sense of routine and discipline, which can be grounding amidst the unpredictable nature of film production.

Healthy Eating:

A balanced diet rich in nutrients provides the energy needed to power through long shoots and demanding schedules. Consuming a variety of fruits, vegetables, lean proteins, and whole grains ensures that the body receives essential vitamins and minerals. These nutrients support vital functions, including energy production, muscle repair, and immune system maintenance. In contrast, a diet high in processed foods and sugars can lead to energy crashes and decreased productivity.

Nutrition has a direct impact on cognitive function. Foods rich in antioxidants, healthy fats, vitamins, and minerals nourish the brain and promote optimal function. Omega-3 fatty acids, found in fish and flaxseeds, are particularly beneficial for brain health, improving memory and cognitive performance. Conversely, poor nutrition can lead to cognitive decline, making it harder to concentrate and make decisions during demanding production schedules.

Long-term health is significantly influenced by diet. By prioritising nutrient-dense foods, film professionals can reduce their risk of chronic illnesses such as heart disease, diabetes, and obesity. A healthy diet supports sustained physical and mental health, enabling individuals to have longer, more productive careers in the industry.

Practical Tips for Staying Fit and Eating Healthy

Incorporate Movement: Even with a busy schedule, find ways to incorporate physical activity. This could be as simple as stretching, walking, or doing quick workouts between shoots. Utilise fitness apps or online workout programs that offer short, effective routines that can be done anywhere.

Plan and Prep Meals: Plan and prepare healthy meals and snacks in advance to avoid relying on fast food or craft services, which often lack nutritional value. Keep healthy snacks, such as nuts, fruits, and yogurt, readily available to maintain energy levels throughout the day.

Stay Hydrated: Drink plenty of water to stay hydrated, especially during long shoots and physically demanding activities. Dehydration can lead to fatigue and decreased cognitive function.

Balance Work and Rest: Prioritise rest and recovery. Ensure adequate sleep and take breaks when needed to prevent burnout and maintain overall health.

Seek Support: Join fitness groups or find a workout buddy within the industry to stay motivated. Sharing goals and progress with peers can enhance commitment to a healthy lifestyle.

In conclusion, staying fit and eating healthy are not just beneficial but essential for anyone working in the film industry. By investing in physical fitness and nutrition, film professionals can enhance their energy levels, mental clarity, and overall well-being, leading to more productive, creative, and sustainable careers.

Personal Mental and Emotional Health Strategies

On top of what we already discussed, the following are summaries of further ideas. If you require professional help, guidance, or counselling, please don't hesitate to seek support.

Working in the screen industry can make it challenging to implement these strategies, but with a conscious decision and a well-thought-out plan, setting boundaries and sticking to them can lead to significant improvements in your life—even if you only manage to incorporate a few of these practices.

Practice Mindfulness and Meditation: Engage in mindfulness practices like meditation, deep breathing exercises, or simply paying attention to the present moment. These practices help reduce stress, increase self-awareness, and promote emotional regulation. Start with just a few minutes a day and gradually increase the time as you become more comfortable.

Build Strong Social Connections: Maintain close relationships with family, friends, or a support group. Social interactions provide emotional support, reduce feelings of isolation, and increase overall happiness. Schedule regular catch-ups with friends or join a community group that interests you.

Set Boundaries and Manage Stress: Learn to say no when necessary and manage your time effectively to avoid burnout. Setting boundaries helps maintain a healthy balance between personal and professional life. Use tools like planners or apps to organise your tasks and prioritise activities that bring you joy.

Practice Gratitude: Regularly reflect on things you are grateful for. This practice can shift your focus from negative thoughts to positive ones, improving overall emotional well-being. Keep a gratitude journal and write down three things you're grateful for each day.

Seek Professional Help When Needed: Don't hesitate to seek help from a therapist or counsellor if you're struggling with mental health issues. Professional support can provide valuable tools and strategies for managing emotions. If you feel overwhelmed, consider talking to a mental health professional to explore your feelings and develop coping strategies.

Engage in Hobbies and Creative Activities: Pursue activities that you enjoy, whether it's painting, writing, gardening, or playing an instrument. Creative expression can be a powerful outlet for emotions and a source of joy. Dedicate regular time each week to your hobbies, even if it's just for a short while.

Ensure Adequate Sleep: Quality sleep is essential for mental and emotional well-being. Poor sleep can exacerbate stress, anxiety, and depression. Establish a regular sleep routine, aiming for 7-9 hours of sleep per night, and create a relaxing bedtime environment.

Practice Self-Compassion: Treat yourself with kindness and understanding, especially during difficult times. Self-compassion involves recognising that it's okay to be imperfect and to experience setbacks. When you make a mistake, talk to yourself as you would to a friend, with encouragement and support, rather than harsh criticism.

Limit Exposure to Stressful Media: Consuming too much negative news or spending excessive time on social media can increase stress and anxiety. Set limits on media consumption and take regular breaks from social media to focus on more positive activities.

Practice Positive Thinking and Affirmations: Replace negative thoughts with positive affirmations and focus on your strengths and achievements. Positive thinking can enhance emotional resilience and overall mental health. Start each day with a positive affirmation or write down positive thoughts about yourself and your life.

Incorporating these strategies into your daily routine can significantly improve your mental and emotional well-being. It's important to find what works best for you and to practice these strategies consistently.

Long-term Career Sustainability

Ensuring long-term career sustainability in the film industry requires comprehensive strategies that include continuous learning, skill development, networking, and personal branding. Here are detailed strategies for long-term career sustainability:

Continuous Learning and Skill Development

Staying updated with industry trends is essential for continued growth and success in the ever-evolving film industry. One of the best ways to do this is by attending workshops, seminars, and conferences that focus on the latest developments in filmmaking techniques, tools, and technology. These events not only provide valuable insights into current trends but also offer networking opportunities with industry professionals. In addition to in-person events, online courses and certifications are a convenient and flexible way to stay current. Many platforms offer specialised courses in areas like cinematography, editing software, and visual effects, allowing professionals to enhance their skill sets without needing to be on set.

Cross-departmental training is another effective way to expand your expertise and adaptability in the industry. Participating in job rotation programs within your organisation can give you hands-on experience in various departments, broadening your understanding of the filmmaking process. For example, someone who primarily works in lighting may benefit from spending time in the sound department, gaining a holistic view of how these areas interact during production. Similarly, attending skill development workshops outside your primary role—such as editing, sound design, or scriptwriting—can enhance your versatility and open new career opportunities.

Advanced education: For those looking to deepen their expertise, advanced education is a valuable investment. Graduate programs in film studies, production management, or other related fields provide an in-depth exploration of the industry's complexities, from storytelling to logistical management. Specialised training programs offered by prestigious institutions such as the American Film Institute (AFI), the Australian Film Television and Radio School (AFTRS), or the National Film and Television School (NFTS) can provide cutting-edge education in specific areas of filmmaking. These programs not only improve technical and creative skills but also build strong industry connections, positioning graduates as leaders in the field.

Networking and Mentorship

Build a Strong Professional Network

Staying updated with industry trends is crucial for anyone working in film, whether you're just starting or are a seasoned professional. One of the best ways to stay in the loop is by attending industry events, such as film festivals, expos, and networking functions. These events provide a unique opportunity to connect with other professionals, exchange ideas, and learn about the latest innovations in filmmaking. Film festivals, in particular, offer a chance to see emerging trends in storytelling, cinematography, and technology, all while building relationships that can lead to future collaborations. Expos, on the other hand, often showcase cutting-edge equipment and techniques, helping you stay ahead of the curve in a fast-evolving industry.

Another great way to stay connected and informed is by joining professional associations. Membership often comes with access to exclusive workshops, webinars, and networking opportunities, as well as industry updates that keep you informed about shifts in the market. Being part of these associations also adds a level of credibility to your career and gives you access to mentoring programs, job boards, and career development resources. By staying active in these communities, you'll not only be better prepared for the changing landscape of the film industry but also position yourself for continued growth and success.

Seek Mentorship

Finding a mentor is one of the most valuable steps you can take in building a successful career in the film industry. Connecting with experienced professionals who can offer guidance, share their knowledge, and provide career advice can make a significant difference in navigating the often complex and competitive world of filmmaking. Mentors can offer insights based on their own experiences, helping you avoid common pitfalls and learn industry-specific skills that you might not get from formal education. Whether it's advice on the technical aspects of filmmaking, career decisions, or simply understanding how to network effectively, having someone in your corner with years of experience can be invaluable.

In addition to seeking out mentors informally, many industry organisations offer formal mentorship programs designed to pair emerging filmmakers with seasoned professionals. Programs like these provide structured opportunities to learn from leaders in the field. These programs offer a more formal framework for mentorship, often including scheduled meetings, specific goals, and development plans tailored to your career. Participating in a mentorship program not only gives you access to expert advice but also opens doors to industry connections, collaborations, and potential job opportunities. Mentorship, whether formal or informal, is an incredible way to fast-track your growth and gain insights that can help shape your career path.

Career Development and Advancement

Set Clear Career Goals

Setting clear short-term and long-term goals is essential for anyone looking to build a successful career in the film industry. Defining what you want to achieve in the next few months, as well as where you see yourself in five or ten years, can help create a focused roadmap for your career. Whether it's gaining more on-set experience, developing a specific skill set like editing or screenwriting, or aiming for larger projects like directing your own feature, having well-defined goals gives you something concrete to work toward. Breaking down those long-term aspirations into manageable short-term milestones will make them feel more achievable and keep you motivated along the way.

It's equally important to regularly review and adjust your goals as you grow and as the industry evolves. The film world is fast-paced and constantly changing, with new technologies, platforms, and opportunities emerging all the time. Regularly reassessing your career plan allows you to stay adaptable and responsive to these changes. Personal growth is also key—your interests or priorities might shift over time, and it's important to factor that into your career path. By periodically reviewing your progress, tweaking your goals, and remaining open to new directions, you'll ensure that your career stays on track while giving yourself room to evolve and succeed in a dynamic industry.

Pursue Leadership Roles

Taking on leadership positions is a powerful way to build your career in the film industry and gain valuable experience. Whether it's leading a project, managing a department, or overseeing a smaller team, stepping into a leadership role allows you to develop critical skills like decision-making, problem-solving, and team management. It's also an excellent opportunity to prove your ability to handle more responsibility and showcase your strengths, which can open doors to bigger projects and more senior roles in the future. Even if you're early in your career, look for opportunities to take the lead on smaller initiatives or volunteer for leadership roles in independent projects. These experiences will help you build confidence and establish yourself as a capable leader.

To complement this hands-on experience, attending leadership and management training programs is an effective way to enhance your capabilities. Many industry organisations and educational institutions offer courses specifically designed to help creative professionals develop their leadership skills. These programs cover areas like team dynamics, conflict resolution, project management, and effective communication, all of which are essential for leading in the fast-paced, high-pressure environment of film production. By investing in professional development and actively seeking leadership opportunities, you'll position yourself for long-term success and growth in the film industry.

Diversify Your Experience

Working on diverse projects is a fantastic way to build a well-rounded career in the film industry. By participating in a variety of productions, from independent films to commercials and web series, you'll gain a wider range of experiences that can help you become more adaptable and versatile. Each type of project brings its own challenges, techniques, and creative approaches, allowing you to learn new skills and understand different facets of the industry. Independent films, for example, often involve smaller budgets and more creative freedom, while commercials may offer fast-paced environments with tight deadlines. Web series can introduce you to new digital platforms and storytelling formats. Diversifying your experience not only makes you a more skilled professional but also expands your network, opening doors to future opportunities in different areas of film and media.

Collaborating with diverse teams is equally important in broadening your perspective and improving your ability to work in a global, multicultural industry. When you work with professionals from different backgrounds and cultures, you gain valuable insights into various approaches to storytelling, problem-solving, and production processes. This exposure to different viewpoints enriches your creativity and strengthens your ability to navigate the complexities of collaborative filmmaking. It also helps build empathy and understanding, which are essential for fostering strong, productive working relationships on set. By embracing diverse projects and teams, you not only enhance your skill set but also position yourself as a more dynamic and adaptable professional in the film industry.

Financial Planning and Stability

Financial Management

Budgeting is a critical skill for anyone in the film industry, where income can often be unpredictable due to the project-based nature of the work. Creating and sticking to a budget allows you to manage your income and expenses effectively, helping you maintain financial control even during periods of irregular earnings. By setting a clear budget, you can prioritise your spending, track your expenses, and ensure you're covering essential costs without overspending. This not only reduces financial stress but also gives you a better understanding of how to allocate funds toward professional development, equipment, or other career-related investments.

In addition to budgeting, it's important to focus on saving and investing a portion of your income to ensure long-term financial stability. Putting aside savings when you can, especially during high-earning periods, creates a safety net for times when work may be less consistent. Wise investing, whether in retirement funds, stocks, or other opportunities, can help grow your savings and provide financial security for the future. By developing strong savings habits and making informed investment decisions, you can build a stable financial foundation that allows you to navigate the ups and downs of a freelance or project-based career in the film industry with greater peace of mind.

Embrace Technology and Innovation

Adopt New Technologies

Adopting new technologies is essential for staying competitive in the ever-evolving film industry. Keeping up with the latest advancements, such as virtual production, VFX, and AI, ensures that you remain tech-savvy and can adapt to modern filmmaking techniques. Staying informed about these technologies not only improves your technical skills but also opens up opportunities for more innovative and efficient ways of working. By embracing advancements like AI-assisted editing, virtual production stages, or cutting-edge visual effects, you can enhance your creative process and bring your projects to life with greater precision and creativity.

In addition to staying informed, gaining hands-on experience with new technologies is key to mastering them. Participating in training programs, workshops, or practical applications allows you to get a feel for how these tools work in real-world scenarios. Whether you're experimenting with new software, learning the intricacies of virtual production, or working directly with VFX, this practical experience helps solidify your knowledge and boosts your confidence in using these tools. By actively adopting and applying new technologies, you'll position yourself as a forward-thinking professional who can tackle the challenges of modern filmmaking with expertise and innovation.

Innovative Storytelling

Exploring new storytelling formats like VR, AR, and interactive films can significantly expand your creative horizons and keep you at the forefront of the film industry. These emerging formats offer exciting ways to engage audiences by immersing them in the story, allowing for a more interactive and dynamic viewing experience. By experimenting with virtual reality, augmented reality, or interactive storytelling, you can break away from the limitations of traditional formats and discover new ways to tell compelling stories. Staying open to these innovations not only broadens your skill set but also positions you as a forward-thinking filmmaker who can adapt to changing audience preferences and industry trends.

Beyond exploring new formats, creative experimentation is key to continuously pushing the boundaries of traditional filmmaking. Embracing innovative techniques and fresh ideas allows you to evolve as an artist, keeping your work exciting and relevant. Whether it's trying out unconventional camera angles, incorporating new editing styles, or blending genres, experimenting with your craft keeps your storytelling fresh and engaging. By taking risks and thinking outside the box, you open yourself up to new creative possibilities, allowing your films to stand out in a crowded market and making your work more memorable and impactful.

Myself as a Case Study for Work-Life Balance

I think it's important to share my personal story and schedule to pass on what I've learned over time. I'm still refining and growing in this area, constantly adjusting as my situation evolves, my daughter's needs change, and I discover new tools and strategies.

For some context, at the time I'm writing this book, my daughter Mia is just over two years old. Right now, I'm not working full-time or permanently; I only take on my own independent productions, and my duties as a mother take priority.

Before Mia was born, I was a workaholic for nearly 20 years, working around the clock. I would juggle several productions at once, often alongside a semi-permanent or contract job. My social life revolved around being on set, and filmmaking was my job, hobby, and top priority. I thrived on the constant hustle, or so I thought. But, as I mentioned earlier in the book, my perspective completely shifted when I became a mother. Suddenly, my primary focus was being a mum, and my passion for filmmaking took a back seat.

I'm not ready to give up the career I've worked so hard for just yet, so my goal is to keep things afloat until Mia starts school and I can return to a more regular schedule. That said, I will always prioritise her, and I'm determined never to fall back into my old workaholic habits. Maintaining a healthy work-life balance is now a top priority, not just for myself but also for my teams and crew working on my projects.

One major thing I've learned is that even though I'm working far fewer hours than I used to, I'm still getting a lot done. While I thought I was organised before, motherhood has pushed me to become even more efficient and my not-so-burned-out brain works more effectively now too! I've also gotten much better at saying no and cutting unnecessary tasks or commitments from my life. It's all about focusing on what really matters and making the best use of the time I do have.

I recognise that I am in a fortunate position. I have a supportive husband who encourages my career as an independent producer, despite the sacrifices it demands. He also supports my choice to prioritise motherhood, and we share the same outlook on balancing family and work. I'm fully aware that I am not a single mother and have the flexibility to choose not to earn a set income at this stage in my life. As a producer, I also have the ability to set my own work parameters. That said, my story is just one example. I encourage you to reflect on your own circumstances—your strengths, limitations, support network, and what is realistically achievable for you. Consider what adjustments you can make to improve your personal situation, and I hope you'll find helpful insights throughout this book to guide you along the way.

At the very least, I urge you to be open and transparent about your circumstances and your needs to your employers. The worst that can happen is that your request is denied, but there's also the possibility that you will be heard, and your wishes granted. Consider some of the advice in this book, such as presenting a solution when approaching your producer or manager.

My Schedule: Below is an example of my weekly plan. It is quite detailed, and everything is pre-planned and micro-planned (in fact, even more so than what I am adding below). Admittedly, having a young child can make it a bit harder to stick to a strict schedule because you can't always control their bodies and minds. However, having this plan gives me something to work toward, providing structure even on chaotic days. If sticking to a plan becomes impossible, I can always swap a few things around to make it work. Generally, this approach works very well, and it's likely to be even more effective for those with older children or no kids at all.

I should note that this plan only works if you stick to it as consistently as possible. For instance, if my toddler doesn't go to bed at the scheduled time, she'll probably sleep in a bit the next morning. This allows me to make up for the lost time by getting some work done early morning, rather than doing it to the evening as originally planned. Staying disciplined with the routine is key to making it effective.

Meetings: I always make sure to book meetings during the times I've allocated for meetings. If that's really not possible, I'll either swap tasks around or ask my parents to look after Mia during that time. I also try not to schedule meetings or activities close to or during nap or sleeping times because it is unpredictable if she will wake up a bit earlier or later than planned.

WhatsApp for Communication: With the exception of pre-production and principal photography times, I try to keep meetings to a minimum to maintain focus and efficiency. I prefer to communicate with my teams via WhatsApp unless something is important or urgent. When meetings are necessary, I usually opt for virtual ones to avoid driving time and to maximise efficiency. However, I'm also mindful of which meetings are best conducted in person and which relationships require face-to-face interaction.

Phone Calls: Firstly, I don't answer calls from unknown numbers. If it's important or legitimate, they'll leave a message. Secondly, I typically make all my phone calls during Mia's nap time since most calls need to happen during the day. I'll answer a call immediately if it's from someone important or difficult to reach, but otherwise, I'll return the call during Mia's nap or at a more convenient time later in the day.

Housework and grocery shopping: I handle the general tidying up and dishes as I go throughout the day, often incorporating it into Mia's playtime. It's been enjoyable for both of us to turn these tasks into fun activities. For example, we play "garbage truck" while picking up trash, or I put on a little performance while folding laundry, naming colours and items as we go. Admittedly, keeping the house tidy with a two-year-old isn't easy, so I don't stress about having everything perfect all the time. The focus is more on making these moments fun and engaging for Mia, which has turned chores into something we both look forward to. (Still, for the record, my house is always a mess now – haha)

Fitness: For fitness, I attend F45, which offers set class times every day. This structure is essential for me and helps me maintain my overall routine. The exercises are trainer-led, so I don't have to think about planning or adjusting my workouts. In the past, I wasted a lot of time planning, tweaking routines, and reading about fitness. Now, I just book the class, show up, and don't think about it before or after. It's a simple, efficient system that saves me time and keeps me on track. Since the classes aren't cheap, they keep me accountable and motivated to stick to my workout schedule.

Night Events: Going out at night is a big disruptor for me because it messes with Mia's sleep schedule, which can throw off the next few days or even weeks. That's why I avoid going out after 7:30 PM whenever possible. If something comes up, I'd rather skip my workout that day than sacrifice our night routine. I'm really selective about evening plans and only go out if it's something truly important—which, to be honest, is pretty rare these days.

This has been a big adjustment for me, as I used to spend most of my nights at industry events, networking, classes, or catching up with people. It's one of the sacrifices I've had to make temporarily, but I'm sure that as Mia gets older, I'll be able to go out more regularly. However, even then, I'll likely limit myself to going out just once a week or two at most to maintain a healthy balance.

Taking Mia everywhere: I take Mia everywhere with me, as long as it's appropriate. She attends my in-person meetings, which I try to arrange in places where I know she'll be welcome, like cafes near parks where she can play. Sometimes, I bring my mom along to play with her nearby while I'm in the meeting. I also take Mia to events and even to set, sometimes with my mom's help. It's important to me that Mia knows she's always welcome in my life and that I'm not constantly leaving her behind to go to work. I'm blessed with a very easy, calm, and well-behaved daughter, which makes it all possible. And I am very blessed to have the support of my mother and father to help where needed, which I try and limit to only an hour or two at maximum a day because I want Mia all for myself!

Social Media: In my schedule, you won't see any time allocated for social media. That's because I now use social media almost exclusively for work-related activities (99% of the time), so it happens during my designated work hours. I'm very strict about not spending more than a minute or two on social media for anything beyond what's necessary for work. By keeping this boundary, I ensure that social media doesn't encroach on my personal time or disrupt my focus on what really matters.

Exceptions: During pre-production, my schedule will shift to accommodate all possible work slots, including those typically reserved for family time. This means that where my schedule usually indicates "family time/work," I'll be dedicating those hours fully to work to ensure everything is ready for production.

Once we move into principal photography, the regular schedule won't be followed, but I'll do my best to keep as much consistency as possible, especially with Mia's routine. As I bring her to set, I'll make sure her eating, sleeping, and play times remain consistent, providing her with stability even in a hectic environment.

During this phase, I'll schedule family and Mia time around the shooting schedule, ensuring I still carve out moments for her. I'll also try to take short breaks during the day to give Mia my undivided attention. Additionally, I'll temporarily sacrifice my exercise time to maximize the time I spend with her and allow my body to rest from the gym.

Of course, if Mia or I get sick, or if there are major life events that disrupt our routine, I accept that we're in a "free fall" period and just focus on getting back on track as soon as possible. Sticking to this schedule as closely as I can is what makes it work, providing the balance and productivity I need in my daily life.

Breaking Down my Work tasks: On a separate spreadsheet, I keep track of all my projects and the specific tasks that need to be completed for each one. I carefully plan when each task should be done, prioritising them based on importance and deadlines. I also consider factors like team abilities, waiting for feedback from others, and any dependencies that might affect the timeline. During each working block, I focus exclusively on one project at a time, ensuring that my attention is fully dedicated to the tasks at hand. This organised approach allows me to manage multiple projects effectively while making steady progress on each one.

Learning to kindly say "no": One of the most significant and positive adjustments I've made is learning to say 'no'. I've realised the importance of saying no to things that don't bring me anything valuable—whether that's work, connections, joy, friendship, or personal growth. By being more selective, I ensure that my time and energy are spent on projects and activities that truly matter. This has allowed me to choose my projects with care, preventing me from taking on too much and spreading myself too thin. Saying no has become a powerful tool for maintaining balance, focus, and overall well-being.

I get asked at least 4 or 5 times a week to read scripts, assess pitch decks or grab coffee and provide advice or mentorship. If I were to say yes to everything, I wouldn't have any time for my work or family, and like I said, everything I say yes to means less time for my work or my daughter. So, without a good reason, I decline these requests. I do however offer consulting services for a fee as then I classify it as "work time". I do also have a couple of people I mentor, I just cannot mentor everyone who asks.

I am not going to lie, this was probably the most difficult change as I feel so passionate about helping others and I also love having too many things on my plate!

Office Jobs: When I take on jobs that require me to be in the office for full days, I stick to a hard rule: no more than two days a week. In fact, I only started accepting these jobs recently, after Mia turned 2. For the rest of the week, I make sure to fully make up for that time away by being completely present and engaged with her when I'm not working. Of course, I still fit in some work when she's asleep or during the evenings, and I occasionally take meetings during those times.

By sticking to this rhythm, I've found a balance that works well for us. It's been getting easier now that Mia's a bit older, and we're both adjusting to the occasional days apart. It's great to see her growing more independent and comfortable with it. It's always a balancing act, but it's becoming more manageable as she grows.

Combining daughter & mother playdates: Playdates with industry friends have been a fantastic way to combine social and professional time. While our children play together, we get the chance to catch up and maintain our industry connections. These playdates allow my daughter to enjoy social interaction, while I also benefit from connecting with friends and colleagues. When I was pregnant, walking meetings with friends were also a wonderful way to stay active, enjoy good company, and keep those professional ties strong. Walking meetings are not as practical at the moment but I would love to return to them later on.

This balance between social time for both our children and ourselves has been incredibly rewarding and it helps me stay connected in both my personal and professional life. Perhaps a working playdate would be the next step.

Weekends: typically reserve one day for catching up with friends (though I don't always have plans) and getting a bit of work done. The other day is strictly for me-time and family time, with no work at all. This could fall on either Saturday or Sunday, depending on how things are scheduled for the week.

"Me Time": Going to the gym and enjoying a long, relaxing bath each night is really all the "me time" I need. Occasionally, I'll treat myself to getting my hair or nails done, but that's about it. If I need a bit of extra time for myself, I usually take a few hours while Mia is with her dad or grandparents. That said, those moments are rare because, honestly, I find nothing more fulfilling than being with Mia and my family.

I also find that walking outside with Mia, spending time in nature, or simply watching her play independently while I take a moment to relax is a perfect escape for me. It gives me that balance without needing a lot of alone time.

However, it's crucial for everyone to understand and respect their own personal needs—how much "me time" they require, how often, and how they want to spend it. It's important to ensure you're getting the time you need for yourself.

Your support network: It's essential to discuss your schedule with the other people who are affected by it. For example, make sure your family or partner is on board with the times you've set for activities that involve them. Whether it's coordinating family time, ensuring they understand your work commitments, or planning shared activities, getting their input and agreement is crucial. This not only helps in avoiding conflicts but also ensures that everyone feels considered and respected in the planning process. Open communication about your schedule helps create a supportive environment where everyone is aligned, making it easier to stick to the plan and maintain a balanced routine. I have been blessed here as well with a very supportive and patient husband.

The Outcome: Even as a full-time mom who prioritises sleeping 8 hours a day, staying fit, and maintaining a small social life, I still manage to carve out roughly 38 hours of work time each week. That's about 8 hours of work spread over 5 days. The difference is that I've scattered and scheduled my work hours differently across the 24-hour period.

Admittedly, I used to work about 70-80 hours a week, which was excessive and an unhealthy habit.

Adjusting the Schedule: As Mia grows and goes through different stages of her life, I have had to adjust the schedule several times, and I am sure that I will need to do so frequently moving forward also, esp. when she starts going to school.

Because I've always been a workaholic, time management has always been a top priority for me, so I'm quite accustomed to this kind of scheduling. However, having a family now means there are more factors to consider in my planning, and I have slightly less control over everything. Balancing work with family responsibilities requires more flexibility and coordination, but it's a necessary adjustment to ensure that all aspects of my life are given the attention they need. While it can be challenging at times, it's also rewarding to find a routine that works for both my career and my family.

	Mon	Tues	Wed	Thu	Fri	Sat	Sun
8.00	Wake up & cuddle with Mia	Wake up & cuddle with Mia	Wake up & cuddle with Mia	Wake up & cuddle with Mia	Wake up & cuddle with Mia	Wake up & cuddle with Mia	Wake up & cuddle with Mia
8.30	Nappy and Breakfast (& VIT Tablets)	Nappy and Breakfast (& VIT Tablets)	Nappy and Breakfast (& VIT Tablets)	Nappy and Breakfast (& VIT Tablets)	Nappy and Breakfast (& VIT Tablets)	Nappy and Breakfast (& VIT Tablets)	Nappy and Breakfast (& VIT Tablets)
9.00	Both Brush Teeth, get dressed	Both Brush Teeth, get dressed	Both Brush Teeth, get dressed	Both Brush Teeth, get dressed	Both Brush Teeth, get dressed	Both Brush Teeth, get dressed	Both Brush Teeth, get dressed
9.30	Drive to Music Class	Home Play/Play Park/ Drive to meeting if in-person	Structured Play with me / arts & crafts	Structured Play with me / arts & crafts	Home Play/Play Park/ Drive to meeting if in-person	Family time with Mia, play or outing	Family time with Mia, play or outing
10.00	Music Class	Meeting/ Playpark with Mia	Meeting/ Playpark with Mia	One-one kids playdate with other	Meeting/ Structured Play with Mia	Family time with Mia / allow weekly to	Family time with Mia, play or outing

					industry mom		catch up with a friends	
10.30	Music Class	Meeting/ Playpark with Mia	Meeting/ Playpark with Mia	One-one kids playdate with other industry mom	Meeting/ Structured Play with Mia	Family time with Mia / allow weekly to catch up with a friends	Me House Clean & Daddy daughter Time
11.00	Drive Home	Meeting/ Playpark with Mia	Meeting/ Playpark with Mia	1-1 kids playdate with other industry mom	Meeting/ Free Play with Mia	Family time with Mia / allow weekly to catch up with a friends	Me House Clean & Daddy daughter Time
11.30	Free play with Mia	Play at home/Playpark with Mia/Drive to meeting if in-person	Play at home/Playpark with Mia/Drive to meeting if in-person	Free play with Mia	Drive/ Free Play with Mia	Family time with Mia / allow weekly to catch up with a friends	Me House Clean & Daddy daughter Time
12.00	Family Lunch time at the table	Family Lunch time at the table	Family Lunch time at the table	Family Lunch time at the table	Family Lunch time at the table	Family Lunch time at the table	Family Lunch time at the table
12.30	Daddy Daughter Time & Me catch up on personal things like paying bills, reading industry news, etc.	Daddy Daughter Time & Me catch up on personal things like paying bills, reading industry news, etc.	Daddy Daughter Time & Me catch up on personal things like paying bills, reading industry news, etc.	Daddy Daughter Time & Me catch up on personal things like paying bills, reading industry news, etc.	Daddy Daughter Time & Me catch up on personal things like paying bills, reading industry news, etc.	Daddy Daughter Time & Me catch up on personal things like paying bills.	Daddy Daughter Time & Me catch up on personal things like paying bills.
13.00	Mia Play/Cuddle Time	Mia Play/Cuddle Time	Mia Play/Cuddle Time	Mia Play/Cuddle Time	Mia Play/Cuddle Time	Mia Play/Cuddle Time	Mia Play/Cuddle Time

13.30	Mia nap Time & My work time (Phone calls)	Mia nap Time & My work time (Phone calls)	Mia nap Time & My work time (Phone calls)	Mia nap Time & My work time (Phone calls)	Mia nap Time & My work time (Phone calls)	Mia nap Time & My work time	Mia nap Time & My work time
15.00	Mia Play Time	Mia Play Time	Playgroup Time if didn't go in morning / Play at home	Mia Play Time	Mia Play Time	Family time (can do a bit of work if need be & if possible)	Family time (can do a bit of work if need be & if possible)
17.00	Gym (incl drive to and from)	Gym (incl drive to and from)	Gym (incl drive to and from)	Gym (incl drive to and from)	Gym (incl drive to and from)	Family time (can do a bit of work if need be & if possible)	Family time (can do a bit of work if need be & if possible)
18.30	Family Dinner time at the table	Family Dinner time at the table	Family Dinner time at the table	Family Dinner time at the table	Family Dinner time at the table	Family Dinner time at the table	Family Dinner time at the table
19.30	Daddy Daughter Time & My work time	Daddy Daughter Time & My work time	Daddy Daughter Time & My work time	Daddy Daughter Time & My work time	Daddy Daughter Time & My work time	Family Time	Family Time
20.30	Mia & My Bath, brushing teeth & Calming Down Time	Cleaning & Nighties on & Calming Down Time	Mia & My Bath, brushing teeth & Calming Down Time	Cleaning & Nighties on & Calming Down Time	Mia & My Bath, brushing teeth & Calming Down Time	Cleaning & Nighties on & Calming Down Time	Mia & My Bath, brushing teeth & Calming Down Time
21.00	Mia Sleep (process)	Mia Sleep (process)	Mia Sleep (process)	Mia Sleep (process)	Mia Sleep (process)	Mia Sleep (process)	Mia Sleep (process)
21.30	My work time	My Bath Time	My work time	My Bath Time	My work time	My Bath Time	My work time
22.00	My Work time	My Work time	My Work time	My Work time	Flexi 50/50 Split of My Work time/Hub by Time (e.g. movie or just catch up)	Flexi 50/50 Split of My Work time/Hub by Time (e.g. movie or just catch up)	Flexi 50/50 Split of My Work time/Hub by Time (e.g. movie or just catch up)

00:00	Go to Bed	Go to Bed	Go to Bed	Go to Bed	Go to Bed	Go to Bed	Go to Bed

* My calendar is actually more detailed with time allocated to even very small things, but you don't need to know when I shave my legs!

How did I do according to the recommended balance split:

> ✓ **Family Life:** A at least 1-2 hours daily.
>
> ✓ **Health and Fitness:** 30 minutes to 1 hour daily, at least 3-5 times a week.
>
> ✓ **Relaxation and Mental Health:** Allocating 30 minutes to 1 hour daily for unwinding.
>
> ✓ **Social Life:** 1-2 hours weekly
>
> ✓ **Personal Development:** A few hours weekly.
>
> ✓ **Leisure Activities:** Allocating **a few hours weekly** for leisure activities such as hobbies, entertainment, or travel. A full day on weekends is often recommended for complete relaxation.

CHAPTER 15

Unions

Unions play a crucial role in advocating for the rights and well-being of workers across various industries, including the film industry. They are instrumental in negotiating fair wages, ensuring safe working conditions, and promoting equitable treatment for all employees. This chapter explores how unions can significantly contribute to improving work-life balance and general wellbeing and ensuring equal opportunities for all in the film industry.

The Historical Context of Unions in the Film Industry

The film industry has a long history of union involvement, dating back to the early 20th century. As the industry grew, so did the need for organised labour to protect the rights of its workers. The establishment of major unions like the Screen Actors Guild (SAG), the Directors Guild of America (DGA), and the International Alliance of Theatrical Stage Employees (IATSE) marked significant milestones in the fight for fair labor practices in Hollywood and beyond.

These unions have been instrumental in setting industry standards, such as regulated work hours, mandatory breaks, and overtime pay. By negotiating collective bargaining agreements (CBAs), unions have secured benefits that are essential for maintaining a healthy work-life balance and ensuring that all workers are treated fairly.

The Impact of Unions on Work-Life Balance

Regulated Work Hours: One of the primary ways unions help improve work-life balance is by negotiating regulated work hours. Unions ensure that crew members are not subjected to excessively long working days and have mandated rest periods. For example, IATSE has established rules that limit the number of hours crew members can work each day, reducing the risk of burnout and fatigue.

Overtime Compensation: Unions advocate for fair compensation for overtime work. This not only ensures that workers are paid fairly for their time but also acts as a deterrent against unnecessarily long working hours. By making overtime expensive for production companies, unions encourage better scheduling practices that align with work-life balance goals.

Health and Safety Standards: Unions are at the forefront of ensuring safe working conditions. They push for health and safety regulations that protect workers from hazardous environments and ensure that productions adhere to safety protocols. This focus on safety contributes to a healthier work environment, which is a critical component of work-life balance.

Benefits and Support Services: Unions negotiate for comprehensive benefits packages that include health insurance, retirement plans, and support services such as counseling and mental health resources. These benefits provide a safety net for workers, allowing them to focus on their work without the added stress of financial or health-related concerns.

The Role of Unions in Ensuring Equal Opportunities

Advocacy for Diversity and Inclusion: Unions play a vital role in promoting diversity and inclusion within the film industry. They advocate for equal representation and opportunities for underrepresented groups, including women, people of colour, and LGBTQ+ individuals. Unions work to ensure that hiring practices are fair and that all members have access to the same opportunities.

Anti-Discrimination Policies: Unions enforce strict anti-discrimination policies and provide a platform for workers to report instances of discrimination or harassment. By addressing these issues proactively, unions help create a more inclusive and respectful work environment.

Training and Development Programs: Unions offer training and development programs to help members enhance their skills and advance their careers. These programs are designed to be accessible to all members, ensuring that everyone has the opportunity to grow and succeed in the industry.

Support for Parents and Caregivers: Unions advocate for policies that support parents and caregivers, such as flexible work arrangements, on-set childcare, and comprehensive parental leave. By promoting these policies, unions help ensure that all workers, regardless of their personal responsibilities, have equal opportunities to thrive in their careers.

Case Studies of Union Impact

IATSE's Fight for Safe Working Hours: In recent years, the International Alliance of Theatrical Stage Employees (IATSE) has been at the forefront of the fight for safer working hours in the film and television industry. Their advocacy has led to significant improvements in production schedules, including the enforcement of rest periods and limits on consecutive work hours. These changes have positively impacted the work-life balance of crew members, though the fight for consistently safe working conditions is ongoing.

SAG-AFTRA's Diversity Initiatives: SAG-AFTRA has implemented several initiatives aimed at increasing diversity and inclusion in the film industry. These efforts include the establishment of diversity committees, mentorship programs, and strong advocacy for more inclusive casting practices. These initiatives have helped create more opportunities for underrepresented groups, contributing to a more equitable industry. However, continuous efforts are needed to sustain and expand these improvements.

DGA's Family Leave Policies: The Directors Guild of America (DGA) has successfully negotiated family leave policies that provide directors with the necessary time to care for their families. These policies include paid parental leave and flexible work arrangements, ensuring that directors can better balance their professional and personal responsibilities. While these benefits represent significant progress, their specifics can vary depending on individual contracts and productions.

Challenges and Future Directions

Addressing Resistance to Change: Despite the significant progress made by unions, there is still resistance to some of their initiatives. Production companies may be reluctant to adopt new policies due to cost concerns or traditional industry practices. Continued advocacy and education are essential to overcoming this resistance.

Expanding Union Membership: Ensuring that all workers in the film industry are represented by unions is a challenge. Some workers, especially freelancers and those in emerging roles, may not be covered by union agreements. Expanding union membership and ensuring that all workers have access to union support is a crucial step forward.

Adapting to Industry Changes: The film industry is constantly evolving, with new technologies and production methods emerging. Unions must adapt to these changes and continue to advocate for policies that protect workers' rights and promote work-life balance and equal opportunities.

Unions play a vital role in improving work-life balance and ensuring equal opportunities in the film industry. Through regulated work hours, health and safety standards, advocacy for diversity and inclusion, and support for parents and caregivers, unions help create a more equitable and supportive work environment. While challenges remain, the continued efforts of unions are essential for the ongoing improvement of working conditions in the film industry.

CHAPTER 16

Future Outlook and Recommendations

As the film industry continues to evolve, the importance of addressing work-life balance and creating a more inclusive and sustainable environment becomes increasingly clear. This chapter outlines a vision for the future, provides a summary of practical recommendations for industry stakeholders, as discussed throughout the book and explores innovative work models that could reshape the landscape of film production.

Vision for a More Balanced Film Industry

Envisioning a future where the film industry prioritises work-life balance involves imagining a world where all professionals can thrive both personally and professionally. This vision includes:

Inclusive Workplaces: An industry that values diversity and inclusivity, providing equal opportunities for all, regardless of gender, race, or background.

Supportive Environments: Workplaces that offer comprehensive support systems, including mental health resources, flexible working arrangements, and family-friendly policies.

Sustainable Practices: A commitment to sustainable work practices that protect the well-being of employees and the environment, including reasonable working hours and environmentally friendly production methods.

Innovative Work Models: The adoption of flexible work models that embrace technology and remote work, allowing for a better balance between professional and personal lives.

Recommendations for Industry Stakeholders

Achieving this vision requires the active participation of all stakeholders in the film industry, including production companies, unions, guilds, and individual professionals. Here are some practical recommendations:

Production Companies:

- Implement and enforce family-friendly policies, including on-site childcare
- Implement or allow flexible scheduling, job sharing, reduced days or hours of work
- Invest in mental health resources and support systems for employees.

Unions and Guilds:

- Advocate for improved working conditions, including limits on working hours and fair compensation.
- Provide training and resources for mental health and stress management.
- Promote diversity and inclusion initiatives, ensuring that underrepresented groups have access to opportunities.

Individual Professionals:

- Advocate for your own well-being by setting boundaries and prioritising self-care.
- Participate in industry initiatives that promote a healthy work-life balance.
- Engage in continuous learning and professional development to adapt to changing industry needs.

- Reevaluate your personal and work schedule and how you manage your life as a whole.

Policy Suggestions for Governments and Unions

Governments and unions play a crucial role in shaping the regulatory framework that governs the film industry. Here are some policy suggestions to support a more balanced and equitable industry:

Regulations on Working Hours: Implement stricter regulations on maximum working hours and ensure fair compensation for overtime. This can help prevent burnout and protect the health and well-being of industry professionals.

Support for Freelancers and Independent Contractors: Establish policies that provide freelancers with access to benefits such as health insurance, retirement savings, and unemployment protection. This would offer greater security and stability for those working outside of traditional employment structures.

Incentives for Family-Friendly Practices: Offer tax incentives or grants to productions that implement family-friendly policies, such as on-set childcare and flexible scheduling. This can encourage more productions to adopt these practices.

Diversity and Inclusion Initiatives: Support initiatives that promote diversity and inclusion, including funding for mentorship programs, scholarships for underrepresented groups, and diversity targets for productions.

Mental Health Wellbeing Incentives: Support initiatives that promote and support mental health awareness and support, including funding for organisations specialising in this area.

Encouraging a Cultural Shift Towards Work-Life Balance

Creating lasting change in the film industry requires a cultural shift towards valuing work-life balance. This involves changing attitudes and behaviours at all levels of the industry:

Raising Awareness: Industry leaders, media outlets, and advocacy groups can play a key role in raising awareness about the importance of work-life balance. This includes sharing stories of successful initiatives and highlighting the benefits of a balanced approach.

Engaging Industry Leaders: Leaders within the industry have the power to set the tone for workplace culture. By prioritising work-life balance and modeling healthy behaviours, leaders can influence the broader industry culture.

Championing Change: Industry professionals can act as champions for change by advocating for policies and practices that promote work-life balance. This includes speaking out about the challenges they face and participating in initiatives that drive change.

Innovative Work Models and Practices

The future of the film industry may see the adoption of innovative work models and practices that better support work-life balance. Some possibilities include:

Gig Economy Principles: The gig economy model, which involves short-term contracts and freelance work, can offer flexibility but also poses challenges related to job security and benefits. Finding a balance that provides flexibility while ensuring fair treatment and compensation is key.

Rotational Schedules and Shift Work: Implementing rotational schedules or shift work can help manage workloads and prevent burnout. This approach can also provide more opportunities for workers to balance their professional and personal lives.

Adapting Successful Practices from Other Industries: The film industry can learn from other industries that have successfully implemented work-life balance practices. For example, the tech industry has pioneered remote work and flexible scheduling, which could be adapted to the needs of film production.

Building Community and Support Networks

Creating a supportive community is essential for sustaining change in the industry. This includes:

Establishing Support Groups: Creating support groups for industry professionals can provide a space to share experiences, seek advice, and find support. These groups can be particularly valuable for underrepresented groups and those facing unique challenges.

Facilitating Peer Support and Mentoring Programs: Mentoring programs can help individuals navigate the industry, providing guidance and support from more experienced professionals. Peer support networks can also offer valuable connections and resources.

The future of the film industry depends on its ability to adapt to changing conditions and prioritise the well-being of its professionals. By embracing innovative work models, advocating for supportive policies, and fostering a culture that values work-life balance, the industry can build a more sustainable and inclusive future. The final chapter will summarise the key points discussed and provide a call to action for all stakeholders to continue pushing for positive change.

CHAPTER 17

Conclusion

As we conclude this exploration of work-life balance and general wellbeing in the film industry, it is crucial to reflect on the key points discussed and the path forward. The industry is at a pivotal moment where change is not only possible but necessary for the wellbeing and sustainability of its workforce.

The journey towards a more balanced film industry is ongoing. While progress has been made, there is still much work to be done. Continued efforts and advocacy are crucial to ensure that the industry evolves in a way that prioritises the well-being of its workforce.

Industry leaders, policymakers, and professionals must work together to implement and enforce policies that support work-life balance and general wellbeing. This includes advocating for regulations that protect workers' rights, promoting diversity and inclusion, and ensuring that all professionals have access to the resources and support they need.

The future of the film industry hinges on its ability to adapt to changing conditions and prioritise the well-being of its professionals. By embracing innovation, advocating for supportive policies, and fostering a culture that values work-life balance, the industry can build a more sustainable and inclusive future.

As we move forward, it is essential to keep the conversation going and continue pushing for positive change. The film industry has the potential to lead by example, demonstrating that it is possible to create a thriving, equitable, and supportive work environment. Together, we can shape a future where every professional in the industry can achieve a healthy balance between their work and personal lives, contributing to a more vibrant and resilient industry.

WORKSHEETS & SURVEYS

EVALUATING PERSONAL WORK-LIFE BALANCE

PART 1 - Reflective Questions:

Satisfaction Assessment:
- What aspects of your current work-life balance are you satisfied with?
- Which areas of your work-life balance need improvement?

Health Impact:
- How do long working hours affect your mental health?
- How do long working hours affect your physical health?

PART 2 - Interactive Exercise
Work-Life Balance Wheel:

1. **Create Your Wheel:**
   - Draw a circle and divide it into segments representing different aspects of your life: work, family, health, leisure, personal development, social life, and any other relevant areas.

2. **Rate Your Satisfaction:**
   - On a scale from 1 to 10, rate your satisfaction in each area (1 = very dissatisfied and 10 = completely satisfied).

3. **Identify Improvement Areas:**
   - Highlight the segments with the lowest ratings. These are the areas that may need more attention and improvement.

EVALUATING PERSONAL WORK-LIFE BALANCE

PART 3 - Practical Activity

Action Plan Development:

1. Set Specific Goals:
    - For each area identified for improvement, set specific, measurable goals. For example, if you rated your health low, a goal might be to exercise three times a week.

2. Outline Steps:
    - For each goal, outline the steps needed to achieve it. For instance, if your goal is to exercise more, steps might include joining a gym, setting a workout schedule, and finding a workout buddy.

3. Monitor Progress:
    - Create a timeline to review your progress. Set regular check-ins (e.g., weekly or monthly) to evaluate how well you are meeting your goals and adjust your plan as necessary.

EVALUATING PERSONAL WORK-LIFE BALANCE

PART 4 - REALWORLD SCENARIO

Peer Mentorship:

1. Identify a Mentor:
- Find a mentor or peer in the film industry who has successfully achieved a better work-life balance. This could be someone you admire or who has openly discussed their strategies.

2. Schedule a Meeting:
- Reach out and schedule a meeting to discuss their approach to work-life balance. Prepare questions about their strategies, challenges, and any advice they can offer.

3. Implement Advice:
- Reflect on the advice and strategies shared by your mentor. Consider how you can incorporate their insights into your own action plan for improving work-life balance.

SURVEY ORM

Work-Life Balance Survey for Film Industry Professionals

SECTION 1

On average, how many hours do you work per week?

- Less than 20 hours (5)
- 20-39 hours (4)
- 40-59 hours (3)
- 60-79 hours (2)
- 80 hours or more (1)

How often do you work on weekends?

- Never (5)
- Rarely (4)
- Sometimes (3)
- Often (2)
- Always (1)

Do you have access to flexible working hours?

- Yes (5)
- No (1)

Are there any on-set facilities to support work-life balance (e.g., daycare, quiet rooms)?

- Yes (5)
- No (1)

SURVEY 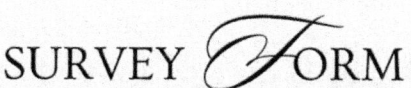ORM

Work-Life Balance Survey for Film Industry Professionals

SECTION 2

QUESTIONS	RATING				
How often ...	Always (1)	Often (2)	Sometimes (3)	Rarely (4)	Never (5)
do you feel stressed due to work?	○	○	○	○	○
do you NOT have time for personal activities and hobbies?	○	○	○	○	○
are you satisfied with your current work-life balance?	○	○	○	○	○
do you feel that your work interferes with your personal life?	○	○	○	○	○
is your workplace supportive in promoting work-life balance?	○	○	○	○	○
do you find it challenging to balance work and family responsibilities?	○	○	○	○	○
do you feel guilty about the time you spend working instead of with your family?	○	○	○	○	○
do you miss important family events due to work?	○	○	○	○	○

SURVEY

Work-Life Balance Survey for Film Industry Professionals

INTERPRETATION OF SCORES

After completing the survey, add up the scores from all your responses. Use the following ranges to interpret your overall work-life balance:

50-60: Excellent Work-Life Balance - You have a very healthy work-life balance, with minimal stress and ample time for personal activities and family. Your work environment is supportive and flexible, contributing positively to your overall well-being.

40-49: Good Work-Life Balance - Your work-life balance is generally good, with manageable stress levels and sufficient time for personal activities. There may be some areas for improvement, but overall, you are maintaining a healthy balance between work and personal life.

30-39: Moderate Work-Life Balance - Your work-life balance is moderate, with noticeable stress and occasional difficulty in managing personal activities and family responsibilities. Some changes may be necessary to improve your overall well-being and reduce stress.

20-29: Poor Work-Life Balance - Your work-life balance is poor, with high levels of stress and significant interference from work in your personal life. It's important to identify the key areas that need improvement and make necessary adjustments to enhance your well-being.

Below 20: Very Poor Work-Life Balance - Your work-life balance is very poor, with constant stress and severe impact from work on your personal life. Immediate changes are needed to address the issues and improve your overall health and well-being. Consider seeking support from workplace resources or professional help to manage stress and create a healthier balance.

Documenting Your Team's Accounts of Working Conditions - EXAMPLE

Title: Balancing Act: A Cinematographer's Journey in the Film Industry

Date: August 6, 2024

Participant Information:

- **Name:** John Doe
- **Role in the Film Industry:** Cinematographer
- **Years of Experience:** 12 years
- **Location:** Los Angeles, California

Introduction: John Doe, an experienced cinematographer, shares his journey navigating the demanding world of film production. With over a decade in the industry, John provides insights into the challenges he faces and how he manages to maintain a semblance of work-life balance.

Work Environment: John typically works on feature films and high-budget TV series, often requiring extensive on-set presence. His average workweek exceeds 60 hours, with frequent weekend shoots. Despite the demanding schedule, facilities like on-set childcare are rarely available, adding to the challenge of balancing work and family life.

Challenges and Issues: John highlights the intense pressure to meet tight deadlines, leading to high levels of stress. The unpredictable nature of film schedules often means missing important family events. He recounts an incident where a 16-hour shoot caused him to miss his daughter's birthday, emphasising the personal sacrifices involved.

Work-Life Balance: John strives for balance by setting strict personal boundaries, such as not answering work calls after 8 PM. However, the lack of flexible working arrangements often undermines these efforts. Support from his production team varies, with some understanding the importance of balance while others prioritise project completion over personal well-being.

Personal Accounts: "Last year, I worked on a project that required us to shoot in a remote location for three months. The long hours and isolation took a toll on my mental health. It was tough being away from my family, and the stress was overwhelming at times," John recalls.

Impact on Career and Personal Life: The gruelling work hours have affected John's health, leading to chronic back pain and frequent stress-related illnesses. Despite the challenges, he remains passionate about his work but acknowledges that the industry's demands have strained his family relationships and personal life.

Solutions and Recommendations: John suggests implementing mandatory rest periods and enforcing maximum work hours to prevent burnout. He also advocates for on-set childcare facilities and flexible working options to support parents in the industry. Personal strategies, such as regular exercise and mindfulness practices, have helped him cope with stress.

Conclusion: John's experience underscores the need for systemic changes in the film industry to promote healthier work-life balance. By sharing his story, he hopes to inspire others to prioritise their well-being while pursuing their passion for filmmaking.

Attachments (if any):

- Photos from on-set locations
- Schedule examples from recent projects

Documenting Your Personal Accounts of Working Conditions – EXAMPLE

Date: August 6, 2024

Participant Information:

- **Name:** John Doe
- **Role in the Film Industry:** Cinematographer
- **Years of Experience:** 12 years
- **Location:** Los Angeles, California

Introduction: I am John Doe, an experienced cinematographer sharing my journey navigating the demanding world of film production. With over a decade in the industry, I provide insights into the challenges I face and how I manage to maintain a semblance of work-life balance.

Work Environment: I typically work on feature films and high-budget TV series, often requiring extensive on-set presence. My average workweek exceeds 60 hours, with frequent weekend shoots. Despite the demanding schedule, facilities like on-set childcare are rarely available, adding to the challenge of balancing work and family life.

Challenges and Issues: The intense pressure to meet tight deadlines leads to high levels of stress. The unpredictable nature of film schedules often means missing important family events. One incident that stands out is when a 16-hour shoot caused me to miss my daughter's birthday, emphasising the personal sacrifices involved.

Work-Life Balance: I strive for balance by setting strict personal boundaries, such as not answering work calls after 8 PM. However, the lack of flexible working arrangements often undermines these efforts. Support from my production team varies, with some understanding the importance of balance while others prioritise project completion over personal well-being.

Personal Accounts: "Last year, I worked on a project that required us to shoot in a remote location for three months. The long hours and isolation took a toll on my mental health. It was tough being away from my family, and the stress was overwhelming at times," I recall.

Impact on Career and Personal Life: The gruelling work hours have affected my health, leading to chronic back pain and frequent stress-related illnesses. Despite the challenges, I remain passionate about my work but acknowledge that the industry's demands have strained my family relationships and personal life.

Self-Assessment Questions:

1. How often do you feel stressed due to work? Often
2. How often do you have time for personal activities and hobbies? Rarely
3. How satisfied are you with your current work-life balance? Dissatisfied
4. Do you feel that your work interferes with your personal life? Often
5. How supportive is your workplace in promoting work-life balance? Moderately supportive
6. Do you find it challenging to balance work and family responsibilities? Often
7. Do you feel guilty about the time you spend working instead of with your family? Often
8. How often do you miss important family events due to work? Often

Solutions and Recommendations: I suggest implementing mandatory rest periods and enforcing maximum work hours to prevent burnout. On-set childcare facilities and flexible working options would greatly support parents in the industry. Personal strategies, such as regular exercise and mindfulness practices, have helped me cope with stress.

Conclusion: My experience underscores the need for systemic changes in the film industry to promote healthier work-life balance. By sharing my story, I hope to inspire others to prioritise their well-being while pursuing their passion for filmmaking.

Attachments (if any):

- Photos from on-set locations
- Schedule examples from recent projects

Exercises for parents to document challenges and solutions

This workbook is designed to help parents in the film industry document the challenges they face and develop solutions to achieve a better work-life balance. By reflecting on your experiences and identifying practical strategies, you can work towards a healthier and more balanced life.

Exercise 1: Identifying Challenges

Objective: To document the specific challenges, you face as a parent in the film industry.

Instructions: Write down the top five challenges you encounter in balancing parenthood and work. Be as specific as possible.

1. Challenge 1: _____
2. Challenge 2: _____
3. Challenge 3: _____
4. Challenge 4: _____
5. Challenge 5: _____

Reflection: How do these challenges impact your daily life and well-being? Write a brief reflection on each challenge.

Exercise 2: Analysing Work Environment

Objective: To evaluate your work environment and its impact on your work-life balance.

Instructions: Answer the following questions about your work environment.

1. Describe your typical work schedule (hours per day/week, weekend work, etc.).
2. What facilities and resources (e.g., childcare, quiet rooms) are available at your workplace?
3. How supportive is your employer or production team in promoting work-life balance?

Reflection: How does your work environment contribute to or alleviate the challenges you face as a parent?

Exercise 3: Documenting Personal Accounts

Objective: To provide detailed accounts of specific incidents that highlight the challenges you face.

Instructions: Write a detailed account of a recent incident that illustrates a significant challenge related to balancing work and parenthood. Include the following details:

- Date and description of the incident
- How it affected your work and personal life
- Your feelings and reactions

Exercise 4: Impact on Personal and Family Life

Objective: To assess the impact of your work on your personal and family life.

Instructions: Answer the following questions to reflect on how your work affects your family life.

1. How often do you miss important family events due to work?
    - Never
    - Rarely
    - Sometimes
    - Often
    - Always

2. How do your working hours affect your relationship with your children and partner?
3. What is the most significant way your work impacts your family life?

Exercise 5: Identifying Solutions

Objective: To develop potential solutions for the challenges you face.

Instructions: For each challenge identified in Exercise 1, brainstorm at least two potential solutions. Write them down below.

1. Challenge 1:
    - Solution 1: _____
    - Solution 2: _____
2. Challenge 2:
    - Solution 1: _____
    - Solution 2: _____
3. Challenge 3:
    - Solution 1: _____
    - Solution 2: _____
4. Challenge 4:
    - Solution 1: _____
    - Solution 2: _____
5. Challenge 5:
    - Solution 1: _____
    - Solution 2: _____

Exercise 6: Implementing Solutions

Objective: To create an action plan for implementing the solutions.

Instructions: Choose one solution for each challenge and develop a step-by-step action plan to implement it.

1. Challenge 1 Solution:
    - Step 1: _____
    - Step 2: _____
    - Step 3: _____
2. Challenge 2 Solution:
    - Step 1: _____
    - Step 2: _____
    - Step 3: _____
3. Challenge 3 Solution:
    - Step 1: _____
    - Step 2: _____
    - Step 3: _____
4. Challenge 4 Solution:
    - Step 1: _____
    - Step 2: _____
    - Step 3: _____
5. Challenge 5 Solution:
    - Step 1: _____
    - Step 2: _____
    - Step 3: _____

Exercise 7: Evaluating Progress

Objective: To evaluate the effectiveness of the implemented solutions.

Instructions: After a set period (e.g., one month), evaluate the progress of your action plans. Answer the following questions:

1. Which solutions have you implemented?
2. What changes have you noticed in your work-life balance?

3. What additional adjustments are needed?

Exercise 8: Seeking Support

Objective: To identify sources of support and resources available to you.

Instructions: List the resources and support systems you can utilise to help manage work and parenthood.

1. Workplace resources (e.g., HR policies, childcare services):

   ----

2. Personal support (e.g., family, friends, babysitters):

   ----

3. Professional support (e.g., counselling, coaching):

Reflection: How can these resources and support systems help you achieve a better work-life balance?

Conclusion: Summarise the key insights you have gained from completing this workbook. Reflect on the progress you have made and the steps you will continue to take to balance parenthood and your career in the film industry.

Templates for creating and documenting job-sharing arrangements.

This template is designed to help film industry professionals create and document job-sharing arrangements. Job sharing can improve work-life balance, increase productivity, and provide flexibility for employees.

Part 1: Job Sharing Proposal

Title: A concise title summarising the job-sharing arrangement.

Date: The date when the proposal is created.

Participants:

- **Employee 1 Name:**
- **Employee 2 Name:**
- **Role/Position:**
- **Department:**
- **Supervisor/Manager:**

Introduction: Provide a brief introduction to the job-sharing arrangement, including the reasons for proposing it and the expected benefits for both the employees and the organisation.

Part 2: Job Sharing Plan

Objective: To outline the detailed plan for the job-sharing arrangement.

Job Description: Describe the job responsibilities and tasks that will be shared. Include any specific duties that each participant will handle.

Work Schedule: Detail the work schedule for each participant, including:

- Days and hours each employee will work

- Overlap time (if any) for collaboration and communication
- Flexibility options (e.g., swapping days, adjusting hours)

Communication Plan: Outline how the participants will communicate with each other and the team, including:

- Preferred communication methods (e.g., email, phone, in-person)
- Frequency of check-ins and updates
- Procedures for handling urgent matters

Performance Metrics: Define the metrics that will be used to measure the success of the job-sharing arrangement, including:

- Key performance indicators (KPIs)
- Quality of work
- Timeliness and deadlines
- Customer/client satisfaction

Tools and Resources: List any tools, resources, or support needed to facilitate the job-sharing arrangement, such as:

- Shared workspace or desk
- Access to software and systems
- Training or professional development

Part 3: Job Sharing Agreement

Agreement Terms: Detail the terms of the job-sharing arrangement, including:

- Duration of the arrangement (e.g., 6 months, 1 year)
- Review and evaluation periods
- Conditions for renewal or termination

Responsibilities: Clearly define the responsibilities of each participant, including:

- Primary tasks and projects
- Shared tasks and projects
- Accountability and reporting structure

Compensation and Benefits: Explain how compensation and benefits will be handled, including:

- Salary distribution
- Benefits eligibility (e.g., health insurance, paid time off)
- Overtime and holiday pay

Signatures: Include spaces for the signatures of all parties involved to indicate agreement and commitment to the job-sharing arrangement.

- Employee 1 Signature: _____
- Date: _____
- Employee 2 Signature: _____
- Date: _____
- Supervisor/Manager Signature: _____
- Date: _____
- HR Representative Signature: _____
- Date: _____

Part 4: Job Sharing Implementation

Implementation Plan: Provide a step-by-step plan for implementing the job-sharing arrangement, including:

- Start date
- Orientation and training schedule
- Initial check-in meeting

Orientation and Training: Detail any orientation or training sessions required to ensure both participants are fully prepared to start the job-sharing arrangement, including:

- Job duties and expectations
- Tools and systems training
- Introduction to team and key contacts

Initial Check-In: Schedule an initial check-in meeting with the supervisor/manager to discuss progress, address any concerns, and make any necessary adjustments.

Part 5: Monitoring and Evaluation

Ongoing Monitoring: Describe how the job-sharing arrangement will be monitored, including:

- Regular check-ins with the supervisor/manager
- Feedback sessions between participants
- Tracking of performance metrics

Evaluation Plan: Outline the evaluation plan to assess the effectiveness of the job-sharing arrangement, including:

- Evaluation criteria (e.g., productivity, job satisfaction, work quality)
- Frequency of evaluations (e.g., quarterly, biannually)
- Methods for gathering feedback (e.g., surveys, interviews)

Adjustments and Improvements: Provide a process for making adjustments and improvements to the job-sharing arrangement based on feedback and evaluation results.

Part 6: Conclusion

Summary: Summarise the key points of the job-sharing arrangement and its expected benefits for both the employees and the organisation.

Next Steps: Outline the next steps for finalising and implementing the job-sharing arrangement, including any additional approvals or documentation required.

Contact Information: Provide contact information for any questions or further discussion about the job-sharing arrangement.

- Employee 1 Email: _____ Phone: _____
- Employee 2 Email: _____ Phone: _____
- Supervisor/Manager Email: _____ Phone: _____
- HR Representative Email: _____ Phone: _____

This template provides a comprehensive guide to creating and documenting job-sharing arrangements in the film industry. By following these steps, employees and employers can ensure a successful and productive job-sharing experience.

Strategies and Templates for Flexible Scheduling on Set

Introduction

This guide is designed to help film industry professionals implement flexible scheduling on set. Flexible scheduling can improve work-life balance, enhance productivity, and increase employee satisfaction. This guide includes strategies and templates to facilitate the implementation of flexible schedules.

Part 1: Strategies for Implementing Flexible Scheduling

1. Assessing Needs and Feasibility:

- **Identify Key Roles and Tasks:** Determine which roles and tasks are suitable for flexible scheduling.
- **Assess Workflow and Deadlines:** Analyse project timelines and deadlines to ensure flexibility does not impact productivity.
- **Gather Employee Input:** Conduct surveys or meetings to understand employee needs and preferences for flexible schedules.

2. Types of Flexible Scheduling:

- **Flextime:** Allow employees to choose their start and end times within a specified range (e.g., 7 AM to 10 AM start, 3 PM to 6 PM end).
- **Compressed Workweek:** Enable employees to work longer hours on fewer days (e.g., four 10-hour days instead of five 8-hour days).
- **Job Sharing:** Allow two employees to share the responsibilities of one full-time position.
- **Telecommuting:** Permit employees to work remotely for part or all of their scheduled hours.
- **Shift Swapping:** Allow employees to swap shifts with one another with managerial approval.

3. Communication and Planning:

- **Clear Policies:** Develop clear policies outlining the options available for flexible scheduling and the procedures for requesting changes.
- **Schedule Coordination:** Use scheduling software or tools to coordinate and manage flexible schedules efficiently.
- **Regular Check-Ins:** Hold regular check-in meetings with employees to discuss their schedules and address any issues.

4. Monitoring and Evaluation:

- **Track Performance:** Monitor productivity and performance metrics to ensure that flexible scheduling does not negatively impact work quality.
- **Collect Feedback:** Regularly collect feedback from employees and managers to assess the effectiveness of the flexible scheduling arrangements.
- **Adjust as Needed:** Be open to making adjustments to schedules and policies based on feedback and performance data.

Part 2: Templates for Flexible Scheduling

Template 1: Flexible Scheduling Request Form

Title: Flexible Scheduling Request Form

Date:

Employee Information:

- **Name:**
- **Position:**
- **Department:**
- **Supervisor/Manager:**

Current Work Schedule:

- Start Time:
- End Time:
- Days of the Week:

Requested Flexible Schedule:

- Proposed Start Time:
- Proposed End Time:
- Proposed Days of the Week:
- **Type of Flexible Schedule:** (Flextime, Compressed Workweek, Job Sharing, Telecommuting, Shift Swapping)

Reason for Request:

_____

Impact on Work: Describe how the proposed schedule will impact your work and any strategies to ensure continuity and productivity.

_____

Employee Signature: _____

Date: _____

Supervisor/Manager Approval:

- **Approved:** Yes / No
- **Comments:**

_____

_____

Supervisor/Manager Signature: _____

Date: _____

Template 2: Flexible Scheduling Policy

Title: Flexible Scheduling Policy

Objective: To provide guidelines for implementing flexible work schedules to enhance work-life balance and productivity.

Scope: This policy applies to all employees eligible for flexible scheduling.

Policy:

1. **Flexible Scheduling Options:**
   - Flextime
   - Compressed Workweek
   - Job Sharing
   - Telecommuting
   - Shift Swapping
2. **Request Procedure:**
   - Employees must complete a Flexible Scheduling Request Form and submit it to their supervisor/manager.
   - The supervisor/manager will review the request and approve or deny it based on feasibility and impact on work.
3. **Approval Criteria:**
   - The nature of the employee's role and responsibilities.
   - The impact on project timelines and team collaboration.
   - The ability to maintain productivity and work quality.
4. **Implementation:**

- Approved flexible schedules will be implemented for a trial period of three months.
- Regular check-ins will be conducted to monitor the effectiveness of the arrangement.

5. **Review and Adjustment:**
   - At the end of the trial period, the flexible schedule will be reviewed.
   - Adjustments will be made as necessary based on feedback and performance data.

Contact Information: For questions or further information about this policy, please contact [HR Department Contact Information].

Template 3: Flexible Schedule Tracking Sheet

Title: Flexible Schedule Tracking Sheet

Employee Information:

- **Name:**
- **Position:**
- **Department:**

Flexible Schedule Details:

- **Start Date:**
- **End Date:**
- **Type of Flexible Schedule:**

Weekly Schedule:

Day of the Week	Scheduled Start Time	Scheduled End Time	Actual Start Time	Actual End Time	Notes
Monday					
Tuesday					
Wednesday					
Thursday					
Friday					
Saturday					
Sunday					

Weekly Reflection:

- **Challenges Faced:**

  _____

  _____

- **Successes:**

  _____

  _____

- **Suggestions for Improvement:**

  _____

Employee Signature: _____

Date: _____

Supervisor/Manager Signature: _____

Date: _____

_____

Conclusion

Flexible scheduling can significantly improve work-life balance and productivity for employees in the film industry. By implementing the strategies and using the templates provided in this guide, organisations can create effective and supportive flexible work arrangements. Regular monitoring and adjustment will ensure that these arrangements continue to meet the needs of both employees and the organisation.

Printed in Great Britain
by Amazon

56871786R10185